T0248253

REVENUE
REVOLUTION

MATT DOYON

REVENUE REVOLUTION

DESIGNING AND BUILDING A HIGH-PERFORMING SALES SYSTEM

WILEY

For general information on our other products and services or for technical support, please contact our Customer Care Department within the United States at (800) 762-2974, outside the United States at (317) 572-3993 or fax (317) 572-4002.

Wiley also publishes its books in a variety of electronic formats. Some content that appears in print may not be available in electronic formats. For more information about Wiley products, visit our web site at www.wiley.com.

Library of Congress Cataloging-in-Publication Data is Available:

ISBN 9781394196371 (Cloth)
ISBN 9781394196395 (ePub)
ISBN 9781394196388 (ePDF)

Cover Design: Wiley
Cover Images: Gears © fotohansel / Adobe Stock

SKY10053691_082223

To my mother, Rose Sergi, who taught me the incalculable power of the written word.

Contents

1

Introduction to Design-Build Modeling

The Case of Virginia Greiman – Boston's Central Artery Tunnel Project

The Central Artery Tunnel Project, known more commonly as "The Big Dig," broke ground on September 1, 1991. An elevated, six-lane highway standing on sun-faded, green, steel girders cut through the heart of downtown Boston, cluttering the cityscape and clogging up traffic. The idea was to bury the highway underneath the tract of land it currently ran on while at the same time expanding traffic lanes, adding new tunnels, and reducing the number of exits to clean up the congestion.

In 1991 The Big Dig was estimated to finish in seven years, in late 1998, at a total cost of $2.8 billion. The project was completed on December 31, 2007, nine years late. The total cost, $14.8 billion. I was starting my freshman year in high school when the first of more than 100 Big Dig job sites got started. I was 30 years old, had been out of college for seven years, and owned my own home in South Boston by the time the last trucks moved out.

Living in and around the city for the entire 16-year era of the central artery tunnel construction, I had a front-row seat to its "evolution." Conversations over Big Dig mishaps were as common and as frustrating as its traffic detours. Neighborhoods were constantly under siege from construction crews. Suspicions of graft or flat-out incompetence filled the air.

So, what the hell happened here? How could the biggest highway project in United States history have been so mismanaged that it took more than twice as long as expected and cost five times as much as its original estimate?

The long answer involves an elaborate decomposition of each of The Big Dig's 118 individual construction sites. A detailed root-cause analysis would investigate all possible contributors that may have caused the overages in time, labor, and material costs. The short answer – poor project management.

Virginia Greiman is the former deputy counsel and risk manager of Boston's Central Artery Tunnel Project. When claims were filed against the project, it was her job to handle them. If a resident filed a complaint because a crane was blocking access to his driveway, Greiman would hear about it. A business owner reporting damages incurred from traffic rerouting would go to Greiman. When an indigenous tribe would ask that a job site be relocated due to the cultural significance of an ancient burial ground, it was Greiman who had to sort it all out. She sat at the intersection of the Big Dig's complications and resolutions for more than seven years. It was her job to know each situation from all angles.

When the dust settled and the people demanded answers for the $12 billion overage, it was Greiman who had the most tangible information on what had gone wrong. As she put it, "Our research on the Big Dig has shown us that no single catastrophic event or small number of contracts caused costs to escalate. Multiple decisions by project management across all contracts contributed to the increases."[1] It was a systems issue at the very heart of how the project was managed across all job sites.

Greiman went on to state: "The most difficult problems on the Big Dig involved the means and methods used to address issues raised in the project's design and drawings, and the failure to properly account for subsurface conditions during the construction process." Failure to properly account for subsurface conditions. The planning and execution were quite literally too superficial.

In defense of those who planned and executed The Big Dig, many of the overruns were due to unforeseeable contingencies which no amount of planning would have taken into consideration: the discovery of uncharted utilities and the unearthing of significant archeological discoveries to name just two. But could they have better planned for the unknown in general? Should they have better expected the unexpected?

Greiman seems to think so. As she wrote years after the completion of the project, "If there is a single cause for the massive cost escalation on the Big Dig, it probably involves the management of the project's complex integration. True integration calls for a design-build model from the beginning of the project. Because contracts were negotiated separately with designers and contractors, there was little room for collaboration among the project's most important stakeholders."

The design-build model Greiman refers to is an alternative to the design-bid-build model that dominated project management at the time. (See Figure 1.1.) In design-bid-build, the blueprinting of the project is done by one team. Once complete, the work is then put out to bid to find a "build" team to do the construction.

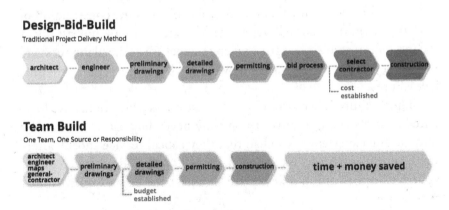

Design-Bid-Build
Traditional Project Delivery Method

architect … engineer … preliminary drawings … detailed drawings … permitting … bid process … select contractor … construction

cost established

Team Build
One Team, One Source or Responsibility

architect engineer maps general-contractor … preliminary drawings … detailed drawings … permitting … construction … time + money saved

budget established

Figure 1.1   Design-Bid-Build vs. Design-Build

Design-build modeling puts the two teams of "planners" and "doers" together from the onset. Want to see around corners? Talk to someone who's been around the block and back. Want to project what might be underground? Talk to someone who works underground all day and can share details about knowns and unknowns.

Ultimately, once construction began on The Big Dig, there was no turning back. As soon as you've gone ahead and ripped a hole through one of the biggest cities in the country, there's no stopping until the job is done, regardless of time or money. Not so in the business world. In the business world, money runs out. The time clock expires.

Miss your delivery time by more than 2x and construction estimates by 5x cost and you're likely not just out of a job, but your business goes under too. Budgets and timelines are far less patient in the private sector versus the public. Rip a hole through the middle of your business, and consequences will be felt.

The Six Systems of a Sales Organization as a Design-Build Model

The Six Systems of a Sales Organization is meant to provide a design-build model for business. After 20 years of working inside the sales teams of small and mid-sized companies, what I've discovered is the same lack of design-build integration that caused massive slowdowns and expenditures during The Big Dig, also plagues the construction of sales organizations today. The failure of leaders to look holistically at the interconnected systems of a revenue structure at the planning stage is causing massive inefficiencies, slowdowns, budget overruns, and project failures.

These failures are costly. Good-fit customers who would have benefited from working with your company never buy. Even worse, they buy, but the experience is so bad that they cancel service shortly afterward, return products, ask for their money back, and complain about your business in the public square of social media and open-source review sites.

And there are high internal tariffs as well. Good-fit employees who would have added to your company are never hired. Worst still, they are hired, but due to misalignment and mismanagement, they fail at their jobs and are fired or quit. The employee public square of Glassdoor tells this story to the candidate market, keeping great talent at arm's length.

Applying the design-build model to business construction diminishes the costs of both the external and internal costs of poor project management. *Revenue Revolution* aims to help business and sales leaders achieve several broader objectives:

- Build a team with a culture of collaboration where employees are aligned with company goals and are encouraged to work as a team in order to achieve them.

- Build a growing base of customers who are delighted by your company, will continue to come back and work with you, and will refer others to do the same.

- Build a business model with consistent and controllable economics, providing predictable security and growth for employees, customers, and owners.

- Build integrated systems with enough sturdiness to withstand the pressures of a scaling business and enough plasticity to flex to an ever-changing world.

To effectively use the design-build model, it's critical to consider the whole before and during the building of the parts. Every sales organization is unique; its own mosaic is made up of individual people and customized processes selling proprietary products and services to a specific market. Taking account of the entire organization at a distance brings the mosaic into focus.

To achieve the broader company-wide objectives, the organization should be examined in six individual yet interconnected subsystems, each one broken down into smaller elements, but constructed with the final organizational picture in mind.

1. The Process System
2. The Demand-Generation System
3. The People System

4. The New-Hire Onboarding System
5. The Ongoing Improvement System
6. The Internal Alignment System

Note that these systems are numbered, not bulleted. There is an order of operations to design-building the six systems of a sales organization. In order to build each system on a solid foundation, the supporting infrastructure of the underlying systems must first be in place.

The Process System is centered around the customer, the problem you solve, and why your business exists. The bedrock of a healthy sales organization is a clear and common understanding of the ideal customer profile, the customer journey, and the appropriate sales motion needed to meet them where they are in their evaluation of market offers. This perspective and focus on the customer informs the documented steps of the sales process, which is then built into customer relationship management (CRM). And from CRM the performance metrics, reporting, and general governance of your revenue organization can be tied together in a single source of truth.

The Demand-Generation System is built on top of the Process System. The Process System informs who your customer is, how they make decisions, and where to find them. The unit economics and sales motion that are determined in the Process System drive the volume and go-to-market choices for sales. Decisions on how to maintain operational efficiency at scale, where new customers will come from, and whose job it is to bring them in are set down and put into motion.

The People System relies on the intelligence provided by the Process and Demand-Generation Systems. Recruiting, hiring, and maintaining a great team requires seller–sales org fit. You need to get process and demand mostly figured out in order to set the sales org expectations and clearly communicate expectations with the team. If you do not know who your customer is and how they buy (the Process System) or how to predictably initiate the conversations to buy balancing volume and efficiency (the Demand-Generation System), you cannot truly understand the right-fit salespeople you need for your team.

The New-Hire Onboarding System pulls together the core knowledge documented in the Process and Demand Systems and delivers it to the People just hired. Process provides the "what, why, and how." Demand-Generation the "where," and People the "who" needed to effectively onboard newly hired sales team personnel.

The Ongoing Improvement System aims to look internally at the Process, Demand-Generation, People, and New-Hire Onboarding Systems with the goal of optimizing performance. As the name indicates, the work of the Ongoing Improvement System is never done. Through effective use of root-cause analysis, group training, team-call review, one-on-one coaching, and an ongoing practice system, performance is measured, analyzed, and iterated upon. Action plans are created to optimize key performance, outcomes are measured against previous performance, and the cycle repeats.

The Internal Alignment System aims to clarify and operationalize the integration of people within the sales team and the sales team with other functional area's teams. This is of particular importance where nodes, communication points, and interdependencies form. Here is where rules of engagement are sorted out, service-level agreements are made and documented, cross-functional collaboration is reinforced, and bottlenecks are addressed. Expectation and communication are paramount when working cross-functionally as a team.

To effectively design-build a sales organization at scale, each of these systems must be created with context. The implications each system has on the other five must be taken into consideration. It's only with this balance of deep work within a system and broad perspective on the impacts of the other core systems – a consciousness of the entire systems blueprint – that you can bring the design-build model of project management into the construction of your sales organization.

There's an old saying every contractor knows: "Measure twice, cut once." The following chapters are intended to help you size up the scope of work inside your company, double-check the plans, and provide you with the best chances of making the right cuts the first time. Bringing designers and builders together early is in effect, measuring twice.

Before diving into procedural details, each system section of the book starts with a principle story. While not every story is derived from sales, or even from business, they are all grounded in the fundamental logic needed to effectively design-build and more importantly execute each system. These vignettes portray extraordinary people working through extreme situations. It's with the backdrop of the extreme that we can see more clearly the basic truths of the system integrity brought out by the character of these systems builders. And from them, and their often-heroic stories of adversity and achievement, are the rest of us able to learn.

Note

1. Virginia Greiman, "The Big Dig: Learning from a Mega Project," *ASK*, Appel Knowledge Services, NASA, https://appel.nasa.gov/2010/07/15/the-big-dig-learning-from-a-mega-project/.

2

The Process System

The Case of Ignaz Semmelweis – Vienna General Hospital

Of the young, healthy women entering the hospital to give birth, nearly 1 in 5 were dying within days of delivery. Each time, there was a last moment to save the girl's life. One final opportunity for the doctor to reconsider. One last moment where he could take the single precaution needed to keep his patient safe. Each time the advice was ignored.

Dr. Ignaz Semmelweis had the cure. Yet, in spite of his pleading, his evidence, and finally his outright demand for change, his colleagues went on as they always had. And the deaths kept piling up. The cure was found, tested, proven, presented, and summarily dismissed. To understand how it came to this we need to examine the situation Semmelweis walked into months earlier.

In the summer of 1846, Ignaz Semmelweis, fresh out of medical school, accepted the position of Assistant Obstetrician in the maternity clinic at Vienna General Hospital. At just 29, his experience was limited to post-grad teaching. But when taking on his role at the maternity clinic he would immediately be confronted with young mothers, in his care, dying every day. New to the hospital, his eyes hadn't adjusted to the sight of death in such regularity. He was outraged.

To get a sense of the sheer scale of the problem, today in the United States, a woman will die as a result of childbirth at a rate of about 1 in every 5,000 births.[1] In Vienna General in the mid-1840s the rate was 1 death in every 12 deliveries. In 1846, the worst year, 4,010 women delivered in the physician's clinic at Vienna General; 459 would die before leaving the hospital.[2] That year new mothers died at a rate of 1 or 2 per day, every day, in a maternity clinic with just 40 beds. Cause of death was known. Puerperal fever, better known as childbed fever, a bacterial infection of the blood.

The physician's clinic represented only half of the hospital's births at Vienna General. The other half took place in a separate ward where only midwives attended to patients. In the midwives' clinic the mortality rate of childbed fever was less than 2%. At Vienna General, you were 8× more likely to die if you were attended by physicians instead of by midwives. And the expectant mothers of Vienna knew it.

Semmelweis wrote in his memoirs recalling patients in labor at the admissions desk, falling to their knees, begging not to be placed in the doctor's clinic. Some opted to deliver in the street, only dragging themselves to the hospital for treatment afterward.

Upon learning of the mortality gap between the two clinics, Semmelweis became obsessed with finding out why patients in the physicians' clinics were dying in such greater numbers than in the midwives'. After only weeks on the job, he went to work aiming to solve the mystery and save the young mothers.

Functional decomposition, simply put, is the process of undoing process. If an auto manufacturing line works through the process of functional composition while assembling your car, the mechanic you go to when the thing won't start is the functional decomposition doctor. Your engine is spread out in 73 pieces on his garage floor like intestines in a hernia surgery.

Childbirth is a process. A step-by-step, documented sequence of events working to yield a specific outcome. Semmelweis pulled apart the physicians' and midwives' processes to see where the breakdown might be hidden. What was the hidden difference that was killing the young mothers in one clinic but not in the other?

He examined the procedures followed at the moment of delivery and found them to be the same. The instruments used – the same.

He looked at the logistics and capacity data recorded from both delivery wards and found, oddly, that the midwives' clinic had more instances of overcrowding than the physicians. He examined patient records, even considered different religious practices observed by the patients as a possible root cause. It wasn't until he turned his attention to the delivery staff itself that he found the answer.

Both the doctors and the midwives spent their afternoons in their respective clinics attending to patients and delivering babies. In the mornings, however, the doctors were busy in the hospital morgue performing autopsies on the most recent victims of childbed fever. Midwives never worked with the dead. That was the deviation.

It wasn't the sight of the physicians working in the morgue that tipped off Semmelweis to the cause of the problem. It was the smell. When the doctors arrived on the floor of the clinic for their afternoon rounds of patient exams and new deliveries, the doctors' hands still carried the smell of the dead they had handled, bare-handed, early that morning. Semmelweis was the first to pose the idea that dirty hands were in some way responsible for transmitting disease.

In the twenty-first century, it's hard to envision a world where doctors would perform an autopsy bare-handed and immediately go to work on patients without thoroughly cleaning up. But in 1846 germ theory was still viewed as superstition. The prevailing belief of the day was that *miasma* or "bad air" was what caused diseases to spread.

Semmelweis himself had been brought up and educated in the era of miasma. Even when he did come to realize there was a connection between a doctor's unwashed hands and a sick patient, he didn't point to germs or bacteria by name. He cited the root cause of the childbed fever epidemic as the transmission of "cadaverous particles." It was particles – evident in the deadly odor the doctors carried with them – that he claimed to be the source of the spreading disease.

His cadaverous particle theory was met with immediate skepticism. His requests for doctors to begin a regimented process of hand washing and instrument cleansing were rejected with hostility. His accusation that a doctor's hands were dirty and infectious was viewed as an insult to the profession.

It wasn't until April 1847, some 10 months and hundreds of deaths after he joined the obstetrics clinic, that Semmelweis's theory received approval to be tested. The previous month, a colleague had suffered a cut on his hand from a scalpel while performing an autopsy on one of the recently deceased mothers. Days later that same doctor died from childbed fever. Hospital administrators caved, and Semmelweis got to test his hand-washing experiment.

Of the 312 women who gave birth at the physician's clinic at Vienna General Hospital in April 1846, 57 died from childbed fever. Nearly 1 in 5. By mid-May, Semmelweis had implemented his process change, requiring doctors to wash up in a choline-lime solution prior to treating live patients. The following month, 268 women delivered at the physician's clinic. Just 6 were lost to childbed fever, 1 in 50. In July just 3 of 250 births. The success was seen, literally, overnight.

The hand-washing process was set and stayed firmly in place for all of 1847. From January to April of 1846 the fewest deaths recorded in a single month was 27. From May of that year through December of 1847 the worst month the hospital saw recorded 12 deaths. The worst month after hand washing had fewer than half the deaths of the best month prior to hand washing.

Semmelweis had done it. He had rooted out the cause of childbed fever transmission, isolated the process flaw, and implemented an action plan to correct it. The desired result was realized almost immediately. And then it all fell apart.

In 1848 doctors began resisting the oversight. Semmelweis became emphatic, sharing his data with them on the declining death rates. The doctors saw it differently, reverting back to the idea of miasma. They claimed that upgrades in the clinic's ventilation system, which took place around the same time that the hand washing started, were just as likely the cause of the drop in the death rate.

Hospital administrators reportedly resented the accusation Semmelweis was claiming. Doctors were the professional aristocracy of European society. They attended the best schools, belonged to the most exclusive clubs, lectured at the most prestigious institutions. To confront them as dirty-handed disease carriers was inconsistent with their status as "gentlemen."

Conceptual conservatism is the tendency to hang on to beliefs in spite of new evidence to the contrary. It holds the answer to how educated people like physicians can reject seemingly obvious truths, like the fact that hand washing reduces disease transmission.

One study that detailed how deep conceptual conservatism can run in a person's belief system examined the "Doomsday Cult" of 1954. This group believed that the end of the world was destined to occur on December 21 of that year. In spite of the prophecy not coming to fruition, the group overwhelmingly maintained their belief system.

That's right. The cult continued to maintain their faith even after the seminal event in their belief system failed to occur. When dawn broke on December 22 and the world was still there, cult members began using a series of angles, circular explanations, and mental gymnastics to explain away the absence of Armageddon. Conceptual conservatism can be far more powerful than the conscientious deliberation of facts and truths.

The driving force behind conceptual conservatism is the psychological phenomenon known as cognitive dissonance – the stress people feel when their perception of who they are is contradicted by whom they believe they are. In a state of conceptual conservatism, the person's self-perception overpowers any evidence to the contrary, and the reaction is extreme defensiveness.

Compared to the doomsday cult, the evidence Semmelweis's doctors had to grapple with was insignificant. Semmelweis was alone, presenting a newly tested theory without the benefit of a completely controlled experiment. There were a number of variables, like the ventilation system, for example, which changed at the same time, effectively giving the doctors an easy out to preserve their belief system and subsequently their self-images.

The physicians quickly disregarded the hand-washing mandate altogether. As Semmelweis predicted, childbed fever began to reemerge. He became even more determined that the process be reinstituted immediately. Hospital administration responded by reprimanding him, demanding that he fall in line with the miasma doctrine. He refused. The doctors and administrators held their ground firmly. Young mothers continued to die at astonishing rates.

Death from childbed fever was painful and prolonged. Within 24 hours of delivering her baby, the woman would begin to feel the effects of the infection taking hold. Her body, exhausted from the natural birthing process, would be overcome with sore muscles, stiff joints, and a spiking fever.

Two days after delivery, rather than breastfeeding her newborn, the young mother would be consumed with pain. A heavy, pounding headache and piercing pains throughout her abdomen and pelvis. Her uterus would become swollen and covered with abscesses, bursting into open sores.

On the third day, the medical staff, desperate to treat an unrelenting fever and alleviate the woman's agony, would commonly administer the treatment of the day. Bloodletting. If miasma was thought to let the disease in through the air, opening the veins was the means by which to drain it back out. Most of the patients would be dead by Day 4.

Furious at his colleagues, Semmelweis accused them of ignorance, later negligence, and finally homicide. He accused them quite literally of premeditated murder. The doctors dug in, refusing to yield. Desperate, Semmelweis went on a grassroots campaign. He took to the streets, seeking out pregnant women, whom he would stop and insist that they require their doctor to wash his hands when they go to deliver. Hospital administrators retaliated. In March 1849, Ignaz Semmelweis was removed from his position at Vienna General, forced out of Vienna, and made to leave Austria altogether.

He spent the next 15 years fighting with the European medical community to implement hand and instrument cleansing as a critical process step inside every patient care facility. He published papers, wrote letters, and submitted data from his repeated trials. His claims continued to be ignored, and deaths piled up.

In 1865 Semmelweis was lured back to Vienna and committed to a psychiatric clinic. According to the medical community, he was insane and had to be put away. Shortly after his admittance, he suffered a cut on his hand wrestling with the guards. He was not permitted to wash his hand or clean the wound. A severe infection took hold. A fever set in, his abdomen became wracked with pain. His own dirty hand had caused a bacterial infection. Within days, Semmelweis was dead.

First Principles of the Process System

Functional Decomposition

Isolation and examination of each element of a process are critical in uncovering the root-cause influencers of a problem. As Semmelweis did with the process of childbirth when design-building and implementing a sales process, it is critical to consider the components at the most granular level. Playbooks, operating manuals, qualification criteria, service-level agreements, tagging, and sorting measures all need to be taken into account. This involves considering the smallest of components that may need to someday be examined, altered, or removed to improve process performance is vital.

A/B Testing

Also, the Semmelweis story underscores the value of science-based trial and error. Key to his ability to act so quickly on his theories to solve the outbreak was in no small part the natural A/B test, which already existed at Vienna General. Having access to two functioning clinics with the same general processes, same patient profiles, and same equipment inside the same hospital at the same time, but with very different results made it possible for the process of elimination to quickly yield findings. It was the perfect side-by-side experiment and a critical aspect of the rapid process improvement he was able to put in place in May 1847. When running revenue experiments, A/B testing with just one variable change to measure impact allows for objective analysis of successes and failures.

Fresh Perspective

We cannot overlook Semmelweis's newness to the process as a clear advantage. Thrust into the hellish situation of the physicians' clinic was a shock to his system. His eyes hadn't the time to adjust to a 1-in-5 mortality rate as "normal." And he had no personal stake in the systems currently in place. He hadn't implemented the existing process or performed the deliveries. His lack of experience freed him from insider biases.

Open-mindedness to challenge any assumptions and a willingness to use positive skepticism in an effort to find objective truth are of the highest order when evaluating processes. Bringing in a fresh pair of eyes from the outside to critique what's working and what isn't helps in the search for truth and offers an example for us to follow when assembling design-build revenue teams.

Data-Driven Analysis

Meticulous data capture is another fundamental takeaway from the Semmelweis case. To the credit of the administrators at Vienna General, they kept detailed records on their patients dating back years, not the least of which was documentation on mortality rates from childbed fever tracked separately in each of their two clinics. As the old adage goes, we cannot improve that which we do not measure.

If Semmelweis had not been furnished with clear data from each clinic, which objectively told the story of two very similar processes with two very different outcomes, if all patient data had been grouped into a single clinic data set, it's hard to see how the process issue would have been discovered. Further, had he not continued this documentation after implementing the hand-washing change protocol, Semmelweis would have been left without the evidence needed to mount such a passionate argument for sweeping change.

Process Buy-In

The change Semmelweis proposed, or rather, his inability to enact it, offers us the greatest learning from this case. Where a process requires people to act out specific tasks, the rational explanation of the necessity of those tasks is by itself insufficient. Fundamentally, people are driven more by emotion than by rational thought.

Semmelweis teaches us that we must take into consideration the more powerful emotional perceptions of those who are asked to carry out a process. Belief in a process and the way a group feels are far more influential to success than any rational justification offers. We must not rest alone on the mere explanation of a critical process, but also get buy-in on the feeling that each step in the process is the right thing to do to achieve effective implementation.

The story of Ignaz Semmelweis is tragic, not because he was a bad scientist or inept physician, but because he was a poor salesman. He failed not due to a lapse in his intelligence, but rather to a lapse in his emotional intelligence. Even a seemingly insignificant change like hand washing with a low cost and high potential return might not be adopted if there is a failure to take into account the emotional impact on those asked to enact it. It is a high EQ, not IQ that's needed to win people over.

Through his pioneering work in the field, psychologist and author Dan Goleman breaks down emotional intelligence into four key skills: self-awareness, self-management, social awareness, and social management.[3] It was Dr. Semmelweis's failure in this last area, social management, where the process change he so passionately fought for failed to be realized.

Social management requires empathy, persuasion, conflict resolution, and tact. Semmelweis, by all accounts, used none of these when working to persuade his colleagues at Vienna General. Had he done so, his efforts might have won them over, saving countless lives.

Tactically speaking, a process, especially a sales process, works best when it is engineered with small, measured elements, and is examined regularly with open-minded objectivity. But none of that matters without also considering the psychological buy-in of the people we rely on as operators. Semmelweis teaches us that we cannot merely implement a process. We need to sell a process.

How does the team feel about what's being asked of them? Do they understand and agree on the value of each task being asked of them? Will there be any resistance, not only to performing the tasks of a process but also to performing them with quality and the intent to make them work? How will even the smallest change to process impact them emotionally as well as practically?

Failure to consider the emotional aspects of the team who operate a process is failure to execute the process itself. So, as we examine the design and implementation of the Sales Process System, let's also consider both the rational and emotional elements necessary for sound process implementation, execution, and iteration over time.

Elements of the Sales Process System

The Buyer Persona and Ideal Customer Profile (ICP)

Everything starts with the customer. Process is the foundation on which a stable sales organization is design-built. A deep understanding of the customer is Job 1 in laying the process foundation. A clear, detailed, and documented description of who your customer is (buyer persona) and the type of businesses that have the best fit for your product or service (ideal customer profile) are the two cornerstones of this foundation.

The buyer persona is a semifictional biographical summary of the best audience for your business. What audience do you want to find you, to engage with you, to buy from you, and ultimately to advocate for you? A well-crafted buyer persona is complete, not just with demographic details, but also with interests, experiences, background, and even an avatar or photograph of someone who looks like your typical buyer.

Design-Building Buyer Persona

The goal when creating a buyer persona is to get your entire customer-facing team – especially marketing, sales, and support – familiar with whom they are aiming to engage, sell, and service. Involving these various teams is key, not only in creating a full, rich picture of your customer persona but also in getting team buy-in on who the audience of the business really is.

When creating the buyer persona, the design-build team should consider:

- A real name for the persona
- Age
- Marital status
- Education level
- Social style
- Hobbies, interests, pastimes

- Motivations
- Pain points
- How you can help
- Common objections

Start by bringing the select sales, marketing, and customer support project members together. Marketing typically leads this design-build project. Define the objective with templated examples of customer persona to create the framework.

Next, have each member build their own customer persona independently, from their own perspective. This allows for contributions from a diverse cross-section of possible persona information. At Rock Content we created a free online tool you can access to help guide your design-build project team through the creation of your buyer persona: https://interactive.rockcontent.com/en/buyer-persona-generator.

The final step is for the design-build project leader (again, typically represented by marketing) to pull together the contributions from each team's representative, reviewing and selecting the elements that depict the clearest picture of the customer. For example, marketing, sales, and support may each have different items on their list of persona pain points. This is a good thing. Talk through them to decide which should be kept in the final copy and which (if any) omitted.

Ideal Customer Profile

Similar in some ways to the buyer persona, the ideal customer profile (ICP) helps salespeople identify and get acquainted with targeted, "good-fit" buyers in the market. Where the buyer persona leans mostly on qualitative information focused on the individual profile that represents your general audience, the ICP layers in more quantitative data. It seeks to nail down the exact type of buyer with whom salespeople should be spending their time.

Where persona answers "who" a potential buyer is in the market, ICP helps to answer "where" they are. ICP criteria are the guideposts salespeople follow for identifying good-fit vs. bad-fit prospects.

Design-Building ICP

When creating an ideal customer profile consider zeroing in on the perfect-fit customers based on criteria such as:

- Company headcount
- Company revenue
- Industry
- Location
- Team structure/roles
- Presence of competitors
- Presence of complementary products/services
- Likely challenges/pain points

It's natural for the design-build team that is assembled for the customer persona project to move directly into the ICP work. Information is gathered through general surveys, one-on-one interviews, and market research – once again led by marketing. Rather than guessing, go right to the audience, pick up the phone and have the conversations.

The final product should be a bulleted-out, organized summary of ICP criteria, all fitting on a single page for easy access and consumption. Salespeople should have persona and ICP intel as an easy-to-use reference guide, not an elaborate operating manual.

The Customer Journey

If the buyer persona is the "who" your business is focused on and the ICP is the "where" you specifically should focus your efforts, the customer journey is the "what" – more specifically, "what" this person needs in order to effectively educate and feel comfortable believing your product or service is the best solution to help them advance. When design-built at the highest level, the customer journey takes into account four sequential steps – awareness, education, action, evangelism.

Design-Building the Customer Journey

Awareness, the first step of the customer journey, is the "why" behind the buy. At the root of any purchase, there is a need for which we are willing to exchange money to solve a problem or capitalize on an opportunity. This is a simple point, but one that is often lost or skipped over too quickly by many sales teams. All purchases are built on the customer's awareness of a problem or opportunity. Understanding and oftentimes creating customer awareness of problems and opportunities is the key first step. The design-build committee must start here.

Once a problem or opportunity has been firmly established, the second step customers take is education. They seek to understand available options to solve a realized problem or capitalize on the newly found opportunity. How and where do your customers commonly educate themselves on their solution options is key. Are they mostly offline or online? If online, are they researching on social media, specific publications, review apps, referrals from trusted advisors or existing partners?

In order to effectively meet ideal customers where they are, find out where they tend to gravitate while researching market opportunities. Each design-build committee member should submit their lists for consideration. This helps in zeroing in on where your customers are gathering.

Action is the third step of the customer journey, when they decide to move out of their current situation and implement a specific solution. By this step, problems and opportunities have surfaced, and the buyer has educated herself regarding solution options to the point where she is comfortable in her market knowledge to make a purchase.

When satisfied with the research done in the first two steps of the customer journey, the third step of actually buying can be made with confidence. The design-build project team should have a refined list of these education points documented as key learning criteria that clients typically have checked off in order to enter this phase. If the value that the purchased product or service delivers ends at the moment of purchase, the journey stops. But that's seldom the case.

When a buyer continues to derive some benefit from a purchase, whether physical or emotional, the journey can continue to the fourth, ongoing step of evangelism. In the age where buyers have more control and influence over brands than ever before, the savviest businesses will continue to enrich customer experience long after purchase. This can yield a lifelong relationship between a buyer and a business, resulting in grassroots, customer-based advocacy for the brand.

Customer-Journey Usage and Upkeep

Joining these four steps of the customer journey lifecycle creates what's commonly referred to as the customer flywheel. (See Figure 2.1.) Proactively putting positive energy into and removing friction from the flywheel is the goal of an integrated design-build revenue organization. Marketing, sales, customer support, and, more than ever today, product teams work to maintain their momentum.

These four teams collaborate to energize prospect awareness, education, engagement, and advocacy, working as a team to get the flywheel spinning faster and faster. Action is taken to make the purchase and the service delivery experience so delightful that customers openly

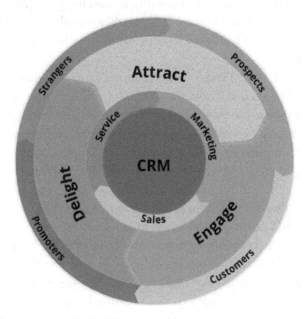

Figure 2.1 The Flywheel

advocate for your business. They volunteer for case studies, introduce you to new potential clients, help raise awareness, and the educate, act and evangelize cycle begins anew, with the next generation of future customers (Figure 2.1).

Let's push the boundaries of a buyer's journey and look at the case of Mongolian restaurants to see how the process flows. The need/opportunity in the market could be the quest for variety in cuisine or a new cultural food experience. The educational step the customer takes would involve an online search for restaurants outside the normal dining experience in the immediate area specifically using a restaurant app. The action stage of the journey is the selection of a Mongolian restaurant based on the customers' wants, needs, and expectations. Evangelism occurs when the customer is so delighted by the quality of the food and service that they tell friends and family, give positive reviews online, and, of course, return for future meals with new customers and possible future advocates.

It is this last step, evangelism, that is often left out of the buyer's journey when it is not considered connected to the original purchase. Businesses ignore this critical step at their own peril. Most customers are willing to evangelize for a business they buy from; most businesses fail to consider this and lose out on setting the table for a long-term relationship with their single greatest asset – their customer base. Design-build teams mapping the journey are advised to consider the long game of customer evangelism and flywheel growth.

With each step of the customer journey, there should be a question to which the buyer answers a definitive "Yes" before moving to the next stage. At Rock Content, where we helped clients design and scale content marketing systems, we would hold ourselves accountable for understanding where our prospective customers were in their journeys by confirming:

- **Awareness:** Is increasing visibility and demand for your business a priority now?
- **Education:** Is implementing an integrated content system the best means to help increase awareness and demand for your business?

- **Action:** Is Rock the best option to help you design and implement your content marketing system?
- **Evangelism:** Would you recommend Rock to a marketing professional in a similar situation as you were in prior to partnering with us?

These questions, and their answers, create the framework for what needs to be accomplished at each step of the customer journey, first and foremost from the perspective of the customer. To accomplish each of these checkpoints effectively, the design-build team will need a complete needs-analysis for each stage – the journey map.

Mapping Customer-Journey Needs

With your customer persona in hand and the skeleton of your step-by-step customer journey framed up, it's now time to put meat on the bones. The design-build committee next works to map in greater detail what your prospective customers need at each stage of their decision-making process. Once again, this is a project best worked on with active participation by marketing, sales, and customer support teams. Here, however, it's typically the salesperson in the project group who leads, as needs assessments and qualifications will mostly be in their realm.

For the sales team, the customer-journey needs map will provide the blueprint on top of which a customer-focused sales process will be built. Matching your buyers' pace and meeting them where they are at each stage of their education flow is the objective. When processes are not built in lockstep with the customer-journey needs, misalignments often occur. Sellers work with prospects through a one-size-fits-all model of customer education, which is often too superficial for some and too detailed for others.

Worse still, if needs by stage are not effectively mapped and matched in the sales process, salespeople can gravitate to moving too fast and presenting products and services based on what they, not the customer, deem valuable. This is the proverbial "show up and throw up" sales presentation style that turns buyers off. People like to be heard. Design-build your journey map to listen.

In the design-build customer-journey project, marketing, sales, and customer-service teams collaborate using the intelligence gathered from your persona and ICP research and follow-on interviews and surveys. They compile a one-page assessment of what your customers' needs and expectations are for each step in the customer education-decision journey. Some sample questions to consider when creating the journey needs map are:

Awareness:

- What common challenges/problems does your customer encounter?
- What changes in the market may be creating problems or opportunities for your customer?
- What changes in the market may have created new opportunities for your customer?
- What are the consequences of the status quo for your customer if problems and opportunities are not addressed?
- What are the broader objectives your customers have both at the business and individual levels?

Education/Consideration:

- What categories of solutions are there to consider (internal and external)?
- What criteria are important to consider when selecting a best-fit solution category?
- What are the internal factors (people, process, performance) that would impact and be impacted by the implementation of a solution?
- What limitations need to be considered (people, technology, budget) when considering solution alternatives?
- How does the client perceive price vs. value when considering solution alternatives?

Action:

- What criteria are important to consider when selecting a best-fit company to work with?

- Who needs to be involved in vendor selection and in what role as part of the buying committee when a new product or service is purchased?
- What common steps are there to consider in the buying process, (demo, trial, proof of concept [POC], etc.)?
- How does the client perceive price vs. value when selecting a vendor?
- How does peer advocacy influence decision making (reference sites, case studies, live recommendations, etc.)?

Evangelism:

- What does the customer need to feel/believe regarding their experience to exceed their value expectations?
- Would the customer buy again if the situation repeated itself? Why or why not?
- Would the customer refer others in their situation to buy from you? Why or why not?
- Has the customer actively endorsed you or referred possible new customers? Why or why not?

The customer-journey map provides the framework for all customer-facing personnel to stay immersed in the customer's world. With each customer interaction, everyone stays on-book, knowing exactly what is most relevant to work on with future or current customers as the journey unfolds.

Syncing the Customer-Journey Needs Map with the Sales Process

Anchoring your sales process to the customer-journey needs map creates the framework for customer-centric conversations to be followed, measured, and improved upon at scale. Customer sync not only maximizes your win rates but also creates a positive perception of your company in the mind's eye of your prospects and customers.

Matching your prospects' pace, you will have the best chance of earning their trust when the deal fits and earning their respect when it doesn't. Not all great-fit prospects buy in the first go-around. Providing a high-caliber, customer-focused experience as a repeatable process not only wins more first-opportunity deals, it also sets up a higher win rate when closed lost opportunities reopen later on.

A quick recap: By now you have documented who your buyers are (personas), where they are (ICP), and how they learn and make purchasing decisions (Customer-Journey Needs Map). Each phase of your buyer's journey warrants at least one unique step in your sales process. You'll need these unique steps to help provide clear and accurate reporting later on.

High-touch, multi-stakeholder sales motions can have multiple process steps for each journey phase. For example, the decision-stage needs for an enterprise prospect could reveal the required steps of (1) a technical demo, (2) a feasibility review, (3) a final stakeholder presentation, and (4) negotiation of terms. That's four individual sales-process steps needed for a single customer-journey phase.

Shorter, more transactional sales motions can often require the opposite process flow, collapsing multiple stages into a single process step. For example, on a single call a sales rep connects with a prospect and runs a light qualification, followed by immediate value education and product presentation, and closes by asking for the business and negotiating the deal. Awareness, education, and decision all in a single process step.

What is most important in the syncing of your customer journey to your sales process is that the conversations provide adequate information exchange to follow the pace of how your potential buyer learns, evaluates, and makes decisions. At each step, your team is set up to be in the right place, at the right time, with the right information on hand to have the most productive conversation.

Using the awareness questions and answers from your customer-journey needs map, design-build a framework for what the salesperson needs to confirm regarding problem/opportunity recognition as step 1. This creates an exit criteria checklist – a set of key confirmation points sales can use to record in order to qualify a healthy deal for each next step in the process.

Problem-Opportunity/Needs Fit

Journey: What common challenges/problems does your customer encounter?

Process: Prospect has confirmed and agreed to a current challenge/problem.

Journey: What changes in the market may be creating problems or opportunities for your customer?

Process: Prospect has confirmed and agreed to the likely value in a market opportunity.

Journey: What are the consequences of the status quo for your customer?

Process: Prospect has confirmed and agreed that now is the right time to act on the problem or opportunity.

Journey: What are the broader objectives your customers have at both the business and individual levels?

Process: The prospect has confirmed their definition of value at either a business or individual level.

At the earliest stage of a sales process, not only do prospective customers need to have awareness about the challenges/problems or opportunities impacting them, but Sales also needs to have confirmed their awareness. You need to get the prospect to tell it back to you. It is the responsibility of the salesperson at this early stage to stay focused on base problems and opportunities and be disciplined to not outrun the prospect.

The Pillars of Change

True change won't occur until a decision is made. If the aim is for that change to be the purchase of your product or service, a profound understanding and alignment on problems or opportunities is critical. You need to get your customer on the record early and align value on their terms. Each subsequent step is built on this. It's best to build on concrete issues solidified by the client early.

In order to earn the right to advance with the prospect to the consideration phase of their process, consultative selling requires a deeper conversation regarding the prospect's situation. This is a discovery step, or sometimes called the diagnostic step, of a sales process. Here the salesperson's work is to involve the prospect in a deep understanding and analysis of their situation.

The common mistake at this stage occurs when salespeople focus the prospect's attention on making a change too quickly. The focus should be on the imperfections of today and the consequences of maintaining a broken status quo. It's a commitment to move away from this current state that makes the necessity to change a foregone conclusion. It is here that most sales are won or lost.

Selling is about the process of change. If someone believes their current scenario is "okay enough" to carry on as is, the change won't happen. It is during the diagnostic stage that a sales methodology is used as a means of structuring the change conversation inside the sales process. We will come back to diagnostic sales methodologies in the next section.

Consideration/Education

After the prospect and sales rep have hashed out all the details of the current scenario and why the need for change is evident, education on the choices available, and the best change to consider, can take shape. It is important to take note here that the process does not specifically call for educating on YOUR solution.

Clearly, if there is a great fit for what your business offers, then purchasing is the next logical step. But often it is not. When appropriate, educating the prospect early in the process NOT to move forward with your solution is just as valid and worthwhile an outcome in the consideration stage.

Once again, referring to the questions and answers from the consideration phase of your customer-needs journey map, you can design-build the sales process step for effective solution education. Sample pairs could be:

Journey: What categories of solutions are there to consider (internal and external)?

Process: The prospect has confirmed the solution category best suited for the needs that have been uncovered (people, process, product, performance).

Journey: What criteria are important to consider when selecting a best-fit solution category?

Process: Sales has confirmed with the prospect what is already known and should know about their solution category options. Based on the prospect's situation uncovered in the diagnostic the prospect has confirmed that they should/should not solve internally with our recommended solution category.

Journey: How does the client perceive price vs. value when selecting a solution?

Process: Based on the value of the problem being solved and the resources needed to yield that value, the effective cost to consider should be between $x and $y. Prospect has confirmed they already have, or are willing to get, the resources necessary to buy a solution like ours.

The Placement Test

Before launching into the education step of your process, it's best practice to gauge where your client's education level is on their solutions options. Conducting a verbal placement test along the lines of "What do you already know about how people in your situation are addressing this today?"

Placement tests not only help qualify the engagement level of the prospect in conducting their own research, but they also invite them to clear as many education items off the list as possible. When educating prospects, less is more. By removing the information already known to the client, you're able to zero in on just the missing info to help them get to the next phase in their decision process.

The most important discipline for the salesperson in the consideration/education step is to focus the conversation on the general solution, not the company's specific product or service to sell. The prospect must first agree to a general solution that is the best choice for them, regardless of what specific product or service is selected. This not only confirms the change action needed, it also isolates and removes potential roadblocks to getting a deal done.

"You need to take this action to improve your current situation and here's why" is a much different conversation than "You need to buy my product or service to improve your current situation and here's why." The former is focused on the customer and their need to change, with or without you. It is the ambition of the consideration/education stage to arrive at this checkpoint. The latter is the conversation about specifically working with your business to help actualize the change with the best possible outcome. This is to be addressed in the next step in the process – action/purchase.

Action/Purchase

Having gained agreement that change is needed, and that the best-fit solution category is defined, the prospect and salesperson can now engage in a grounded conversation regarding specific products, services, and company choices. This is the final decision to act, make the purchase, and implement the specific solution. If the salesperson has earned the prospect's trust as an advisor on the change needed, and the general solution to be implemented, the work of now earning the business becomes much easier.

Returning once more to the journey evaluation, the process elements detailed below are best delivered alongside an internal champion that has been developed through the awareness and education stages of the customer journey.

Journey: What criteria are important to consider when selecting a best-fit company to work with?

Process: Prospect/champion has explained the decision criteria including feature analysis, services support, customer specialization, and overall credibility (relevant success cases) and confirmed your solution as the best fit for their needs.

Journey: Who needs to be involved in vendor selection and in what role as part of the buying committee when a new product or service is purchased?

Process: Prospect/champion has explained the process of presenting to decision stakeholders. Users, influencers, technical buyers, and economic buyers have confirmed your solution as the best fit for their needs.

Journey: What common steps are there to consider in the buying process (demo, trial, POC, etc.)?

Process: Prospect/champion has explained the buying process steps, and each one has been completed, and agreement has been gained from the buying committee.

Journey: How does the client perceive price vs. value when selecting a vendor?

Process: Prospect/champion has confirmed that the cost-benefit analysis for specific products/services of your offer is positive and that any competitive analysis on where your company sits regarding the value spectrum (low-cost, competitive-cost, or premium service) is the best suited for their needs.

Journey: How does peer advocacy influence decision making (reference sites, case studies, live recommendations, etc.)?

Process: Sales has collaborated with the prospect/champion on providing required case study/reference information if needed to secure stakeholder consensus that your company is the best-fit option and has been confirmed.

Putting all the pieces together, you've now clearly defined who your customer is, where they are, and what they need to know at each stage of their decision process. You have the documented steps to align your salespeople to usher prospects through their problem/opportunity awareness, solution-evaluation education, and decision to take action and make the purchase with your company.

The sequence, whether collapsed into a single meeting or spread out over 10+ individual interactions, allows customer-facing personnel to present prequalified offers directly to customer needs.

Everyone loves to feel heard. The way salespeople like to say, "I love you" to prospects and clients is by using the phrase "You told me . . ." We earn the right to present our products and services to clients as best-fit solutions only when we present them with the context of what they have already told us is valuable for them. "You told me . . ." anchors the conversation in the customer's world.

Evangelism

More than 70% of buyers report that they conduct research on a product, service, or company on social media before making a purchase decision. Even businesses that don't live by Pareto's 80/20 revenue law are deeply impacted by this phenomenon. In the age of peer review sites and online product evaluation directories, salespeople need to consider how customers perceive the long-lasting value delivered to them by your company.

Following the flywheel cycle, many of tomorrow's sales are started by or are influenced by how today's customers are feeling about your company. Closing the loop on the customer flywheel, Evangelism helps kickstart the next cycle of customer interaction by following through on process checkpoints.

Journey: What does the customer need to feel/believe regarding their experience to exceed their value expectations?

Process: Confirm and document positive customer sentiment regarding the value perception you/your company provided (case study, recommendation).

Journey: Would the customer buy again if the situation repeated itself? Why or why not?

Process: Customer has confirmed they will continue to work with you, buy again, buy new offers, renew purchases when terms expire.

Journey: Would the customer refer others in her situation to buy from you? Why or why not?

Process: Sales rep/customer support/account manager maintains a regular cadence of mining for referrals and asking customers for introductions to other ideal customer prospects.

Journey: Has the customer actively endorsed you or referred possible new customers? Why or why not?

Process: Customers who have referred are more likely to refer. Reward, recognize, and reconnect frequently.

With persona, journey, needs, and process stacked (see Figure 2.2), it's important to consider how much, or how little, of an investment (time and budget) you can reasonably make in working with prospects through their customer journey. The process outlines what the progression steps should be that match the customer-journey needs. It is the sales motion and methodology that customize the sales process to the number of interactions and level of detail needed to earn the customer's business.

Sales Motion and Methodology

A quick recap: Your buyer persona is the "who" your business is centered around. The ICP is where your potential customers are found. The journey these customers progress through when making purchasing decisions and the associated steps of a sales process matching this journey is the "what" that needs to happen to win new customers. The "how" this journey and process develops is the sales motion and the sales methodology.

If childbirth is a process, then the methodologies possible are natural, C-section, water birth, and so on. A well-crafted methodology becomes the checklist of must-haves Sales uses to qualify opportunities during the process.

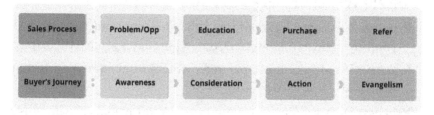

| Sales Process | Problem/Opp | Education | Purchase | Refer |
| Buyer's Journey | Awareness | Consideration | Action | Evangelism |

Figure 2.2 The Process System Stack

Sales motions are defined by three key elements:

1. The level of interactions needed to win the prospect's business.

2. The level of detail these interactions require in order to effectively guide the prospect to the next step in their journey.

3. The level of investment that can justifiably be invested in the effort to win a prospect's business.

Sales motions can be segmented into four broad categories: account-based sales (sometimes called field sales or outside sales), high-touch inside sales, low-touch inside sales, product-led/Sales-assisted.

A sales methodology provides the guardrails to a sales process. It outlines the checklist of information needed at each step in the buyer-seller conversation to effectively move deals forward. Methodologies provide a framework of intel for each step and help to keep your team all following best practices to move conversations along with healthy qualification criteria.

Your sales methodology brings consistency to your messaging, measurability to process, and accuracy to pipeline forecasting. If each deal is qualified using the same objective criteria at each specific step in the sales process, over time you will be able to trust conversion rate and sales cycle projections, giving your business a higher degree of future revenue predictability. Creating (or more commonly selecting) the right sales methodology is a function of the level of detail and type of qualifying information needed throughout your sales motion.

Purpose

You've taken the time to deeply understand who your customer is, what they care about, and how they research and evaluate purchase decisions. You've used all this valuable intel to craft a very customer-focused sales process and sales motion to meet each prospective client where they are in their decision journeys. It's a good time to stop, reflect on, and write down where your company fits into the conversation. What is the purpose of your business?

Why you exist is the critical ingredient in your corporate narrative. It inspires customers to buy, investors to underwrite, and, most of all, employees to stay and work hard. Connecting your team to the deeper purpose of your business pays off both emotionally and bottom line.

Customer Relationship Management (CRM)

Customer relationship management (CRM) has become so commonplace today that the core meaning of why we use it and what value we look to extract from it often gets lost. You only get out of CRM what you put into it. CRM set-up presents another key area where using a design-build model is supremely valuable. Let's start by putting context around this important tool with a quick refresh on its impact.

Customer relationship management is the name, so let's start there. More effective management of the relationships you aim to have with your customers is the goal. Critical information you need to know about your customer is gathered, stored, and shared with key stakeholders within your company. This allows everyone to continuously enrich the customer's experience with each new interaction.

Your customer expects you to be up to speed and intimately aware of their situation the first time, without having to be re-told again and again. From the details of the customer's business, whom they've previously spoken with at your company, what was talked about, purchase and payment history, to why they are working with you, your people need to have it all top of mind and ready to reference. When the "you" in your company is a collective "you" (i.e., a team), you need a source of truth everyone can rely on.

When CRM is used effectively, everyone in your company is in the know with critical customer info to help deliver a seamless customer experience at every interaction. Remember the flywheel and the design-build model. CRM should be constructed WITH, not FOR, your teams in a format that helps each customer-facing team member add more momentum to the value cycle.

CRM is also your single source of truth for data. Performance measures on marketing, sales, services, and customer types like size, industry, and geography are all in there. Data provide visibility into how the business, the sales, and especially the Sales Process System are operating. Without it you are blind to issues and bottlenecks are localized and lack the clarity of intel needed to effectively build sustainable countermeasures to improve performance.

Design-Building Your CRM

When setting up CRM, it's critical to have data specialists (design) and front-line sales personnel (build) in the room. With only the data specialists' voice, CRM is created with the stages, fields, and formatting that theoretically gather what's important to know at each stage of the sales process, but CRM often lacks the operation clarity of when, where, and how to capture it.

If the job is left only to sales personnel, broader, more contextual information is often missed. Let's face it, we in sales often need to have guardrails and info-capture checkpoints to require clean systemic info gathering. Sales needs to do this work, as the data is too valuable to be missed, but doesn't like to do it. I've never heard a sales rep ask to have the CRM stages locked requiring a data entry before moving to a new stage, which is exactly why design-side team members are needed on the project team.

During the design-build process, the build-side (sales) takes the micro view of process and design (sales ops) the macro. Sales brings context on what good customers and conversation look like on an individual basis. Ops takes this and, thinking long-term, helps create the broader stages, fields, and flow to cover all conversations.

In design-building a CRM, it's critical to consider not only what metrics, stats, and reporting you'll need today, but what information you will need in the months and years to come. For example, cataloging the reason you lost a deal in a CRM notepad can be good enough for a single opportunity, but after you've lost hundreds, thousands, maybe tens of thousands of deals, you're going to want to know what's going on. To do that you'll need data collected in a way that allows filtering and reporting – fields with standardized options versus a sales rep's shorthand. (We'll dive more into data in the Sales Process System Health Reporting.)

Package stock-keeping units (SKUs) and plans are built inside CRM assuring that company guidelines are met and communications with clients by phone and email are filed for future reference. Your customer-facing teams are the orchestra; CRM provides the sheet music they need to follow to stay in harmony.

The biggest value CRM offers a sales team is as the control panel for the sales process. Once the buyer persona is defined, the journey mapped, and the process detailed, the operating system to reflect that process needs to be re-created inside CRM in the form of pipeline stages. The benefits to syncing your pipeline stages to your sales process and sales process to your buyer's journey are many.

- CRM acts as guardrails for salespeople to follow the buyer's journey-build sales process maintaining customer-centricity.
- Salespeople have a tool to help them stay on point with what's expected at each process step.
- Data-recording over time allows for process analysis and iteration for the total sales team, sub-teams, and individual reps.
- Pipeline tracking over time allows for insights into forecasting predictability.
- Continuity across the sales team allows for broader comparisons with larger sample sizes, consistent data sets, and the ability for salespeople to learn from one another as they all strive to accomplish the same outcomes inside the same documented process.

There are a number of questions to ask and answer to effectively design-build version 1 of your CRM, including:

- What unique steps in the sales process need a unique stage in CRM?
- What information needs to be recorded inside a CRM at each stage (exit criteria) to effectively qualify and record critical intel?
- What is the right format for information to be gathered – checkboxes, drop-down fields, open text boxes, given not only what we want to learn, but how we will need to report on data and trends over time?
- How can integrations to other data sources (marketing automation, lead enrichment, company enrichment, playbook tools, etc.) help add value and save time?

The ambition of pipeline stages inside CRM is to clearly track the milestones of progress in your deal flow. As a shorthand, we will refer to deal stages with the simple chronology of S1, S2, S3, and so on. As deal stages move forward, the buyer is progressing through their decision journey. How many pipeline stages you have is a reflection of how many significant steps there are in the sales motion to justify a unique stage.

The Sales Playbook

The phrase "sales machine" is commonly used to describe revenue teams, and for good reason. Like any other machine, processes aren't just mapped, they're "diagrammed." Customer conversations are broken down and analyzed as "components." We have roles like sales engineer and sales operations. And, like any machine, from a household blender to an F-22 Raptor, an operator's manual is required to ensure that anyone using or working with the machine knows exactly how to get the most out of it. Enter the sales playbook.

Even elite professionals need a playbook to optimize performance and work as part of a greater team unit. Think of a topflight professional athlete changing teams. He may have had it all figured out with his last squad, but joining a new system requires a renewed clarity regarding performance expectations, play-by-play direction, guidance for what he should do to get the best results when playing, and, above all else, coordination with the other players on the field.

The creation of a sales playbook is best viewed as the building of a product. Once again, we turn to the design-build model where sales leadership (build) and operations leaders (design) are the product developers.

The key to a well-crafted playbook is context. In high school, the only cars I ever drove had automatic transmissions. It wasn't until I got to college and had to borrow my roommate's manual Honda Civic that I first learned to drive stick. Like most rookies, I revved the engine, let the clutch out too slowly, jerked the car back and forth, then too fast, and stalled out. Tried again, revved, jerked, stalled. Again – revved, jerked, stalled. In an effort to save both his clutch and our friendship, my roommate shut off the ignition and explained the mechanics happening beneath my feet.

The crankshaft creating all the power in the engine is connected to the transmission with a flywheel and a circular clutch plate. It's called a transmission as its job is to transmit power from the engine to the wheels. Different gear sizes are needed in the transmission to adjust the rotational power level (torque) depending on how much power is needed, given the speed of the car. Pressing the clutch pulls a plate away from the flywheel, disconnecting the power altogether, allowing you to change the gears while the engine is running. This is why you feel the car start to glide when the clutch pedal is pressed.

With the clutch pressed and power in the flywheel disconnected from the transmission, you can change gears with greater ease. The gear teeth can line up and connect smoothly before the clutch is released allowing power to start spinning them again. Shift without the clutch fully engaged, and the misaligned teeth trip over one another, creating that unmistakable grinding noise.

Once I understood WHY I was clutching and shifting, it all clicked. I could visualize what was going on when I pressed the pedal and shifted the stick. On my very next attempt, my hand and foot worked in sync knowing the role each step played in lifting the plates and moving the gears. Behind the wheel operating the car, I was in the "build" role. After my roommate's very basic system explanation, I also understood the "design-side." I've been able to drive a stick shift ever since.

Poorly written sales playbooks document what salespeople need to do. Good playbooks cover what they need to do and how to best get it done – providing examples of how to word questioning and links to sample calls on the realities of doing the job. Best-in-class sales playbooks will explain the *what* and the *how* on the backdrop of *why* each task needs to be done.

Design-Building Your Sales Playbook

A best-in-class sales playbook is a constant work in progress. As best practices develop, offers change and markets evolve, your playbook too flexes to the new situations, always adding, deleting, and changing the content. Having this in mind, it's wise to create your playbook in a flexible format that invites ongoing iteration by a diverse group of contributors.

At Rock Content, we evolved through a number of platforms for our sales playbook, each catering to regular scrutiny, contribution, and internal sharing. We first wrote it out in a collection of Google docs, later with an internal wiki to allow greater searchability of subject matter, and finally recreated again right inside CRM using the digital adoption tool Spekit.

Like any piece of content, when outlining your sales playbook, it's best to think of the audience at every turn. In this case, the front-line salesperson. To create the most comprehensive playbook, consider the least knowledgeable member of the audience. Create your playbook to match the experience of the newest, least-experienced new-hire you can conceive. What would this person need to know about the job you've hired them to do, and how can you document it?

Your documented sales process provides the outline for the body of your sales playbook. Each stage is a heading, each field to be filled or critical piece of information to be learned, a play. Each play a subject item inside your playbook. When fully developed, a sales playbook explains in easy-to-navigate detail every aspect of what a salesperson needs to know about every task required of them. Items that commonly emerge as headings are:

- Using the playbook effectively (yes, a manual about how to use the manual)
- Company core value statement/Why we exist (mission)
- Compensation plans (detailed in System 3)
- Promotion/minimum performance plans (detailed in System 3)
- Sales/marketing SLAs (detailed in System 6)
- Sales/CS-Services SLAs (detailed in System 6)
- Persona/ICP documentation
- Using CRM effectively
- Prospecting leads

- ICP (good fit/bad fit qualification)
- Initiating conversations
- Discovery (think of all the possible subheadings under here!)
- Product/service information
- Building offer packages
- Presenting/demoing
- Negotiating/discounting guidelines
- Processing an order/signing a new customer
- Getting referral introductions

These items are by no means a complete list, but a window into how broad playbooks need to be in order to provide the required value to your intended audience. Creating this from the point of view of your least-knowledgeable audience member not only maximizes its coverage, but it also sets you up for the foundation of your new-hire onboarding system (System 4).

In the design-build model of playbook creation, the headings outline is developed with a build-side leader (head of sales) owning the project and including from day 0 a select feedback/contributor team of sales operations analysts, sales managers, and sales reps to provide feedback. Once outlined, the specific headings are then claimed by, or assigned to, individual members of the contributor group for content creation. A unified format for the content layout is agreed upon to provide guidelines to the writers, and deadlines are committed for draft submission to the project leader.

Design-side (typically IT or sales ops) owns the tool or medium where the playbook lives. They set the rules of the game on where and how information is to be added and cataloged. Again, considering the user experience, information needs to be easy to access. (This is why we implemented Spekit. It put our playbook material right inside CRM where and when our people needed it most.)

One way to help maintain ongoing momentum and multiply the value of playbook creation is to make the playbook sub-headings an ongoing line item in weekly team meetings. Invest five minutes of each meeting to present a new or updated playbook guide to the sales team to discuss, learn from, or help improve. This ritual helps to keep production in motion and deadlines met, while also improving sales adoption of the content. Even the best-written playbook is useless if nobody is accessing it.

The discipline of playbook creation rests on the concept of compounding time investment. As a sales leader, it's easy to be seduced into more in-the-moment activities like jumping on sales calls, reviewing activity reports, running spiff incentives, or running a pipe review call. All of these activities have their value, of course, but none of them have the same long-term payout as playbook creation. Sitting down and investing the effort to craft a high-impact, design-build model playbook has a high multiple on time and value creation.

Health Check Reporting Inside the Sales Process System

The Sales Process System is System 1, as it forms the foundation on top of which all other systems are to be built. Similarly, the reporting on, and analysis of, the health of the Process System will inform the performance measures of each of the other five systems developed on top of it. Embedding the analytics, reporting, and analysis tool into the Process System early will enable the tracking, measuring, and extracting of valuable data over time. As the saying goes, "In God we trust, all else bring data."

The design-build model informs the data infrastructure by voicing their two very different objectives. Design is commonly more consumed with larger data sets, systems checks, and a comprehensive sense of understanding what's working or not working at the business or team levels. Build wants greater insight into what variables impact their day-to-day and what they can do about them to see maximum results with minimal friction (work smarter, not harder). Both objectives are important and needed in the design-build data model.

Design-Building Your Health Check Data and Reporting

First consider the design-side objectives for data and reporting, looking at health check reporting from the macro point of view. How do you know if the Sales Process System as a whole is healthy? Moreover, what levers do you have available to pull that can help positively impact the team predictably to achieve its global targets?

To answer these questions, start by listing out the sub-questions you'll need to answer at each level for all the various inputs that contribute to the health of the Process System.

- How many total leads are being generated?
- How many sales-qualified leads are being generated?
- How many sales opportunities are being generated?
- How many sales opportunities are moving to each stage in the sales process?
- What are the average conversion rates between each stage in the sales process?
- What is the average number of days in between each deal stage?
- What is the average conversion rate from stage 1 in the process to a won deal (win rate)?
- What is the average number of days from stage 1 in the process to a won deal (sales cycle)?
- What is the average contract value of won deals?
- What are the most common reasons logged for losing deals?

This is just a small sample of the types of data points commonly needed to track the Process System's health. Ultimately, it's necessary to have a detailed understanding of how many opportunities at each stage you'll need (and by when) to deliver the global sales number and which of these numbers you should focus on to positively impact quota attainment. Snapshot data sets offer little strategic decision-making value. The real learning comes from reading trends in the grouped data points over weeks, months, quarters, and years.

Consider early on the level of granularity you'll need to understand valuable trends over time at each critical stage of the sales process. For example, in the discovery stage of your sales process one of your exit criteria is "competition," where you ask sales reps to learn if the prospect is actively considering any of your direct competitors.

To run global reports and measure trends regarding the influence that specific competitors have on win rates, you'll need to create a "Competition" field inside CRM with a dropdown list of all competitors that are worth tracking (including "none"). Most CRMs allow you to lock fields like these at each stage, requiring sales reps to fill out the information before moving the deal forward in the process or to close lost.

Building out a cadence of global reporting helps to see KPI trends over time. While snapshot data sets are too isolated to extract strategic value, analyzing reports too infrequently allows poor performance to fester and bad habits to form. The balance is struck when short-term reports are issued and analyzed next to each other over a series of weeks, months, and quarters. A story develops in pieces of data, viewed side by side.

At Rock, I had a regular Monday morning meeting with my sales ops leader, during which she would review the same KPI data criteria from each sub-team in the sales org. We looked at that week's snapshot data alongside previous weeks and months with the trend lines clearly delineated and quantified with performance shifts – a 27% increase here, 13% decrease there. The routine gives clarity to the trends, and the trends dictate where to focus your attention on performance optimization. The weekly cadence allows for fast action.

Turning now to the build-side objectives for data, the perspective is bottom-up. Much of the data infrastructure work is the same as in design-side ops; however, the answers sought after and reported on are focused much more on the individual rather than the team. The big question here is, how does a single sales rep need to perform on every variable in order to predictably hit quota?

You'll need answers to subquestions like:

- How many stage 1 opportunities does each individual rep need to achieve quota?
- How does each rep's performance at each conversion point compare to the team averages?
- How do each rep's sales cycle and average ticket compare to team averages?

- How does each rep's quota attainment percentage compare to team averages?
- What is the minimum performance and promotion track status of each rep (more on these in System 3)?
- What are the end-to-end unit economics for each rep from lead, through sale, through the ongoing relationship for the lifetime of the customer?

I refer to these build-side stats as "business-of-one" reporting. Global sales performance is made up of a collection of individual sales team members performing smaller process steps to achieve their goals. In business-of-one reporting, when you have a sales team of 10 reps working deals through a 7-step sales process, your team report consists of 70 data points.

Setting up business-of-one reporting is critical for building and maintaining individual accountability. Tracking sold-customer stats by each individual sales rep provides a clear picture of the true value each player on the team is providing. Do you want a sales rep who brings in eight clients a quarter or five? The correct answer is "need more information."

Even if we assume the average contract value is the same for these two sales reps, what happens downstream matters. What if the eight-client sales rep sees half of his clients complain, ask to cancel, and demand their money back within six months, whereas the five-client sales rep's customers love what they bought, are well aligned with expectations, rave about your business on social media, and refer other clients like them? Failing to track business-of-one stats could lead you to backing the wrong horses on your sales team and reinforcing toxic behaviors that look good early but have steep costs later on.

Root-Cause Analysis

A common scenario when using data and reporting is the see-problem-solve-problem approach. Rev Ops has provided a detailed, end-to-end sales process report. In it, you clearly recognize that the conversion rate from the discovery stage to demo stage is dropping. The trend has shown a steady decrease from 50% three months ago, to 40% two months ago, to 33% last month. The strong leader that you are, you jump in with a sales incentive where any rep who brings his or her conversion rate back to 50% or more earns a cash bonus. It works, and every rep is now back above 50% discovery to demo conversion. Great work, right? Wrong!

You've successfully made the number on the spreadsheet bounce back, but how? You motivated the sales reps to convert more discovery ops to demo stage, but completely ignored how they should do that. Or why they should do that. Or if they should even be doing that at all. Is it possible that the 17% drop is a result of a more mature sales team focusing their efforts on higher-value opportunities and better screening out bad fits? Is the drop actually a good thing? You've designed an incentive without considering build-side knowledge.

To put a check in place on superficial solution-building consider applying root-cause analysis (RCA) as part of your standard operating procedure when building action plans. This invites build-side input that is valuable to design-drafted remedies. There are a number of RCA tools in the market to select from. I'm partial to the logic tree.

Logic Tree for Root-Cause Analysis

Let's use the example of the drop in discovery to demo deal conversion rate to map out how a logic tree can be used for better decision making.

Step 1. Write out the problem statement that describes the deviation from expected performance, the timeline of the issue, and its impact on results. "Over the last three months, the conversion rate of deals has steadily dropped from 50% to 33%, reducing the total number of late-stage opportunities in our pipeline."

Step 2. Map out primary elements contributing to the cause of the decline.
  • Lower opportunity quality
  • Higher screening standard
  • Poor value building
  • Poor momentum building

Step 3. Map all the secondary elements contributing to the primaries, the tertiary elements contributing to the secondaries, and so on until all variables have been diagramed. (See Figure 2.3.)

With the tree now done, it's time to add the logic. Once more the design-build model plays a key role. Bringing in a diverse group of perspectives from both the design-side (experienced leaders and ops specialists) and the build-side (front line salespeople conducting the discovery calls) helps to add valuable insights into what's really happening.

The axiom is wrong. Numbers do lie. Or rather, the misinterpretation and misuse of numbers can make unintentional liars when RCA checks aren't put in place. After deeper analysis, listening to call recordings, looking into ops quality, info quality inside CRM, reviewing sales process adherence, and interviewing the reps, you determine that the drop in the conversion rate is actually a positive trend. Sales is working smarter, not harder, focusing more effort on better-fit, winnable deals.

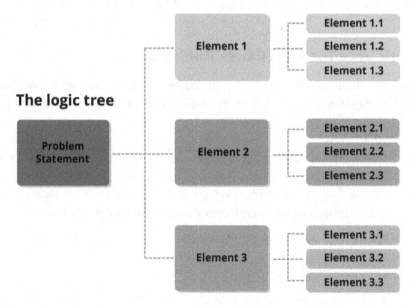

Figure 2.3 The Logic Tree

Rather than running an incentive to pay reps for adding lower-quality deals back into the late-stage pipeline, you invest your attention (and your incentives budget) elsewhere.

Like any teamwide, repeatedly used process, whatever you settle on for your root-cause analysis should be added to your playbook. Descriptions of what RCA is, why you use it, and how to use it all with the supporting docs linked in. Creating a reusable template to streamline the process and keep everyone using the same format is a must-have.

Sales Process System Rituals

Systems are built to standardize and optimize repeated actions. Rituals help to reinforce standardized actions building positive habits. Let's review a few rituals that can help to create awareness, adoption, and optimization with the Sales Process System.

Reporting

Building a cadence of what stats will be looked at and at what frequency is a communication tool. It sends a clear message to the team regarding which performance measures the company values, what the expectations are, and how everyone is tracking. In sales, the ritual of sending out metrics sheets, bar charts, mountain graphs, and stack rankings is standard practice, but choose wisely. Distributing detailed reports is a form of content marketing. Overdo it, and the reports become spam, and your team will soon tune them out like any other spammy email.

Mitigate this by limiting the sends to a single, consolidated daily stats report. That is, one comprehensive ranking that covers the essential performance data needed by the team. Reserve weekly, monthly, and quarterly reports for live presentation in team meetings and kickoffs.

Publicizing Wins

Never waste an opportunity to let everyone know they're on a winning team. Hitting the gong has its place, but I prefer a more elaborate explanation than a simple *cha-ching*. It's a learning moment for the team to better understand what success looks like.

Whether through a dedicated email folder, Slack group, or some other means, have a channel for distributing when a new customer signs, who the new customer is, what they bought, and most importantly why they bought. Salespeople gobble that stuff up. Over time they get a really clear sense of the ICP, high-conversion industries, popular packages that do well in the market, and common pain points and narratives that drive the *why* behind each customer's buy.

Shout-Outs

Commissions and incentives are powerful motivators, but nothing replaces recognition. People want to know their work matters and that they are making a difference. Especially salespeople. So, give it to them.

Regular, public displays of recognition go a long way toward energizing the team. Top reps who are recognized for their superior work pull up the performance of the next generation of reps who aim to be recognized. Try coupling the shout-outs as a "reply all" on the daily stats ranking email thread to help bring eyeballs back to KPIs that matter most.

You can make recognition the gift that keeps on giving by providing top performers with a physical status symbol of what they've earned. The most common of these are the ubiquitous President's Club trophies lining the desks of top-flight reps. Make these status symbols of excellence a more common occurrence than the annual P-club award.

At Rock, we used these very tall, thin bottles of tequila. They were the trophies awarded to 8–10 of the best reps on a monthly basis. Reps would keep the bottles stacked up on the back of their desks like the bar at a Guadalajara nightclub. Status. Ongoing recognition. High-performance culture.

Kickoffs

Everyone loves a good party. Especially when they have energy, enthusiasm, takeaways, and a shot at being the guest of honor. This is made possible in a sales org through regular parties in the form of weekly team meetings, monthly kickoffs, and quarterly all-hands. What turns a stuffy sales meeting into a sales performance party?

- **Music.** Sounds out of place, but never start a sales meeting with dead air. Energize the base.
- **Message.** Slide 1 (use visuals) is a reaffirmation of the company's purpose. Bring everyone back to the power of the *why* and the deeper purpose of their work.
- **Sharing.** Help everyone get a little bit better while together. Multiply the value by cross-training, and have high-performance reps teach a session. This mixes up the training content with fresh voices and emphasizes your all-stars, giving them a voice to share their individual value with the group.
- **Recognition.** Call people out for exceptional performance in front of the group. These become role models for the rest of the team and help build engagement and reduce turnover among top performers. (Cue the handouts of the regular recognition awards mentioned earlier in the "Shout-outs" section. Viva la tequila!)
- **Evangelism.** You've got your team feeling great about being part of an exciting organization. Seize the moment and ask for referral intros to possible new hires.

Mistakes I've Made When Constructing the Sales Process System

The learnings for how to best design-build the Sales Process System were born more out of mistakes and false starts I made along the way than from the time I guessed right on the first try. In an effort to help you avoid repeating these mistakes, let's dig into a few of the most egregious here.

Superficial Documentation of the Customer

It's easy to get lost working inside your sales machine once it gets going. So much so, in fact, that the people you built the thing for, your customers, often get lost along the way. At scale, new people will join your team who may not have the same level of intimate knowledge regarding who your customers are, what they care about, and why they should spend time and money to work with you.

Investing in documenting detailed customer personas, ICP, and journey maps early pays huge dividends late. Customers are more educated and less patient than ever. Give your team a head start in knowing the customer in detail to help build rapport and alignment. My documentation at Rock was thin in the early days. As a result, new team members' customer knowledge was superficial. And it showed on calls and in performance.

Missed Data Fields in CRM

Live sales calls offer a treasure trove of customer intel. Some salespeople take great notes. Most do not. Some salespeople log their notes meticulously in CRM. Most do not. Of the salespeople who do log notes in CRM, none organize the information in a way that is searchable at scale. This is a result of having builders off a building without the design-side infrastructure in place.

I failed to set up the info-gathering system early enough. My team carried on like this for years, not entering their information in sortable, searchable fields into the CRM. The cost was that valuable information evaporated as soon as each sales call ended. You never get that info back.

Avoid this fate by bringing design-side thinking into the conversation early and mapping out in detail all the stuff you want to know about deals at every stage in the process. With that, do the work to set up CRM with the stages, fields, and locking systems that require salespeople to enter all the detail in order to do their jobs.

No Root-Cause Analysis Process

In case you were curious the answer is "yes." The earlier example in the "Root-Cause Analysis" section of a sales leader paying an incentive to reps who increase their discovery-to-demo conversion rates only to later learn that he was just paying reps more to work bad deals was all me. Not a great use of the valuable incentive budget. And even worse, a waste of valuable rep time.

Unless there is a valid reason for moving lightning fast (and there almost never is), slow down the implementation of new action plans. Bring a diverse crew of both design and build people into the conversation about performance issues. Use a root-cause analysis framework and make the investment to dive deep into understanding symptoms and underlying diseases and to weigh out all possible remedies. Always keep in mind the side effects from remedies that can sprout up as second- or third-order effects of a change. The butterfly effect is real.

Abandoned Playbook

Everyone loves the idea of a sales playbook. Nobody loves the work that goes into building and maintaining one. Certainly not me. An incomplete playbook leads to an incomplete sales team. Playbooks that are not updated and not regularly promoted go unused. I personally have poured out subject line after subject line of future playbook content that sat idle for years (literally years) like cement foundations for homes that are never built.

Delegation is the key, and it was here that I failed early in my playbook creation. I tried to own the entire playbook design and build myself. It takes a village to raise a playbook.

Assign a global owner of the playbook – not you if your sales team is 10+. You won't give it enough ongoing attention. That owner should have a successor as backup and play conductor, assigning competent owners for the creation and maintenance of the individual playbook sections. Section owners help run new-hire (System 4) and follow-on training (System 5) for their owned area. If section owners leave or fail to keep their playbook areas up to date, it's the global owner's responsibility to replace them.

Checkpoint – System 1

Sales Process is System 1 in the six-system methodology as it is the ground floor on which the other five systems are built. The customer profile, journey, and sales motion inform the type of personnel you will need (System 3). Playbooks and CRM guardrails inform and enrich the process of onboarding new personnel to the team (System 4). Without standard operating procedures and adequate reporting, ongoing improvement of team performance would not be possible (System 5). An architecture for documentation, data collection, and the use of a CRM as a single source of truth for customer engagement is the bed-rock of internal alignment with other functional areas in the company (System 6).

And the Sales Process System is also critical in understanding where your potential customers are, and how to reach them in the appropriate go-to-market strategy for business. It informs where to spend time and budget, how to pull prospects into the sales process, and who owns the various responsibilities associated with filling the pipeline with ICP opportunities and getting the flywheel spinning. It is the platform on which to design-build System 2, The Demand-Generation System.

Notes

1. National Center for Health Statistics, "Child Health," Centers for Disease Control and Prevention, https://www.cdc.gov/nchs/fastats/child-health.htm.
2. Wikipedia, s.v. "Ignaz Semmelweis," last modified April 5, 2023, https://en.wikipedia.org/wiki/Ignaz_Semmelweis.
3. Daniel Goleman, *Emotional Intelligence*, 10th ed. (Bantam Books, 2007).

3

The Demand-Generation System

The Case of Cate Castillo – Neivor

The company was brand new. No sales team. No marketing team. No customer base to mine for referrals. No website traffic to convert into opportunities or lead lists to prospect from. There was zero. Less than zero for Cate Castillo, who not only had to manufacture revenue off a blank page but do it while learning a new industry from scratch.

Neivor, a PropTech (property technology) company, based in Mexico, launched in 2019. The software application serves property managers, helping them to automate and digitalize the administration of their businesses: rent collection, building security, managing amenities, and reporting all in one place. Castillo was brought in at the founding of the company as CEO.

There's a subtle steadiness to Cate Castillo. She sits up straight when she talks. Chin tilted slightly up, her straight dark-brown hair that never manages to make its way over her cheeks. Her clothes are a blend of formal and relaxed. Her lips seemed fixed in a slight smile, but not so much inviting friendship and more communicating "I got this." Just over five feet tall, wiry, and athletic – her voice is disproportionately bigger than her physique. Cate Castillo is heard when she speaks.

Upon assuming the leadership role at Neivor, she had no time to waste. The startup had raised a small round of seed capital, but with no revenue, would burn through it fast if property managers didn't start buying. The clock was ticking from day 1.

"I needed to build a network and make sure people knew Neivor," Castillo explains. "The first thing I did was create a network list. Associations, so we could build partnerships and journalists."

Real estate associations held the contact information that was ideal for an early list of potential Neivor clients, but signing a membership subscription was cost prohibitive in the early days. Castillo had to get creative. She had no PropTech experience or direct contacts in the industry, but she did know people in media. She reached out to her contacts at magazines and newspapers, contacting the reporters who wrote about the real estate industry. In a bit of a role reversal, she asked to interview them.

It turned out to be a goldmine. Journalists knew the ecosystem intimately. They knew the heads of the condo complexes and rental conglomerates by name. They knew how the organizations were structured. Who managed the day-to-day operations and who were just the names on the building. Which businesses were tight, family-owned operations, and which ones were major conglomerates. The information was detailed and contextual, which delivered far more value to Castillo than a simple mailing list.

Contacts list in hand, the next challenge was how to get the property managers to engage. Castillo was not a career salesperson. Prior to Neivor, she had held leadership roles in marketing and product. Cold-calling prospects was *terra incognita*. On top of that, she joined Neivor just as the Covid-19 pandemic was shutting down normal business operations. Options for starting conversations with strangers were limited.

She settled on launching a webinar series focused on market trends or changes in regulations impacting property managers and invited anyone she could find from the businesses her media contacts indicated were worthwhile. Lawyers, facilities managers, bookkeepers – it didn't matter as long as they were associated with potential clients. "In the beginning, I just wanted to create a database of potential clients and have them know the brand and what we're doing," Castillo said.

More than 1,000 attendees showed up to her early webinars. For a business looking to sign single-digit clients, that level of early engagement was huge. The first client Castillo sold came through her early webinar campaign. She got revenue on the board, but not for the product value she anticipated.

"They had a big problem related to amenities. It was during the pandemic, they needed to manage amenities. They were having trouble with the neighbors. They needed a booking system. We provided a solution and started to work. That gave me a very important insight. So then we tried another strategy based on that client."

Neivor's early value proposition focused squarely on rent collection and streamlined financial management for property owners. Little focus was put on helping manage the internal conference rooms, event salons, or gyms that condominiums offered as perks to their tenants. As it turned out, this was the most pressing challenge for the property managers during Covid-19. Castillo ran with it.

Now with a clear pain identified that Neivor could solve and some money coming in from her newly sold client-validating potential return on investment (ROI), she bought data about buildings that had amenities. Any condo complex with event spaces, gyms, or pool areas was on the target list. The purchased contact base had the names of the condos, but nothing on the property managers specifically. Information for that role in that market simply didn't exist.

Castillo solved this with a low-tech, high-impact solution. She went door to door and asked for it, first all on her own, then later hiring field salespeople. They went individual properties, assembling lists of names, numbers, and emails of the property managers of the target condos, one building at a time. Slow, methodical, but effective.

Starting in the same neighborhood where the customer she had just sold was located, Castillo used her new client's name as a point of reference to open conversations, build credibility, and convert other property managers to the platform. As she tells it, "We got other customers like that because they all had the same pain point. And they were all located in the same areas."

With each new customer signed, her case to prospects grew stronger. "This building is working with me, now this other one. We wanted to create this [network] effect."

And they did. Castillo was able to sign a number of new customers using the newly learned pain point and referencing recently sold customers to build credibility. When she exhausted the opportunities in the first neighborhood, she hired additional field salespeople to work new neighborhoods.

Then things started to break down. New customers were signing, but not at a high-enough ticket size to justify the costs of the field team. Monthly cash burn skyrocketed. In mid-2020, Neivor had 75 months of runway. A year later, it dropped to just 12 months. Neivor was selling, but if the economics didn't change quickly, they would run out of money fast. Digital was the answer.

Castillo bet first on paid media campaigns to test the online maturity of the customer base. Results came fast, and she increased the digital ads budget and added content marketing, focusing on SEO, blogging, and social media promotion. By the middle of 2022, organic search and social media were the top channels of customer acquisition at Neivor. The field sales team was disbanded and replaced with inside sales reps built to work inbound leads.

Two years into the business, Neivor had developed a diverse, multi-channel customer-acquisition strategy. Inbound marketing, outbound prospecting, and online events all contributed to revenue flow. The efficiencies driven by the digital channels had rebalanced the acquisition economics, and Castillo was able to add higher-cost, in-person events to the mix. Conferences were often hosted by real estate associations that catered to the wealthier, "old line" clientele in the industry.

Throughout the journey of scaling Neivor's demand-generation system, there was an underlying challenge Castillo had to face. There existed a persistent drag on productivity, like having to swim against a current. She was reluctant to spend much time on the topic but answered me directly and somewhat matter-of-factly.

"Were there times when clients or business partners were treating you differently and making things more difficult, purely because you are a woman CEO?" I asked.

"About 1,000 times," Castillo said without much emotion like she was answering a math problem. I pressed her for an example. She didn't need any time to think.

The previous week, she and her head of sales entered a conference call with a real estate association Neivor was eager to partner with.

The president of the association, an older man, opened the call with "I didn't know that start-ups hire 'niñas' to run companies." *Niñas* is Spanish for "little girls."

Castillo is 35, has an MBA in marketing, a second MBA in international business, has held C-level roles for more than a decade, and has successfully scaled a start-up through series A growth. She nodded, smiled (her smile) at the president of the association, and moved on with the meeting. Business as usual.

Women make up just 4.2% of all CEOs in Latin America.[1] When Castillo attends C-level events, she is the only woman. It's not unusual for the other company execs to ask, "Are you married? Where is your husband?" She never brings her husband for risk of looking weak and dependent. These are things male CEOs never need to spend energy or attention on.

Affinity bias is when people show preference in favor of people like themselves. The more like you someone is, the more natural preference you are likely to afford them. Even when overt prejudice does not exist, the subconscious gravitation toward people with a similar background, ethnicity, and, of course, gender can result in unfair treatment. Even among people who actively make an effort to be fair, the deck is stacked against the outsider, simply due to the subconscious discomfort that differences have on the human psyche. Castillo described this in one of her interactions.

"It's like in poker. When I play poker, I almost always end up at the final table. One time, at the final table, the guy shuffling the cards didn't put any in front of me. I was sitting right there, but in his mind I was nonexistent."

Castillo didn't sit by quietly. She asked to be dealt in. "The first hand I made a great move and won the money. The second time, the third time the same. After I proved myself, showed that I knew how to play and I was there to win, he started to take me seriously."

She has no illusions about the world she is working in. "I expect it that way every time now. When I get into business conversations, I am not kind."

Cate Castillo makes no excuses and refuses to be the victim. She's earned a seat at the table. And when required, she will command attention, get dealt into the game, and take the money on the table.

First Principles of the Demand-Generation System

To build a winning demand-generation system, it's important to approach the tasks of customer acquisition as a business owner. Each salesperson on the team is in fact the owner of their own business. When we look at the case of Cate Castillo, we see this in its purest form as she not only owned all of Sales in the early days of Neivor, but also the business at large.

Chess Game Approach

Castillo did not have a clear line of sight to the property managers. There were no contacts in a database or connections on LinkedIn for her to mine in her initial demand-generation efforts. She had to go to the people she did know (journalists), who could direct her to the right companies (condominiums) where she used a blanket approach (webinars) to initiate conversations. She had to think three moves ahead.

Sales teams often encounter the same challenge. Direct access to the target client is not always within reach. Who are the influencers? Who sits on the periphery? What is the two- or three- or four-step path to get to your prospective client? All too often demand generation is a game of chess, not checkers.

Meet Prospects Where They Are

Castillo knew where her prospects were, but not who they were. There were no lists of names and contact information for Mexican property managers for her to simply buy for direct call and email campaigns. She had to build it. She sent out a street team to go to the buildings and collect names and numbers, lead by lead. The plan was not scalable, but in the short run, when building the first customer base and getting early traction, anything goes.

Business owners do whatever they need to in order to initiate customer conversations. Salespeople who own their businesses must do the same. Call, email, social, events, in person, direct mail, carrier pigeon. Whatever bridges the communication gap between you and your clients is open for discussion.

Learn and Adapt

Mike Tyson famously said, "Everyone has a plan until they get punched in the mouth." Neivor's plan, as their leading value proposition, was to help property managers reduce costs and improve the tracking of rent collection. After talking to clients, Neivor got punched in the mouth. The more urgent pain was not in collection. It was in amenities. Castillo heard it, pivoted her messaging, and opened new channels of demand generation.

Darwinian logic often applies to demand generation. It's not the strongest who survive, but those who are most adaptable to their environment. Markets change, economics change, competitors change, customer needs change. If we in sales don't learn and adapt to the ever-changing environments in which our clients live, we face the risk of extinction.

Mind the Economics

Castillo launched a field sales motion early in Neivor's growth evolution. The property manager clients were hidden behind the walls of their condo admin offices. Putting boots on the ground to go directly to them had worked from the onset, so she built satellite teams across Mexico. But the economics broke. They could sell, just not sell enough to justify their costs.

Castillo's finance background trained her to keep a close eye on the economics of her demand-generation system. It's a lesson we can all benefit from. Short-term losses are not only acceptable in sales, they're virtually required. Demand-gen investments take time to cycle through and yield revenue results. But they do need to eventually pay back enough to make sense for the business. Scaling broken demand-gen economics can quickly lead to peril, if performance just isn't there.

There's No Crying in Demand Gen

Cate Castillo had limited resources from the onset. No brand awareness or aircover from marketing, no network or lay-up clients waiting with checkbooks in hand. She had to create something out of nothing and do so as in high heels, backward as a female CEO in Latin America. Her attitude in light of this? No excuses. Find a way to make it work. Ask to be dealt in. Work hard to take the pot and earn success.

This no-excuses mindset may be the most valuable of demand-generation first principles. Any number of non-controllable factors can adversely impact the ability to build pipeline. The only viable response is to focus on what you can influence. All energy focused on what you can control, moving right beyond the external roadblocks . . . and if possible, with a smile of "I got this."

Elements of the Demand-Generation System

Demand-Generation Economics

How you generate demand for your company is ultimately governed by economic principles. Spend too much on acquiring a customer, and you'll go out of business. Spend too little and you'll risk missing valuable opportunities for growth . . . and potentially go out of business. The key is finding the middle ground? Get out your spreadsheets! It's time to run the numbers.

There are three fundamental questions you need to answer before launching into a demand-generation strategy to know what you can afford.

1. How much net value does a new customer bring to my business?

2. How long does it take to actualize the total value a new customer brings to my business?

3. How deep in debt am I willing to go before recovering the total costs associated with acquiring a new client?

The answers to these questions aren't always cut and dry. Take Facebook, for example. They ran their demand-generation machine for years before having a clear plan for monetization. How much net value did a new user bring to their business in the early days? Unknown. How long did it take to actualize that total value? Unknown. How deep in debt were they willing to go to continue acquiring new users? A lot.

Your business likely operates on more earthbound financial governance than Facebook. Spreadsheeting this cost-benefit analysis should offer you more clarity on the financial parameters you need to place on demand generation. The key here is extrapolation. Without extending the model out until capital recovery, you run the risk of digging yourself into a demand-gen hole so deeply expensive that you cannot recover.

Figure 3.1 shows a sample sheet provided by David Skok, partner at Matrix Ventures.[2] This analysis applies to a software as a service (SaaS) business paying a rep $70,000 base and $70,000 on target commission per year and asking the rep to book $700,000 per year in new business (two new customers per month at $29,000 each). The demand-generation assumption in this scenario is eight opportunities to convert one customer at a cost of $700/op – over $11,000/month in demand gen to feed this rep.

This sheet details the rep's business-of-one economics, which we covered in the Process System. Notice the highlighted net profit line. This rep's individual business does not start making money until month 11 of their tenure, assuming they are averaging 90% quota attainment (best to be conservative with attainment projections).

Expenses	Month 1	Month 2	Month 3	Month 4	Month 5	Month 6	Month 7	Month 8	Month 9	Month 10	Month 11	Month 12
Base Salary	$ 5,833	$ 5,833	$ 5,833	$ 5,833	$ 5,833	$ 5,833	$ 5,833	$ 5,833	$ 5,833	$ 5,833	$ 5,833	$ 5,833
Variable Compensation	$ -	$ -	$ -	$ 2,917	$ 5,833	$ 5,833	$ 5,833	$ 5,833	$ 5,833	$ 5,833	$ 5,833	$ 5,833
Overhead	$ 2,083	$ 2,083	$ 2,083	$ 2,083	$ 2,083	$ 2,083	$ 2,083	$ 2,083	$ 2,083	$ 2,083	$ 2,083	$ 2,083
Cost of leads required	$ -	$ -	$ -	$ 5,576	$ 11,152	$ 11,152	$ 11,152	$ 11,152	$ 11,152	$ 11,152	$ 11,152	$ 11,152
Total Expenses	**$ 7,917**	**$ 7,917**	**$ 7,917**	**$ 16,409**	**$ 24,902**	**$ 24,902**	**$ 24,902**	**$ 24,902**	**$ 24,902**	**$ 24,902**	**$ 24,902**	**$ 24,902**
Cumulative expenses	$ 7,917	$ 15,833	$ 23,750	$ 40,159	$ 65,061	$ 89,963	$ 114,864	$ 139,766	$ 164,668	$ 189,570	$ 214,471	$ 239,373

Breakeven Analysis	Month 1	Month 2	Month 3	Month 4	Month 5	Month 6	Month 7	Month 8	Month 9	Month 10	Month 11	Month 12
Net profit	$ (7,917)	$ (7,917)	$ (7,917)	$ (14,659)	$ (19,652)	$ (16,152)	$ (12,652)	$ (9,152)	$ (5,652)	$ (2,152)	$ 1,348	$ 4,848
Cumulative Net Profit	$ (7,917)	$ (15,833)	$ (23,750)	$ (38,409)	$ (58,061)	$ (74,213)	$ (86,864)	$ (96,016)	$ (101,668)	$ (104,820)	$ (102,471)	$ (97,623)

Figure 3.1 Skok Analysis #1

More critical to the overall fiscal health of the business, it high-lights month 10 in the cumulative net profit line. Assuming you collect cash from customers monthly, you're going into debt more than $100,000 with a single sales rep. Hire 10 reps in a month and be pre-pared to go more than $1 million in the hole before you start digging out.

The costs in this scenario are balanced out by the value the new clients bring to the business. In this example, the assumptions are that the revenue from these customers carries an 80% gross margin and the customer base has 100% net dollar retention (zero churn). Effectively there is infinite value generated from these customers, so most SaaS businesses would jump on these economics and raise the funds to cover these losses.

What happens when the demand gen costs are doubled to $1,400/op?

Not only have you pushed out the breakeven point of the business-of-one economics by three months, you've now created a scenario where an individual sales hire digs you into nearly $200,000 debt. Get-ting your demand-generation economics wrong can have expensive consequences.

At Rock Content, *Skok* is a verb. Understanding "how" the business-of-one economics extrapolate over time before making an investment in a new team, geography, or channel of customer acquisi-tion always needed to be Skoked first. Skoking each individual rep's actual performance month-over-month provided the framework for our business-of-one reporting.

Skok can also be converted to apply to business models without recurring revenue models. Let's look at a business with a one-time revenue-collection model. We'll apply the same scenario of a $70,000/$70,000 comp, $700,000 revenue target, and 90% attainment and productivity ramp. In this non-recurring revenue business, the gross margin is 50%, and all revenue is collected up front at the time of purchase.

The good news here is that the rep breaks even on month 5 and only digs the business into a $27,000 debt hole. The bad news is that the individual rep never generates very much in the way of profit. Because revenue does not compound with each customer, net profits stay flat at just $1,348/month versus the SaaS example where every month after breakeven profit grows.

In this scenario, if your demand-generation cost forecast is off even slightly, it can have a dramatic impact on the bottom line. Essentially, you're only $1,348 in the black each month. If your rep needs 16 ops to convert 2 customers (as is the case in these scenarios) and your cost/ opportunity is off by even $100/op, you can go from a profitable rep to a rep, team, and business that loses money every month with no means of recovering.

Demand-Generation Options

Once you've run your numbers and determined how much you're able to spend on generating demand, it's time to look at your choices of where and how to generate demand. There are many.

Online

- Content marketing
  - Blogs
  - Search engine optimization (SEO)
  - App store optimization
  - Social media
  - Downloadables (e-books, whitepapers, checklists, etc.)
  - Interactive tools (calculators, assessments, graders)
  - Video
  - Podcasts
  - Webinars
  - Email marketing
  - Public relations/earned media
  - Syndicated content
  - Content-led referral program

- Paid media
  - Search engine ads
  - Social media ads
  - App store ads
  - Banner/display ads
  - Video ads
  - Retargeted ads
  - Native ads
  - Sponsored content
  - Referral/product recommendation (Capterra, G2, etc.)
- Product-led growth (PLG)
  - Free trial
  - Freemium – feature gates
  - Freemium – usage limits
  - Freemium – support limits
  - Product-led referral
- Channel
  - Resellers – brand-labeled
  - Resellers – white-labeled
  - Referral partners

Offline

- Events/trade shows (hosting sponsoring or speaking)
- Networking (groups/associations)
- Print media ads
- TV ads
- Radio ads
- Billboards
- Flyers/door hangers
- Direct mail campaigns

- Couponing
- Gifting campaigns
- Cold calling
- Warm calling for referrals

Offline marketing is dead. Actually, all outbound channels for marketing and sales are dead. No, wait, inbound is dead. SEO is too crowded and paid media is too costly. Social selling is dead, as everyone has flooded the chamber and drowned out your ability to connect. Wait, all human selling is dead. PLG is here and the robot armies have taken over.

None of these statements are true of course. Each of the above-mentioned channels is very much alive and, when used in a design-build execution strategy, can be quite effective.

The above is meant to be not an exhaustive list, but merely a window into the vast landscape of demand-gen options available to businesses today. Selecting the right mix to help feed your flywheel with a rich flow of opportunities is an ongoing process of trial and error. A never-ending process of experimentation and iteration.

The cost-benefit assessment run earlier should immediately start to eliminate unrealistic or illogical venue options. If you're scaling a B to C offer with mass market appeal, TV ads may be a great option, but unrealistic based on budget. If you sell a complex software solution to government agencies, product-led growth may look great on a balance sheet, but an impossible choice given the security and implementation needs of a customer to even test drive the tool.

To select the right mix, consider the overlay of two data sets:

1. Where and how your customers do research and educate themselves on market trends, new opportunities, answers to problems they need to solve and their associated solutions – online, events, social media, apps (see the Process System for more detail).

2. The short list of demand-gen go-to-market options based on your budget constraints.

And these demand-gen options are not mutually exclusive. (See Figure 3.2.) The best demand-generation systems get the different

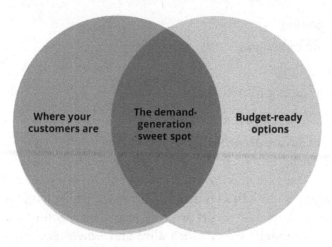

Figure 3.2   The GTM Sweet Spot

instruments they select playing together in harmony. The best demand-generation systems consider the full complement of marketing and sales teams, tools, and techniques available to maximize the total value. The best demand-generation systems see the whole strategy together as greater than the sum of its parts. The best demand-generation systems are design-built.

Design-Building Your Demand-Generation System

To maximize the value of the demand-generation system, it needs to be constructed with both the holistic view of your marketing, sales, and service delivery goals as well as your team's capabilities and limitations. Here is where the System 1 work that was done documenting the elements of your sales process provides a foundation for the demand-generation system. And it's many of those same project representatives who should serve once more on the design-build project committee.

As covered in System 1, the size and complexity of a customer journey drive the sales motion needed. Larger, higher-value, more complex journeys are met with longer, more detailed sales motions. Those sales motions require – and customer values justify – a wider range of demand-gen tactics. As customer size diminishes and customer journeys shorten, the go-to-market options for demand gen simplify.

Design-Build Demand-Generation Case: Account-Based/Field Sales

Going after the biggest client accounts in the land justifies the investment of significant resources, but to pull it off and see results, you'll need significant resourcefulness. Throwing money at enterprise clients does not by itself return contracts. This is particularly the case with the most sought-after clients. For that you need to design-build a cross-function, coordinated approach.

Each business works within its own market with its own product or services and is constrained or empowered by its own unique set of resources. Laying down a specific blueprint as a one-size-fits-all approach to go-to-market demand-gen strategies seldom pays off. But to help better visualize how to design-build a high-ticket demand-generation system, let's workshop an example.

Case: The business sells a software platform for government agencies at the state and municipal levels. The persona targeted are senior public officers (mayors and city managers) of smaller municipalities and IT professionals in government agencies in larger cities and at the state level in the United States. The average first contract value of a single client is $250,000 with a lifetime customer value well into the seven figures.

First the design-side: You've Skoked your sales economics and analyzed your customer persona and how to best meet them. Budget has been approved, solutions evaluated and decided, and resources allocated for the following demand-gen investments to help build early-stage pipeline.

- Two business development representatives (BDRs) for every account exec to help set appointments with key accounts
- Lead-sourcing software to help build lead lists with email, phone number, and date
- Sales automation software to help organize and track outbound calling and emailing
- Intent data tracking to alert sales when visitors from government offices visit site pages

- Daily blog publishing of awareness, consideration, and decision-stage content
- Paid media campaigns on Google and IT-specific networks for display ads
- PR campaigns aimed at branded article placement (earned media) in target municipalities
- ebooks and whitepaper materials to create early-stage lead conversions
- Marketing automation that is used to help maintain visibility with valuable contacts and pull early-stage leads into late-stage conversions
- An interactive assessment tool and agency ROI calculator for lead conversion and lead nurturing and sales enablement
- Radio ads in targeted municipalities
- $25,000 events budget for each account exec

The significant lifetime customer value has armed demand gen with a heavy complement of tools, tactics, and personnel to build awareness and convert pipeline. Each of the above-listed investments has merit as a stand-alone effort. But the assumption here is that your competitors have all the same capabilities and are using them. How do you get an edge if they've leveled the playing field?

Here is where design-build acts as a force multiplier. By putting together a design-build project workstream, we bring marketing and sales together to collaborate on how to maximize the value of all investments. This is where design-minded cross-function coordination and build-minded execution come together to construct a holistic go-to-market strategy.

- Two BDRs for every account exec (AE) to help set appointments with key accounts. Intent data localize their efforts on which contacts to prioritize: ebooks, whitepapers, and interactive tools are all used as value-adds in cadences to elicit conversion.
- Daily blog publishing of awareness, consideration, and decision-stage content. Select blog articles are ghost-written for account

execs and published in their names, helping build individual thought leadership and sales enablement. BDRs invite select prospects to be interviewed for the blog as part of their connect-and-engage cadence campaigns. Blogs are automatically published on every BDR's and AE's social account using marketing automation software, helping to maximize reach.

- PR campaigns aimed at branded article placement (earned media) in target municipalities. Articles from select media are published on the social media accounts of the BDRs and AEs in corresponding geographies.

- $25,000 events budget for each account exec. BDRs and account execs collaborate with marketing and customer success to promote attendance at geo-specific events. Current customers make up the initial list. Targeted prospects are approached by BDRs and AEs with the value of meeting current clients to network and share industry knowledge. The PR team is involved to get media coverage to add value for elected officials to attend the event. Photos, videos, and testimonials are recorded to be used for later sales and marketing campaigns.

Here you can see the power design-build can have when teams collaborate using a holistic strategy. A blog article isn't just a means to add content to your website and build SEO authority. A blog is a tool for account executive brand building and an open invitation to prospective clients to help them share ideas, be recognized, and build their own thought leadership, used as a conversion offer by BDRs. An event isn't just a lead-generation tool. It's also a venue for community building, a means for current clients to help advocate for you, and a content engine for future geo-targeted campaigns.

Fields sales and account-based marketing live or die through collaboration and communication. The teams need to have clear lines of sight into what each of the others are planning to do before they start construction. Putting stakeholders from each of these teams together, who go through each investment line item being considered, and ask the simple question, "What is everything we can do to maximize the impact of this effort?" is a solid place to start.

The Demand-Gen Productivity Flywheel

In the Process System, we covered the concept of the customer flywheel. The customer-value motion perpetually creates more and more energy as opportunities convert into customers and customers into advocates. Customer advocacy brings the energy input around full circle, creating new opportunities and energizing the revenue organization. Working in parallel to this is the demand-gen productivity flywheel powered by the deliberate efforts of the sales team.

Like with setting up a go-to-market demand-generation strategy, each productivity flywheel needs to be design-built to the specs of each company's sales motion. In order to help visualize the process, let's once again workshop a case.

Design-Building the Productivity Flywheel Case: SMB Inside Sales

Case: A 200-employee marketing agency offering web design and development services to small and mid-sized (SMB) clients. The go-to-market is primarily inbound marketing fueled by content marketing and paid media as the top lead-gen sources. The sales motion is a three-step, inside sales process with a 30-day sales cycle from stage 1 to Deal Won. The average contract value is $25,000, non-recurring revenue, and sales reps are given five months to reach full ramped quota.

The sales process in this agency is as follows.

Stage 1 – Connect. Make live contact with leads and complete a light qualification for the current interest in investing in website design or redesign and confirmation of authority figures needed to evaluate service vendors.

Stage 2 – Site assessment/scoping meeting. Evaluate site needs, current state/shortcomings, and company goals for the website. Educate on general services offers and qualify budget range, decision process, and timeline.

Stage 3 – Present a formal website redesign package offer, send the contract, work through objections, or close.

You've Skoked the economics and determined that an individual sale rep needs to deliver $50,000 in top-line revenue every month to maintain a healthy efficiency. Operations, marketing, and sales leadership have collaborated to determine the realistic productivity measures for a rep to achieve on-target performance.

To hit $50,000/month a rep must generate 14 stage 1 ops, convert 50% to qualified stage 2 Qualified Ops, convert 70% of Qualified Ops to stage 3 Scope Presentation, and win 40% of opportunities presented with a package. The conversion metrics are fairly basic. Where build-side sales personnel inform the design-side dashboard planners is with the reality check on how reps will actually hit the 14 stage 1 live connect ops.

In Figure 3.3, you'll see that the rep is forecast to hit her $50,000/month in month 5. Her channels of opportunity generation, however, do not reach full maturity until month 7. Designers have provided what needs to get done and by when. Builders fill in the details on the how.

Month 1 – The rep is in full new-hire onboarding and has not yet been added to the new inbound leads rotation. She starts practicing her outreach with the old inbound leads and outbound leads bases. S1 goal is four from old inbound and one from cold outbound.

Month 2 – The rep has now completed new-hire onboarding and is added to the new inbound leads rotation where she is expected to generate six S1 ops. She does not have any new leads in her contacts base carrying over from the previous month or expert-level skills to convert, so expectations run at 60% of full productivity. The old inbound leads and outbound leads bases are expected to contribute four and three ops respectively. The first stage 2 ops appear in month 2 as the sales cycle matures.

Expenses	Month 1	Month 2	Month 3	Month 4	Month 5	Month 6	Month 7	Month 8	Month 9	Month 10	Month 11	Month 12
Base Salary	$ 5,833	$ 5,833	$ 5,833	$ 5,833	$ 5,833	$ 5,833	$ 5,833	$ 5,833	$ 5,833	$ 5,833	$ 5,833	$ 5,833
Variable Compensation	$ -	$ -	$ -	$ 2,917	$ 3,833	$ 5,833	$ 5,833	$ 5,833	$ 5,833	$ 5,833	$ 5,833	$ 5,833
Overhead	$ 2,083	$ 2,083	$ 2,083	$ 2,083	$ 2,083	$ 2,083	$ 2,083	$ 2,083	$ 2,083	$ 2,083	$ 2,083	$ 2,083
Cost of leads required	$ -	$ -	$ -	$ 5,576	$ 11,152	$ 11,152	$ 11,152	$ 11,152	$ 11,152	$ 11,152	$ 11,152	$ 11,152
Total Expenses	$ 7,917	$ 7,917	$ 7,917	$ 16,409	$ 24,902	$ 24,902	$ 24,902	$ 24,902	$ 24,902	$ 24,902	$ 24,902	$ 24,902
Cumulative expenses	$ 7,917	$ 15,833	$ 23,750	$ 40,159	$ 65,061	$ 89,963	$ 114,865	$ 139,767	$ 164,669	$ 189,571	$ 214,473	$ 239,375

Breakeven Analysis	Month 1	Month 2	Month 3	Month 4	Month 5	Month 6	Month 7	Month 8	Month 9	Month 10	Month 11	Month 12
Net profit	$ (7,917)	$ (7,917)	$ (7,917)	$ (3,284)	$ 1,348	$ 1,348	$ 1,348	$ 1,348	$ 1,348	$ 1,348	$ 1,348	$ 1,348
Cumulative Net Profit	$ (7,917)	$ (15,833)	$ (23,750)	$ (27,034)	$ (25,686)	$ (24,338)	$ (22,990)	$ (21,642)	$ (20,294)	$ (18,946)	$ (17,598)	$ (16,250)

Figure 3.3 Skok Analysis #3

Month 3 – The rep is now working with carryover leads from the previous month, and her connect stage skills are beginning to mature, expecting them to deliver 80% of her S1 conversion capacity. The ops pipeline is filling out more with two deals reaching stage 3.

Month 4 – The rep is now expected to be working at full conversion capacity with new inbound leads, pulling 10 of the 14 S1 ops she needs for the month from that queue. Old inbound leads are providing the remaining four S1 ops and with later-stage deals now consuming time, low-value outbound prospecting has been eliminated from the rep's routine. Of the five S3 ops she has presented to in months 3 and 4, she is expected to convert her first Won deal. She shows a lower than optimal conversion rate (20%) due to immature late-stage conversion skills and opportunities originating from lower-value channels.

Months 5 and 6 – The rep's conversion metrics are now fully mature, and she is generating her full quota of $50,000/month.

Month 7 – The final transition of the rep's channel maturity takes place. She is now generating two high-quality opportunities per month from older, closed lost ops coming back or referral-generated opportunities from recently sold clients. Time spent working lower-quality old ops is cut in half.

Month 7 is when the flywheel comes full cycle. A well-treated opportunities base, nurtured and followed up with, comes back to life. Well-sold clients advocate and help make introductions to new S1 opportunities. The $50,000 revenue delivery is maintained, allowing the rep the reward of a more achievable goal as long as she puts in the work of conversion-skill maturity and invests her time in the channels indicated to yield the best results over time.

The Demand-Gen Productivity Calendar

Time management is self-management. Handing a new rep the itemized opportunity-conversion expectations for each available channel offers clear guidance on where to focus and what is expected as a return on time invested. For greater clarity on when and how much to work, consider offering a sample calendar.

There's a fine balance here that needs to be struck between constraining reps with too rigid an agenda versus completely open, make-it-up-as-you-go scheduling. There are objective best practices that help maximize productivity in the areas of bucketing tasks together, time-to-lead attempts, or high-conversion times to prospect. Conversely, over-structuring a rep's agenda is a fast way to kill their morale. They'll feel a lack of trust and autonomy to run their own businesses.

Design-build modeling is key here. Not only is this balance critical during the construction of a productivity calendar, but also when messaging its value. The goal of a demand-gen productivity calendar is to arm sales with a roadmap for working smarter, not harder. Through data-driven optimized scheduling, it should be understood at each level that structure will provide more freedom, not less.

Let's break down the elements of a sample productivity calendar. Once again, we will use the web design agency example. The time blocks you'll see are grouped by specific activities. Batching the work promotes focus on a specific set of tasks, optimizing performance (the quality of work done on the tasks) and efficiency (the time needed to perform the tasks).

A productivity calendar like this is created by the rep (build-side) on their terms, with their manager guiding the process (design-side) with an experienced and trained eye. (See Figure 3.4.) The best way to maximize productivity, and minimize micro-management, is to design-build a productivity calendar early with the rep owning the process. Time invested in collaborating on this early saves spending time on establishing and re-establishing productivity expectations later on.

Connect Blocks – 10.5 hours/week. The agency rep needs to hold 14 stage 1 live connect calls in a month for on-target productivity. New opportunities feed this business's flywheel so the rep needs to stay on top of prospecting and connect activities like calling, emailing, and social selling. Connect blocks are spread across every day, maintaining the regular cadences needed to stay in front of leads and to maximize conversion into new opportunities. Blocks are scheduled in both mornings and afternoons, varying the attempts to reach leads, further maximizing connect rates.

Daily Practice, 8am	Daily Practice, 8am	Daily Practice, 8am	Daily Practice, 8am	Daily Practice, 8am
Email Triage, 8:30am	Email Triage, 8:30am	Email Triage, 8:30am	Email Triage, 8:30am	Email Triage, 8:30am
List-building, 9am	List-building, 9am	List-building, 9am	List-building, 9am	List-building, 9am
Weekly Team Meeting 9:30 – 10:30am	Flex 9:30 – 10:30am	Connect Block 9:30 – 10:30am	Connect Block 9:30 – 10:30am	Weekly 1-1 9:30 – 10:30am
Connect Block 10:30am – 12pm	Connect Block 10:30am – 12pm	Flex 10:30am – 12pm	Flex 10:30am – 12pm	Connect Block 10:30am – 12pm
Lunch 12 – 1pm	Lunch 12 – 1pm	Lunch 12 – 1pm	Lunch 12 – 1pm	Lunch 12 – 1pm
Email Traige, 1pm	Email Traige, 1pm	Email Traige, 1pm	Email Traige, 1pm	Email Traige, 1pm
List Building, 1:30pm	List Building, 1:30pm	Flex 1:30 – 2:30pm	Flex 1:30 – 2:30pm	List Building, 1:30pm
Connect Block 2 – 3pm	Connect Block 2 – 3pm	Email Triage, 2:30pm	Email Triage, 2:30pm	Flex 2 – 3pm
Email Triage, 3pm	Email Triage, 3pm	List Building, 3pm	List Building, 3pm	Email Triage, 3pm
Flex 3:30 – 4:30pm	Flex 3:30 – 4:30pm	Connect Block 3:30 – 4:30pm	Connect Block 3:30 – 4:30pm	Reserved for Co. 3:30 – 4:30pm
Email Triage, 4:30pm	Email Triage, 4:30pm	Email Triage, 4:30pm	Email Triage, 4:30pm	Email Triage, 4:30pm
Next Day Prep, 5pm	Next Day Prep, 5pm	Next Day Prep, 5pm	Next Day Prep, 5pm	Next Day Prep, 5pm

Figure 3.4 The Demand-Gen Productivity Calculator

List-Building – 5 hours/week. Effective connect prospecting requires clean, prepared lists of contacts to work on. Contact lists are constantly changing, with new leads coming in, progressing through cadences, and moving out of connect sequencing. To maximize the value of a connect block, reps need to allot time to prepare lists of leads that will yield the best returns on their time investment.

Flex Time – 9 hours/week. Just as it sounds, flex time is there for the rep to fill out her calendar as she sees fit. At full ramp, she'll need to hold seven stage 2 and five stage 3 calls every month, consuming an average of three hours/week of flex time. Each of these calls will require preparation time, follow-up time, and CRM note-taking time. The rep also needs to hold two closed won calls and have time available to work through the order processing of those deals. Mental breaks, mid-day workouts, impromptu meetings, pipeline updates, training and practicing sessions, content creation, and social media promotion are all possible uses of open flex time for the rep.

Email Triage – 10 hours/week. Either you manage your inbox, or your inbox manages you. In a well-structured productivity calendar, the diversion, attention-killing email inbox upkeep is contained in four 30-minute time blocks spread out throughout the day. This allows a rep to stay on top of replies to her prospecting emails, which are vital to her demand-gen productivity. The discipline to productivity is going all-in on an activity with full attention, then switching it off completely when working on the next task. Nowhere will your attention be more tested than in your inbox.

Company, Team, and 1-1 Meetings – 3 hours/week. Investing regular time for company updates, team-building exercises, performance reviews, and 1-1 coaching is a must. In order to not eat up hours where reps have the highest hit rate for connecting with prospects, scheduling these meetings during low connect hours is best. In the calendar shown here, these meetings, by design, are set for early Monday, early Friday, and end-of-day Friday. (More on this in System 5 – The Ongoing Improvement System.)

Daily Kickstart Training – 2.5 hours/week. Skills are perishable. If they go unused, they wither and die. And even when used with great regularity, they often become corrupted by bad habits. Cars that are regularly on the road start to pull and need occasional realignment. Such is the case for each of the hundreds of micro-skills needed to perform in a sales role at the highest level. At Rock, we used triplesession .com for daily organized micro-skill training. It's the first activity of the day to help build the habit of waking up the brain and getting skills strong for the challenges of the day.

Midday Lunch – 5 hours/week. Seems obvious, but too many people who work in a completely open, unstructured schedule end up skipping lunch. Don't. Even from a pure business benefit perspective, nutrition helps performance. Intermittently stepping away from the work helps nourish the mind. Take a midday break and eat something, if not right at 12 noon, during one of the flex blocks.

Next-Day Prep – 2.5 hours/week. Like so many aspects of sales, performance is only as good as the preparation that preceded it. Finishing one day by looking ahead at the next lays down the tracks to successful outcomes. What preset calls are on the calendar? Has each one been prepared for? How much demand-gen work will be in tomorrow's diet? Are lists ready, or will contact prospecting be needed? Next-day prep is also where many reps take a few minutes to write down learnings from that day and micro-goals for the day ahead. A process of daily reflection is the cornerstone of building self-awareness. Greater self-awareness strengthens emotional intelligence.

When introducing the productivity calendar it's important to explain the why behind the model to earn the rep's buy-in. Bucketing tasks, maintaining organized time blocks, and staying disciplined about small accomplishments each day yields long-term value, but only when the team sticks to the plan. It's easy to overwrite a prospecting and connecting block to take a demo request. It's harder to work with prospects within just flex blocks.

The reality is that it's highly unlikely that a rep ever loses a client due to scheduling that works around prospecting blocks. But it's guaranteed that you'll lose demand-gen ops if a rep is not on top of new conversions fast and does not stay disciplined to a connecting cadence. Consistency is key when building the Demand-Generation System.

To achieve buy-in, rather than constructing a rep's agenda and forcing a rigid timetable on them, stay disciplined in design-build. (Heed the learnings of Ignaz Semmelweis.) Offer inputs, best practices, and data on optimal outreach times (design-side) and ask reps to write the script of how their days should unfold (build-side). The end results when buy-in is achieved and productivity calendars are followed are optimization with ownership and a happier, more effective team.

Funnel vs. Flywheel

Each demand-generation strategy is a school of thought unto itself. It's not the focus of this book to dive deeply into a specific demand channel. Inbound, Outbound, ABM, and so on – each warrant not just their own books but their own libraries. There is, however, a broader division worthwhile to explore. The demand-gen funnel vs. the demand-gen flywheel: Between the two, there's a clear winner, and it's available (to some extent) to every sales organization.

The demand-generation funnel has a beginning and middle, and when the customer buys, a definitive end. When the customer is in, the sales rep is left to start the pipeline building over again at the top of the funnel from zero. Leads prospecting, whether from inbound requests or outbound attempts are initiated without any association from the existing base of opportunities or customers.

In a flywheel system, each opportunity and customer that enters the system opens up a potential new source of leads. The new leads fuel the early-stage demand and the next generation of opportunities. The opportunities mature, deals are won or lost, and from them new leads are created. More opportunities and customers produce more opportunities and customers, who produce more opportunities and customers.

The flywheel system feeds off its own energy, growing bigger over time. It's not to say the external demand gen of net new opportunities should be ignored. It's not either internal OR external demand gen but internal AND external.

The funnel demand-gen strategy fails to incorporate internal demand-gen tactics. The flywheel, when done right, incorporates both. But this compounding effect of snowballing demand generation rarely happens by accident. You need to plan and execute on a number of fronts. You need to design-build a demand-generation flywheel.

Design-Building a Demand-Generation Flywheel

To construct a demand-generation flywheel inside your sales organization, start by bringing marketing, ops, sales leaders, and select frontline reps together for the design-build project committee. Identify all the possible lead-gen nodes in the sales and marketing processes (design-side).

After mapping all nodes, reps and managers should weigh in on the practicality of executing an internal demand-gen approach at each point of the conversation (build-side). Not only does this add context and foresight to plan, it also gives the builders a voice and accountability for the eventual execution. This is the reason you want some frontline salespeople in the room. They provide context and also act as ambassadors to the plan with the rest of the build team.

Let's examine four of the most common nodes operated within a sales organization to power a demand-gen flywheel.

The Early-Stage Ops Node

Early-stage opportunities that enter your sales pipeline have already cleared a number of quality hurdles. They've shown initial interest in the problem or opportunity you helped to raise awareness on. Many come in already interested in your solution specifically. They are often within or associated with ideal customer-profile businesses (when outbound generated they always are). The contact frequently has professional connections to other contacts who do fit your ICP.

Especially when working with bigger ticket, land, and expand type sales motions, working to get introductions from early-stage opportunities can be a great source of demand energy for your flywheel. Design and build need to collaborate on the right messaging to contacts this early in the process. It's important to maintain primary attention to the active prospect while still working to source the introduction.

A common approach is to ask for invitations to high-value contacts connected to a prospect after a rep has delivered value (say, on an initial consultation/advisory call), especially if it was determined that fit or timing weren't there. In this case, there is no immediate loss to that specific conversation, and it opens an opportunity for a rep to get some value back for his time investment in the opportunity rather than just moving to close-lost with nothing to show for it. Also, the largest volume of opportunities in most sales pipelines are early-stage close-lost. The sheer volume of shots on goal in the early stage can make a significant difference to your demand-gen engine.

The Late-Stage Ops Node

When working with late-stage ops, the risks are higher, but so are the possible rewards. Late-stage ops are all qualified ICP (you wouldn't have invested the time to work with them to the late stage otherwise). They're also more engaged with possibly buying your product or service, and the value you have delivered through your consultative process is much greater than in the early stage. The likelihood of getting a targeted introduction is often greater late-stage, and the quality can often be higher (great-fit prospects tend to know other great-fit prospects).

With late-stage referral prospecting, I personally lean away from introducing this subject until the opportunity is closed won or closed lost. When a late-stage opportunity is engaged in the process and still moving toward purchase, I focus all efforts on that outcome, moving the referral conversation to post-purchase.

The best salespeople I've ever known didn't achieve great results by selling hard to win deals. What they did best was to do well-focused work on the most-qualified opportunities and hit the high-percentage shots. Just like with early-stage ops, when late-stage ops are lost, squeeze a return out of the time investment with the ask for introductions, especially when you've developed a strong champion.

The Customer Node

Working with your existing customers is the most obvious example of flywheel demand gen, and sadly the most overlooked. Dale Carnegie is famously quoted as saying "91% of clients will give a referral, but only 11% of salespeople will ask [for] one." In my experience the 91% is right on, and the 11% is optimistic in today's sales world. Except in the teams who have design-built a referral motion as a fundamental step in their process. This is the flywheel opportunity that virtually every sales team has available to them.

The keys are design implementation in CRM and build execution and reinforcement. Design needs to do their part by creating the process infrastructure like CRM fields that are specific for referral inquiry outcomes tied to monthly productivity reports. Example:

- **Required Field for Closed-Won Deal Stage:** "Asked for Referral"
- **Drop-Down Options:** Yes. No.
- **No Selected:** Open Text Box: "Why not?"
- **Yes Selected:** Drop-Down Options: Got referral. Asked to send email. Asked to revisit later. Declined to refer.

For the builders, sales leaders need to create the playbook guides for the team to follow for this step of the process and hold their people accountable. For reps, execute. Understand the value of asking for introductions to high-value leads from your customers who trust you enough to buy from you. Be consistent. Practice. Ask your managers for help through coaching to hone your skills. The results will follow.

The Closed-Lost Node

As previously mentioned, closed-lost opportunities can be a great source of demand gen at the moment when the initial decision is made not to move forward. It's no surprise that revisiting lost opportunities at a future date can be a means of reactivating a valuable pipeline. What is a surprise is how few sales organizations appropriately plan to do just that.

Too often closed-lost deals are revisited at random intervals and typically with little information recorded from the previous conversations with the sales team. It's a breakdown resulting from builders building day-in, day-out, without proper design infrastructure in place to create long-term value inside deal records. Design-build organizations take this very seriously. Particularly design-side.

I started my career building, first as a BDR, later a rep and then a front-line manager. But even when I began investing more time in design as VP of Sales and later CRO, I still missed the boat on long-term data value on closed-lost deals.

In 2019 I looked inside our closed-lost column inside CRM to find we had accrued more than 20,000 records – all with little to no valuable data recorded to filter or reflect on. I asked myself, "What if we had collected the critical data on these deals that would tell us of all the lost deals, which is the 1% most likely to buy if we called them today?"

Having that intel would have added 200 high-percentage ops to the pipeline. They were in the CRM, but buried inside a list of 19,900 other ops of lesser quality and impossible to find without reworking each one from zero again. At the time, the team was selling between 80 and 100 deals/month. The way I saw it, we could be confident that at least 1% of the old base would buy on a second go-around; then we were sitting on about two months of revenue in our closed-lost base. And that number would grow with each new month as we added more lost opportunities to the heap.

To stop the bleeding, Rev Ops (design) stepped in, working with sales reps and managers to map the critical info needed to qualify a deal, and then built that into the CRM. They created fields with drop -downs, open texts, and locks. The locks helped to ensure that reps would leave each stage of the sales process having recorded the valuable data they would need later on to find the gold in the closed-lost mountain.

Fields with drop-down selections are key for reporting and filtering. Open text boxes are important for reps to add context and detail that cannot be captured in a pre-set option. Some stuff to consider for field capture and format:

- **Problem/Opportunity** – Checkboxes to select one or multiple answers to the problems your solutions solve followed by an open text box requiring more detail.
- **Champion Level** – Drop-Down Options 1 – High, 2 – Mid, 3 – None. (Measures how passionate the champion was as your internal advocate fighting to get approval to buy from you.)
- **Budget Available** – Drop-Down Options – Yes, Needs Approval, No. When yes is selected, a secondary drop-down with confirmed budget ranges.
- **Current Provider** – Drop-Down Options with list of competitors, also with internal, broad terms like "agency" and "none" as selection options.
- **Competition Engaged in Process** – Drop-Down Options with list of competitors.
- **Closed-Lost Reason** – Drop-Down Options with list of common reasons for losing a deal followed by an open text box requiring more detail.

This is just a short list of the types of information you may want to consider when revisiting a closed-lost base of opportunities. Combine this information with the deal stage at the time of loss and deal value information and you have a powerful weapon in the fight against pipeline erosion. Imagine how your approach would change considering the three very different lost deal samples shown in Figure 3.5.

Lost Deal 1	Lost Deal 2	Lost Deal 3
High Value Problem Identified	High Value Problem Identified	Low Value Problem Identified
Champion Level 1	Champion Level 2	Champion Level 3
Budget Available - Need Approval	Budget Available - Yes	Budget Available - Need Approval
Current Provider - None	Current Provider - Competitor	Current Provider - None
Competitor Engaged in Process - No	Competitor Engaged in Process - Yes	Competitor Engaged in Process - Yes
Close Lost Stage - Negotiation	Close Lost Stage - Negotiation	Close Lost Stage - Demo
Closed Lost Reason - Econ Buyer Declined	Closed Lost Reason - Chose Competitor	Closed Lost Reason - Disengaged
Deal Value - $75k	Deal Value - $55k	Deal Value - Undefined

Figure 3.5 Closed-Lost Deal Analysis

Lost Deal 1 is a great flywheel opportunity. The filters alone tell you that the deal was lost late with a champion who fought hard to get the budget to buy but was not able to get the economic buyer on board. As there was a high-value problem identified and a level 1 champion, the chances of winning the deal on a second or third attempt are higher. If the champion switched to another ICP company, you want to have had a regular conversation along the way to open that opportunity.

Lost Deal 2 was also lost late but to a competitor. This is a classic case of a deal that should be nurtured by marketing for most of the year, then revisited by sales before the competitor's contract comes up for renewal. With the open text box associated with the closed-lost field, the rep can review the details behind why the competitor was chosen and if they were effective in solving the identified problem.

Lost Deal 3 is thin. No real problem was identified, no champion established, and the deal never matured to the point of a proposal as the buyer disappeared. This deal would likely best be nurtured by marketing and never looked at again by sales unless the contact reconverts or if used for practice when ramping new reps.

Every sales call offers valuable learning. Recording sales-gathered information inside your CRM provides demand-gen value, not just to sales, but to marketing and product as well. With closed-lost reports, marketing can glean valuable insights as to what messaging is hitting, what channels high-value prospects are coming from, competitors to be ready for, and objections to creating sales-enablement material to combat. Product and services teams can learn more about what problems are prevalent that need solutions built and which competitors are winning clients and the differentiation they are offering.

Design-building demand gen is the gift that keeps on giving. It's the silver lining to losing deals. We all want to win on the first attempt. But the more deals we lose means the more lost opportunities you will have to revisit down the road to help add value to the pipeline. As the opportunities-base grows the flywheel spins faster . . . but only when built right.

Health Check Reporting Inside the Demand-Generation System

Many key components are soldered together when making a demand-generation machine, and any one of them can break down, causing the entire engine to come grinding to a stop. Catching inefficiencies, substandard productivity, and wasteful investments early is paramount. Some health-check stats to consider tracking closely and reporting on regularly are:

- Total contacts created
- Total MQLs (marketing qualified leads)
- Total SQLs (sales qualified leads)
- Time to first attempt
- Number of attempts
- Days in status
- Total accounts created (product-led sales)
- Total accounts activated (product-led sales)
- Opportunities created
- Cost per contact
- Cost per MQL
- Cost per SQL
- Cost per account created (product-led sales)
- Cost per activation (product-led sales)

- Cost per opportunity created
- Cost to acquire a customer (CAC)
- Cost to acquire a dollar of revenue
- CAC vs. lifetime value (LTV) of the customer

All of the above should be tracked and cross-referenced by channel and individual salesperson to offer a clear picture of the health of the system. Referring back to the root-cause analysis methodology in System 1, you will need data capture and trend reporting to effectively uncover the source of demand-generation system breakdowns.

Along with the daily productivity scorecard, it's common practice to distribute daily reports to the team that tracks their productivity. Stack ranking reports that show total active contacts by rep, the average number of attempts by rep, days in stays by rep, and so on help reps stay on track and in line with their peers on early-stage productivity measures.

Not only does daily productive reporting build greater awareness and accountability with reps, it also serves as a valuable coaching and training tool. When sales leaders see performance starting to dip in an individual rep's activity or conversion, a data-driven action plan can quickly be put in place to help rebound. Should teamwide or channel-specific productivity drop, teamwide training and collaboration with marketing can be quickly initiated to reverse the trend. Visibility creates accountability, and accountability creates action.

Monthly/Quarterly Retrospectives

Daily demand-gen reports help add accountability and agility to performance but lack the broader trends and insights needed to clearly see patterns of performance. Sales teams work in cycles. Teams on a monthly sales goal look very different in week 1 than in week 4. On a quarterly cycle, months 1, 2, and 3 all take on a personality of their own. This is where grouping demand-gen data into monthly and quarterly data sets adds value.

Numbers DO lie. Or rather, we often compile numbers in untruthful ways. Retrospectives that look holistically at longer and broader ranges of data sets help surface the truth. Let's look at two examples of this:

Example 1: Short-term vs. long-term view

- Paid media generates a large volume of low-cost MQLs. Conclusion: Paid media is high value.
- Paid media MQLs have a low conversion from lead to opportunity. Conclusion: Paid media is low value.
- Opportunities created from paid media MQLs have a high conversion rate and short sales cycle. Conclusion: Paid media is high value.
- New customers generated from paid media MQLs have an average contract value 30% lower than the average. Conclusion: Paid media is low value.
- Existing customers that originated from a paid media MQL conversion have the highest lifetime value of all channel segments.

As you can see here, the devil is in the details when it comes to data range. The demand-gen channel (in this case paid media) can be seen as high-value or low-value depending on when you cut off the data set. Zooming out and looking at the widest range of data helps provide the truth, the whole truth, and not just a partial truth.

Example 2: Narrow vs. broad view

- Sales rep Mike Jones creates almost no referral leads. Conclusion: Mike Jones has substandard referral prospecting skills and needs to increase the quantity of prospecting, quality of prospecting, or both.
- Sales rep Mike Jones converts 80% of referral opportunities to new customers, 30% higher than the team average. Mike Jones has high-quality referral op conversion skills.
- Sales rep Mike Jones records above-average prospecting and opportunity-creation performance compared to the team when viewing all available channels. Conclusion: Mike Jones has high-quality prospecting and op creation skills.

- Sales rep Mike Jones is historically in the top 10% of total new revenue sold compared to the rest of the sales team. Conclusion: Mike Jones has a healthy overall sales performance.

- Sales rep Mike Jones has a below-average lifetime value of his deals sold compared to the rest of the sales team. Conclusion: Mike Jones has substandard ICP selection or expectation-setting with his clients.

Once again, the perception of performance changes based on the limits of the data set. The global analysis of Mike Jones is likely that he is overall an above-average rep but isn't great at getting referrals. Also, referred customers may have a higher lifetime value, which may be contributing to his under-performance there.

Why this nuance matters comes down to what information you will use when creating action plans. And who Mike Jones is matters. Working with Mike on getting more referrals may help take a B player to A player status. It may also tank his performance in the areas where he is already performing at an above-average level. Remember, Mike is selling in the top 10% of the team. That is an important stat to help inform what action his leader should take or if any action should be taken at all.

At Rock, the sales cadence was monthly in the early days and then transitioned to a quarterly cycle. My rev ops leader and I met every Monday, looking at data that was updated weekly but consolidated in month-over-month and quarter-over-quarter views. This allowed us to zoom out and recognize patterns and trends more readily.

One example was early-stage deal volume. I personally love hustle and seeing reps highly active, working hard to create a lot of opportunities. When we looked at longer-term retrospectives, though, high-volume deal creation turned out to be a predictor of low performance in revenue attainment. What we learned was that the reps who did high-volume work were also the ones who did high-velocity work. They moved opportunities through the process too quickly, missed vital details, failed to plan and execute key elements of the dialogue with prospects, and as a result sold less.

Demand-Generation System Rituals

Demand generation never stops. And if you're building a flywheel, not only does it never stop, it grows. But like all machines, maintenance is required, and upkeep is needed in order to keep everyone on track. Here are a few rituals that can help keep demand-gen momentum moving in a positive direction.

Reply-All Recognition to Reporting

Reporting itself is a ritual. Combining that with reply-all recognition goes a long way to building morale. For most salespeople working leads, making outbound calls, asking for introductions, and reactivating old opportunities is a grind. Even the reps who do it effectively or BDRs who are hired exclusively to do that work often view it as a necessary evil to the job.

Sales leaders can help take the edge off with occasional shout-outs. A reply-all to a report calling out the hustle of one rep who hit the phones hard one day sets a tone of appreciation and achievement. That rep's spirits will likely be uplifted from the recognition, reinforcing the positive behavior, and the rest of the team can take notice that their performance, strong or weak, is not going unnoticed.

Smart sales leaders don't limit the demand-gen recognition to sales alone. Marketing, we all know, is instrumental in feeding the pipeline. Let them know it. If it's hard to localize to just one person for a solid MQL performance or an increase in the quality of leads from a specific channel, put the whole team on the reply-all thread. Take care of the people who take care of you and let marketing know their work matters.

Demand-Generation Cross-Training

At scale, teams become diverse groups of different reps who excel at different areas of the job. If the sales team leader is doing his job, he is hiring people who are better than he is in a number of areas or who grow to be better than he is over time. Superior demand-gen skills in certain reps emerge, often quickly due to the volume of practice. These reps are powerful allies in the effort to help better the performance of the entire team.

A great routine is to have the top-demand-gen performers train their peers. We'll discuss more on the overall practice and benefits of cross-training in System 5, but the benefits of the Demand-Generation System are worth noting here. When reps hear directly from one of their own regarding best practices in approaching and opening up new opportunities, it goes a long way toward building their confidence in the system. It also provides a lot of contextual knowledge as high-performing demand-gen reps can offer real examples of the "how to" conversation.

For the optimistic, coachable reps, cross-training provides great role models. For those less open-minded, hearing success cases from their own ranks helps undo some of the skepticism they may have when the message comes from a manager. For the reps who do the cross-training, it's a great motivator to continue with their high-grade performance. They become the reference on the team for demand-gen skills. The recognition reinforces the positive action.

Mistakes I've Made When Constructing the Demand-Generation System

Failures made when building out the demand-generation system don't always reveal themselves early. Insufficient or non-scalable demand gen is often a downstream effect. You sometimes won't see the negative repercussions of poor decision making for months, quarters, or even years. And the corrective actions needed can take just as long. Let's look at some of the biggest demand-gen missteps I've made over the years.

Failure to Skok

Starting my career in the sales trenches prepared me well for build-side thinking. I was weak on the design-side. In the early years of Rock, I moved fast and loose, growing the sales team from just 5 in April of

2015 to more than 20 by the end of that year to more than 40 by the end of the following year.

I was able to get away with this without much long-term planning since we had exceptional inbound demand generation, short sales cycles, and a strong talent-acquisition machine. Great talent can cover a lot of weak spots in your sales team and a company at large. (More on this in System 3.)

It wasn't until my business partner, a much stronger design thinker, introduced me to the Skok sheet that economics and long-range thinking came into focus. I look at the failure to Skok as a root cause for many of my other demand-gen mistakes. As the saying goes, prior planning prevents poor performance.

Failure to Diversify Demand-Gen Channels

As a company delivering a content-marketing solution, Rock ate its own dog food and was very inbound-marketing savvy. When I started with the company, we had five reps sharing more than 1,000 new inbound leads per month. And marketing was maturing faster than sales, so as quickly as I could hire, the inbound leads were growing. This was good news of course but also left me myopically focused on building an inbound-only team.

Eventually, the sales team scaled headcount to catch up with inbound demand, and we hit equilibrium and stopped growing through inbound alone. Moreover, we began to move our focus up-market where contract size and LTV were greater but lead flow lower. In our business, outbound sales and channel partnerships with marketing agencies would later prove to be valuable sources of customer acquisition, but I started too late.

Outbound and partner programs take time to warm up. The revenue gains from these efforts come months after you go live. They are, in effect, businesses unto themselves that you need to hire for, train, ramp, and work through their own, sometimes longer, sales cycles. I didn't take any of that into account soon enough and looked at diversification only when growth from inbound started to flatten. Revenue growth suffered as a result and hurt our overall performance as a company.

Failure to Specialize the Team for Demand-Gen Optimization

As a build guy, it was crystal clear to me early that specializing in customer focus was a no-brainer. I had worked in a number of sales teams throughout my career where reps focused on a specific customer type, and I was intimately familiar with those advantages. But specializing as a team by role is much more a design side skill and one which I failed to address early enough (failure 1) and when I did, I set up the processes poorly due to superficial planning (failure 2).

My initial take was to follow my own personal experience where inbound reps did all their own prospecting and deal creation. No sales development reps (SDRs) should be needed. This proved to be wrong on a number of fronts. The pure productivity gains of specializing in these roles made the split in job responsibilities worthwhile. Financially speaking, the team had a clear pathway for greater efficiency with an SDR than without one.

There were also gains in team morale and rep retention. AEs tend to enjoy their work more when they are focused on customer conversations and not prospecting. Happy AEs stay longer. More-tenured AEs, trained, ramped, and hitting quota with consistency are highly valuable to a sales organization. Turnover is expensive.

And possibly the biggest gain was that SDRs can be hired with little experience, trained and ramped quickly with little cost to the business, and provide a farm system for staffing the next generation of your AE ranks. Building an SDR team is tantamount to building a staffing engine inside your sales org.

When I did finally get around to building the SDR team, I failed to consider each component of this new process. How do we set up the CRM to require SDRs to collect and pass vital information to AEs? How do we divide up the leads to keep SDRs in their own lanes and not run into one another working on the same prospects? Can SDRs work with older, cold leads that haven't been touched in months? Should they?

This is where I needed to ask for design help to balance my build perspective of "just go sell." I didn't ask until much later, and as you can guess, problems ensued. SDRs fought over account ownership as they didn't have clear, documented guardrails. Some SDRs were great about setting up their AEs with solid info about the prospect. Others scheduled meetings without warning or preparation of what to expect. There were no standards, no playbooks unique to the SDRs, and no design.

Failure to Design-Build a Demand-Gen Flywheel

As detailed earlier in this chapter, there are two key levers a sales organization can pull entirely on its own to create a demand-gen flywheel: (1) setting up stalled or lost opportunities to effectively be reactivated later and (2) asking for referral introductions. I failed on both counts when initially setting up Rock's sales demand-gen processes.

As previously mentioned, it wasn't until more than 20,000 opportunities had been moved to the Close Lost column inside our CRM that I woke up to the importance of capturing searchable data from each sales interaction. In a perfect world, much of this is baked into the process system setup and incorporated early – every lost deal, complete with searchable data spelling out the quality of the opportunity, sets up future opportunities to rework later.

Regarding the process of asking for referral introductions, for years the demand-generation system I set up was part of Dale Carnegie's 91% statistic. Salespeople typically just won't make this effort unless it's part of a required process or it's ground into their personal sales habits. Like the lost op fields, referral asking and tracking should be included as part of the Process System setup and set as a day 1 expectation with reps, accompanied by playbooks, followed up with training, and tracked with regular performance reports. Referral opportunities are just too valuable for most businesses to consider only as an afterthought or not at all.

Checkpoint – System 2

It's a good time to explain the order of operations for the Six Systems of a Sales Organization. There's a logic to when each system is design-built and launched. Demand gen is System 2 only behind the setup of core processes and tracking.

Many sales leaders, myself included, have suffered the slings and arrows of scaling too fast, particularly in staffing up sales headcount ahead of figuring out predictable demand gen. This is a high-risk bet and one for which I have never seen the payoff.

How many salespeople should be hired at a given moment? What productivity metrics do they need to achieve their targets? What expectations should be set for where and how they will start conversations with potential clients? All of these are must-have questions to be answered with confidence before adding people to the team. None can effectively be answered before setting up the Demand-Generation system.

Clearly, if you hire too slowly, your team will lose efficiency, and the demand already generated will fall by the wayside. The perils of hiring too fast, ahead of demand gen, however, are far more grave. Rep efficiency is low. Nobody earns commissions. Morale tanks. People start complaining, believing you sold them a dream that never materialized (which unintentionally you did). Reps eventually jump ship, sometimes leaving a bad review on Glassdoor or other career or company ranking sites.

The greatest capital in any business is human capital. Scale up a sales team ahead of demand gen and you run the risk of burning that precious capital at a very high premium. But figure out the Demand-Generation System, at least on the small scale, and now it's time to hire. It's time to take action in the People System.

Notes

1. "Latin America and the Caribbean: More Women Business Leaders but Still Room for Progress at the Top," International Labour Organization, May 23, 2017, https://www.ilo.org/global/about-the-ilo/newsroom/news/WCMS_554702/lang--ja/index.htm.
2. David Skok, "SaaS Metrics: A Guide to Measuring and Improving What Matters," For Entrepreneurs, https://www.forentrepreneurs.com/saas-metrics/.

4

The People System

The Case of Arthur T. Demoulas – Market Basket

Lowell, Massachusetts, about 30 miles northwest of Boston, was once renowned as the birthplace of America's industrial revolution. In the first half of the nineteenth century, Boston industrialists bought up the farmland along the banks of the Merrimack and Concord Rivers. They built mammoth red-brick factories and fitted them as textile mills, turning cotton into the fabric a growing America needed for clothes.

The mills created a hiring boom. Immigrants, mostly Irish, Greek, and French-Canadian along with young women from across New England farming communities, flocked to Lowell for the opportunity of modern work in a state-of-the-art new city. From 1840 to 1880 Lowell's population tripled from 20,000 to 60,000.[1]

Demand for consistent labor was so great that for the first time in American history, the power dynamic tipped in favor of employees over management. Lowell workers routinely banded together to advocate for better working conditions, higher pay, and limits on the number of hours the company could mandate that employees put in each week. Many labor rights that exist today were either drafted or influenced by the efforts of nineteenth-century Lowell mill workers.

By the mid-1950s, New England mill towns were dying. Cheaper labor in southern U.S. states and overseas was pulling jobs away and shuttering the old factories. Lowell's economy, so dependent on the mills, was hit particularly hard. But fortunately, another revolution was about to take off: the supermarket boom. Many of the displaced mill workers would find employment at new, all-in-one grocery stores, which for the first time put produce, meat, fish, dairy, and dry goods all under one roof. At the center of this boom in Lowell was Market Basket.

Market Basket grew out of modest beginnings. Founded in 1917 by Greek immigrant Athanasios Demoulas, he began as a small grocer aiming to provide fresh lamb and other foods to the growing Greek community. By the mid-1950s, when Lowell mills were crashing, Demoulas's Market Basket was thriving. Then run by two of Athanasios' sons, George and Mike, the original store was rebuilt and expanded to several times larger, and additional stores were opened across Lowell and in neighboring towns. Growth took off, and a supermarket empire was born.

In high school, I worked at store 19 on Wood Street, in Lowell, collecting shopping carts from the parking lot, bagging groceries, and later stocking shelves. It was the late 1990s, and Mike Demoulas was running the day-to-day operations of the now 50+ stores across eastern Massachusetts, southern New Hampshire, and Maine. Mr. Demoulas ran a tight ship. Checkout stations had to be clean and dry, shelves full and well-organized, and floors spotless. Even bottom-of-the-pecking-order baggers like me had to be clean-shaven and show up to work in a white button-down shirt and tie.

There was no new-hire orientation or code of conduct form to be signed when starting (at least, none that I ever saw). But soon into my Market Basket tenure, the unspoken culture governing the business became clear to me. There were three core character elements the company held as required for all who work there.

1. There's no substitute for hard work.
2. Take care of the customer.
3. Market Basket takes care of its own.

In a Market Basket store, everyone has individual responsibilities, but with the expectation of contributing to a larger team. Both positive and negative work quality is felt and seen by all. When a cashier or bagger is slow or makes mistakes, it slows down the checkout lines, and work piles up for everyone else. When a stockboy fills his assigned section of canned goods or boxes of cereal fast and organized, he moves on to help with another coworker's section, lightening the load for a teammate. Scheduled performance reviews aren't needed. Performance at Market Basket is transparent and perpetual. Effort and quality of work are under constant review.

Market Basket's motto is "More for Your Dollar." You see it printed dead center on their shopping bags and emblazing the sides of their delivery trucks. The original store was founded in "The Acre," a particularly rough neighborhood in a generally rough city. As each new store opened, they tended to serve under-resourced communities, lower- and middle-class families. Market Basket's value proposition was centered on price and personalization. Lower prices and rebates to all customers, helping with the economics of feeding families in working-class areas. The average household income in Lowell is $62,000/year, 11% lower than the national average in an area of the country where the total cost of living is considerably higher.[2]

One study by the Strategic Resource Group compared Market Basket's prices to those of other area competitors. They found that the average family of five saved $1,500 per year on the grocery bill.[3] For lower- and middle-class families an additional $1,500/year is significant. Market Basket customers see this difference. That's why they shop there. That, and the personal touch.

Market Basket employees don't turn over. When customers go to their local store each week, they see the same faces again and again. Not just for months or years, but for decades. Market Basket takes care of its own, paying above market-value wages, cutting generous bonus checks twice per year for full-time employees, and only promoting from within.

The internal promotion path is one of the key ingredients to Market Basket's success. One study indicates that it costs a company one-third of a worker's annual salary to replace that employee should they leave.[4] Harder to measure, but potentially more valuable are the costs high turnover has on customer service. When you know the name of the guy slicing cold cuts at the deli counter and he knows yours, the personal touch of the experience helps to build brand loyalty. When there is constant change in personnel, no connections. Trust equals consistency over time. Market Basket builds trust with its customers.

Saving money with lower turnover means Market Basket can reinvest back into the business, building loyal employees with better pay and loyal customers with lower prices and personal attention. It's the virtuous cycle of playing the long game with customers and employees versus short-term penny-pinching of the marginal percentages of pork chops or cost-cutting on benefits packages. Higher costs today for built-in efficiencies that save money and improve workforce morale, and customer loyalty tomorrow.

Market Basket only promotes from within. This mandate means that a Market Basket store manager typically has 25, 30, and sometimes 40+ years with the business, starting out collecting shopping carts and bagging groceries or working on the front lines stocking shelves or produce. Managers and executives at Market Basket have to earn their way up. This guarantees they not only have an intimate knowledge of store operations but a proven track record of doing quality work and building a reputation of being a team player. They have built-in credibility with the people whom they lead.

But in the summer of 2014, a split at the highest level of Market Basket management nearly drove the 97-year-old company out of business. Rumors that the customer-focused/employee-focused philosophy was about to change. In order to make the business more efficient in the short run, talk of cutting benefits, eliminating bonuses, and opening executive hiring to outsiders began to circulate.

Gradually, and then all at once, Market Basket came apart. A chain of events was triggered that resulted in employees walking off their jobs, picketing outside of stores and in the parking lot of the company's corporate headquarters. They stopped stocking the shelves and working the cash registers. They exited the corporate office at the highest levels and the back-office warehouse. Some left voluntarily, some were fired for their unwillingness to go along with the sea change in policy.

Possibly the biggest blow to the operation, company truck drivers stopped delivering the pallets of groceries needed to restock supplies at Market Basket's 71 stores. Their strike shut down the supply chain of the entire business. There was virtually no food on the shelves, meat in the cases, or fish in the coolers. Within a matter of weeks, the shutdown was costing the company an estimated $10 million a day in lost revenue.

To understand what happened, you need to look at how the transition of power evolved over the years at the board level of the company. By 2014, Market Basket was massive. More than 70 stores, 25,000 employees, and $4 billion in annual revenue.[5] The supermarket chain had now been passed down to the third generation of Demoulas management, Arthur S. Demoulas (son of George) and Arthur T. Demoulas (son of Mike). Despite the similarity in their names, the cousins would aim to take the family business in two very different directions.

Arthur T. Demoulas was overseeing the day-to-day operations of the business, as his father Mike had before him. Like all Market Basket execs, Artie T., as many employees call him, worked his way up through the ranks. Name only gets you so far at Market Basket. Even the name Demoulas. Everyone has to put in their time and earn their position on the team.

Artie T.'s management style was a continuation of the founding principles centered on the customers and employees. A continuation of the principles of his father and grandfather before him. More than mere policy, Artie T. got personally involved with his people. He knew their names and the names of their children. When they were sick, he showed up at the hospital. Funerals when they died, churches when they got married. He was among them.

One story captured in *We Are Market Basket* describes a conversation Demoulas had with Terry McCarthy, one of his store directors. McCarthy's 20-year-old daughter had suffered a traumatic brain injury. He was at the hospital with her when he got the call.

> "Mr. D got on the phone call, very reassuring, very professional like he always is," McCarthy recalls. Demoulas asked about the situation. Where was she being treated? How was she? How were McCarthy and his family holding up? After learning how serious the injury was, Demoulas probed further: "Terry, is that hospital able to handle her injury?" McCarthy thought so, but he was still unsure if she would make it.
>
> Then Demoulas asked a question that forever changed the relationship McCarthy has with the company. He asked, "Do we need to move her?"[6]

We.

Board minutes document Artie T.'s unwillingness to bend his employee-focused principles. In one such meeting, he announced to the board that he had approved approximately $20 million in bonuses to be paid out to thousands of full-time employees. He had requested no board approval for this and delivered the news as a decision within his authority. But Artie T. and his team held 49.5% of Market Basket shares. His cousin, Arthur S. Demoulas, and his team held the controlling shares of the company. They were the decision-making authority in the business.

By the summer of 2013, it was clear Arthur S. Demoulas, and his team had a different vision for the future of Market Basket than Arthur T.'s side. The company had accrued a war chest of $300 million in working capital. There was a push by the controlling members of the board to deploy this capital, not as bonuses to employees but as dividends to shareholders.[7]

In order to tap into the capital reserve of the company for dividend payments, but maintain enough cash available on the balance sheet, the company would, for the first time in its history, take out debt. Artie T. and his team opposed the moves by the board but did not have the votes to stop them.

To pull off this change, outside leadership would need to be brought in. In mid-2013 it was leaked that Market Basket's board was actively seeking a new CEO to replace Artie T. His resistance was an obstacle to the shareholder-focused plans of the board.

Market Basket employees caught news of the board's ambition to remove their CEO and revolted. In July of that year, hundreds of them descended on the hotel where the board meeting was held, stopping board members on their way in to voice their disagreement over the possible removal of Artie T. and the fallout they could expect if they moved forward with the plan. The meeting closed with board members stating the CEO search was suspended and Artie T. would remain in his role.

The management and policy changes planned by the board had been halted, but only briefly. As it would turn out, the employee intervention in the summer 2013 board meeting was a dress rehearsal, a small flare-up. By comparison, the summer of 2014 would be a five-alarm blaze for what would ensue a year later in the summer of 2014.

On June 23, 2014, the board went through with their plan to replace Artie T. as Market Basket CEO. He, along with several other long-standing members of the Market Basket executive team, were fired and two co-CEOs were brought in from the outside to take over. The move sent shockwaves throughout the Market Basket workforce.

Upon hearing the news, several other executives loyal to Artie T. resigned, effective immediately. Arthur T. Demoulas had led Market Basket to record growth and prosperity in his seven-year tenure as CEO. Key leaders who stayed on the job after his firing asked the new leadership for a clear explanation of why the popular and, by all accounts, effective leader was fired. They were not satisfied with the answer and asked for him to be reinstated.

What happened next can best be summarized in the incredible timeline of events that unfolded in rapid succession.

- July 13 – Employees at the Burlington store hand out fliers to customers asking them to help voice concerns to the new leadership.[8]
- July 15 – Employees at the Tewksbury store formally demand Arthur T. be reinstated.[9]
- July 18 – 300 warehouse workers, 200 front office workers, and 65 truck drivers walk out on their jobs.
- July 18 – Employees take to social media asking customers to join them in a rally to reinstate Artie T.
- July 20 – Several employees associated with leading the movement to reinstate Artie T. are fired.
- July 21 – Artie T. releases his first public statement asking that the recently fired employees be rehired.[10]
- July 23 – Artie T. and his allied shareholders announce their willingness to buy out Arthur S. and his side of the board.
- July 25 – Approximately 7,000 Market Basket employees, customers, and vendors hold a rally at company headquarters demanding Artie T. be reinstated.[11]

- July 30 – Market Basket's newly appointed co-CEOs announce that any employees who have walked off their jobs must return by August 4 or risk being replaced.[12]
- August 1 – The managers fired on July 20 announce they will sue Market Basket.[13]
- August 3 – Artie T. announces he is ready to return to work and reinstate his team should his request to purchase the controlling shares be approved.[14]
- August 4 – Market Basket's current leadership follows through with its deadline and announces they will host a job fair to fill the positions of employees who have not returned to work due to the protest.[15]
- August 5 – Approximately 6,000 Market Basket employees, customers, and vendors hold another rally at company headquarters demanding Artie T. be reinstated.[16]
- August 8 – Artie T. declines an offer from Market Basket's board to return to the company, but not as CEO.[17]
- August 9 – Arthur S. announced he is willing to sell his shares to Artie T.
- August 27 – Market Basket announces that a deal had been reached where Arthur T. Demoulas will assume sole ownership of the company and return to work as CEO effective immediately.[18]

In two months' time, the employees of Market Basket, along with loyal customers and vigilant suppliers, banded together to impose their will on the decision-making authority of the business. Within a matter of weeks, they had forced an ultimatum: Restore the leadership they trusted or go out of business. A group of mostly working-class people, banding together to get a billionaire his job back from the billionaire who fired him.

Key to the Market Basket movement was that customers got involved. Formerly loyal shoppers would buy groceries at competitors, save receipts, then drive over to the Market Basket store they used to patronize and tape them to the door in protest. Market Basket's board had turned their customers into modern-day Martin Luthers, calling them to task for their indulgences of shareholder gluttony.

Possibly the final blow to the new management team came in the first week of August. A group of loyal Market Basket customers banded together, pooled their money (more than $20,000), and took out an ad in the *Lowell Sun*. They were angry about how employees whom they had come to know and built relationships with over the years were being treated. It read:

> To the Current CEOs of Demoulas Market Basket,
> Board of Directors, and Shareholders:
> A full boycott does not depend on Associates:
> It depends on CUSTOMERS.
> It is YOUR CUSTOMERS who are
> Boycotting your stores.
> It is YOUR CUSTOMERS who bring in the money.
> It is YOUR CUSTOMERS who
> Are your bottom line.
> It is YOUR CUSTOMERS who will not shop at
> Market Basket until Artie T. is back as CEO.
> It is YOUR CUSTOMERS who paid for this ad.
> #YouCan'tFireCustomersWeQuit

After taking over as sole owner of the company Arthur T. Demoulas issued the following statement.

The success of Market Basked is the result of two things: a business model that works and the execution of it by a dedicated and impassioned team of associates. Their fierce loyalty to the company and its customers has always been deeply valued. In the final analysis, this is not about me. It is about the people who have proven their dedication over many years and should not have lost their jobs because of it.

Market Basket pays its people more. Market Basket invests more in employee benefits. Market Basket retains employees longer and promotes from within. Market Basket gives every customer the best price.

Market Basket, more for your dollar.

First Principles of the People System

What occurred at Market Basket in 2013/2014 was a pressure test and testament to its century-old culture. Fundamentally that culture was built around people, namely customers, vendors, and, most of all, employees. Market Basket offers a clear example of a design-build model of a People System. When stakeholders, not just shareholders alone, are empowered and given a voice, the results can change the course of not only businesses, but entire communities.

Playing the Long Game

Core to Market Basket's culture is their long-term focus. It's hard coded into the structure of their People System. They pay above-market wages and offer generous bonuses. They set up far-reaching career plans for their associates and work with them to move up the ladder. They offer tuition reimbursement for employees working toward a degree.

Where some businesses look at employees as cost centers contributing to inefficiencies, Market Basket sees them as investments. The returns on these investments come in lower employee turnover and higher-quality customer service. They don't show up on the balance sheet in the short term but pay higher multiples down the road.

When design-building the People System, it's important to ask what will motivate the team to give all they've got to their roles, both today and in years to come? How are you setting people up to mature within the company? What will the career paths look like of highly valuable employees? What cultural characteristics are you looking to base your People System on? Would they put their careers on the line to maintain that culture?

Culture Through Action

Market Basket doesn't have any posters on the walls of their stock rooms with words like INTEGRITY or TEAMWORK. They don't need to remind employees of how to act. Employees police themselves. Everyone's work is out in the open, and the effects of the quality and quantity of their efforts are felt and recognized accordingly. Both positive and negative.

The People System at Market Basket is built of, by, and for the people who work there. And because of that its culture is transparent and ubiquitous. The company and culture are the people. Should employees not live up to Market Basket values, they aren't violating a logo, motto, website, or stock ticker – but their co-workers.

Communication

The new co-CEOs of Market Basket installed to replace Artie T. were not immediately rejected. The most consequential actions that ground the company's operations to a halt did not begin in earnest until three weeks after the firing. The new management team had that time (not to mention any time they had to prepare before the transition was announced) to control the narrative and limit the damage. They failed.

Clear, forthright communication is one of the most essential ingredients to a healthy People System. Poor communication can quickly lead people astray. No communication will create an information vacuum. When an employee's career security and livelihood are on the line, the vacuum can quickly be filled with a worst-case scenario of what to expect.

Personal Leadership

The clearest examples of Market Basket's People System came directly from the actions of Artie T. himself. Slide decks and speeches can help reinforce a culture, but there is no substitute for leadership in action. Trust in a culture means consistency over time in the carrying out of that culture. Artie T. showed up for his people, again and again, reinforcing the value system on which Market Basket's culture was built. His leadership transcended the professional and reached into the personal. And because of that, his removal and the greater existential threat to Market Basket were felt by employees on a personal level.

A lesson all leaders can take when design-building the People System is the commitment to act it out and see it through. To lead not merely by words, but through actions. Saying you value work–life balance for employees is not personal leadership; remembering the names of co-workers' kids is. Creating a policy of unlimited time off when family crisis strikes is not personal leadership; calling when an employee's family member is in the hospital and asking what "we" need to do about it is.

In the final analysis, the success of a People System does not rest on what a company thinks about its leader, but rather how a company's leader makes people feel about themselves and the greater purpose they have within the organization as a whole.

Elements of the People System

The Culture Deck

The first step in design-building the Process System centered on a deep understanding of who the customer is, your customer persona. Similarly, the People System begins with creating and documenting a clear vision of your ideal co-worker, their character, values, and how you expect them to interact with everyone else in the company. This is crystallized in the company culture deck, available not just for employees, but broadcast to the world at large, making clear the expectations set for norms and behaviors for all who join your team.

So many issues can be sourced back to poor communication or poor expectation setting. A well-built culture deck diffuses both of these risks. It's a marketing tool to attract the type of people you want on your team, by clearly stating the type of people your team values the most.

There is possibly no bigger design-build project inside a company than the creation and iteration of a culture deck. The completed deck is the foundational design of who should be working at the company. It's only as valuable as it is (1) accurate and (2) used. Company-wide collaboration, at least at the leadership level, across all areas of the business is key. No design-build project is ever purely democratic, but the construction of a culture deck may be as close as it gets.

A culture deck is a great primer, letting early-stage candidates know what's in store for them should they end up getting a job at your company. If transparency is a core value your company lives by, and a candidate is averse to having their productivity numbers made public for all the team to see, that's going to be a problem. Culture decks help to prevent these issues from ever arising before an offer is made or accepted.

The granddaddy of all culture decks is Netflix's 125-slide masterpiece,[19] first released back in 2009. In it, one of the value norms they set very directly is regarding exceptional performance. "Sustained B-level performance, despite 'A for effort' generates a generous severance package, with respect." This is just one line from the deck spelling out exactly what the company values and what you should expect (and what's expected of you) if you work there.

A documented culture code not only has alignment benefits with candidates and new hires but also realignment value with the existing team. Over time it's inevitable that co-workers will disagree and have disputes and differences of opinions on judgment calls. In such cases, the culture deck can be looked upon like the company constitution to revert back to for enlightenment on the ethos of the team when tough calls need to be made.

A culture deck should be revisited with regularity to maintain its relevance. As business evolves, so too must a business's culture deck. A small start-up with few documented processes and no historical best-practice data to look back on may value qualities like agility, creative problem-solving, or flexibility. As the business grows, procedures get more and more defined with experience, and specialized execution is needed, a culture of organization, communication, or accountability may take precedence.

Ideal Candidate Profile (the Other ICP)

Much like customer persona offers a preamble to the creation of an ideal customer profile, company culture provides the foundation for the more refined ideal candidate profile – the other ICP. The process is driven by the build-side, typically hiring managers who write out what the perfect-fit candidate looks like, then work with ops and HR to design the process and measures for finding, recruiting, screening, evaluating, and hiring perfect-fit candidates for open spots on your team.

Mapping ideal-candidate profile qualities for your sales team can be organized by hard skills and soft skills. Some look at hard skills as clearly defined measurable abilities, whereas soft skills are more obscure personality traits. I look at hard skills as stuff I'm willing to teach or work on with the right candidate, and soft skills as core characteristics the candidate must bring with them to qualify for consideration.

Examples of Sales Hard Skills

- Knowledge of the industry
- Experience selling to a similar customer
- Experience selling in a similar sales motion
- Experience selling at a similar average contract value
- Proven track record of strong performance achieving quota
- Demonstrated ability to prospect, run discovery, present, and handle objections
- Demonstrated understanding of the business
- Time-management skills
- Note-taking ability

Examples of Sales Soft Skills

- Strong work ethic
- Curiosity
- Coachability
- Intelligence
- Performance-driven
- Accountability

- Grit
- Purpose
- Emotional intelligence
- Communication skills
- Active listening ability

The above is not a complete list. Each of the different roles on your team would have its own set of ICP skill requirements. You likely wouldn't require an entry-level BDR to come to the job with expert-level discovery skills. Similarly, when hiring a sales manager, you're likely to look for hard skills like demonstrated coaching and training experience and soft skills like leadership ability and conflict resolution.

It becomes clear when reviewing the examples listed, particularly in the hard skills category, why defining your ideal candidate profile is a System 3 project. Without first deeply understanding your customer persona and sales motion (the Process System) and your go-to-market strategy and customer acquisition channels (the Demand-Generation System), it's hard to have a clear picture of what a perfect-fit salesperson looks like. You need to have clearly defined whom you sell to, how you sell to them, and where the first conversation will get started to know who the best-suited salesperson for the job is.

The Ideal Candidate Interview Scorecard

I derive from the Mark Roberge sales leadership tree, having had the opportunity to work with him at HubSpot from 2012–2015 and received the benefit of his advice throughout my journey at Rock. One of my key learnings from Mark, detailed in Chapter 2 of his book *The Sales Acceleration Formula*, is the use of an interview scorecard. This is a classic design-build construct.

The scorecard method that Roberge describes engineers a structured process for how sales candidates will be measured in a consistent methodology (design-side), grading them on the known skills and attributes needed for success in that specific role (build-side). At Rock, we scaled our sales hiring efficiency with this model but modified the formula with one key addition to better fit our success criteria and hiring process. First, let's quickly summarize the fundamentals.

The scorecard allows you to organize the predefined ICP characteristics on a sheet for interviewers on the team to follow. This ensures that the screening process is being followed and the essential ICP checklist info is being captured for analysis. The characteristics are weighted based on the level of importance for success on the job.

New sales teams weigh characteristics based on hypotheses. More mature teams with a sample size of experienced rep performance will run a regression analysis on the top-performing reps to see how they scored during original interviews, and the weights will reflect the indications of actual performance. So, if the most proven reps tended to score well on coachability but inconsistently on industry knowledge during their initial interviews, coachability would receive a higher weight and industry knowledge a lower weight.

The addition we made to the core scorecard to help us more accurately screen for ideal fit was the addition of a social style assessment. This helped give us a clearer picture of how rep personality impacted performance.

Social Styles

Pioneered by Tracom Group,[20] social styles assess and categorize people by specific characteristics of how they learn, communicate, and interact with others. Drivers are very direct, fast-paced, and results-oriented. Expressives are spontaneous, seek personal approval, and love a good story. Amiables focus on relationships, building rapport, and maintaining harmony. Analytics go deep into the data, are risk averse, and value being right more than being liked.

We initially started qualifying social styles through interviews and the personal opinions of the interviewer and later installed a formal test into the process. Understanding the type of social style that most comfortably fits into a specific role in a specific team is important in gauging overall fit.

At Rock, the Driver social style outperformed the others. The biggest predictor of success or failure regarding social style assessment was how extreme the person was on the social style register. The extremists typically lacked the flexibility to read and adjust to social styles other than their own, both within the team and with customers. This ultimately hurt performance.

Figure 4.1 shows what the scorecard structure looked like. Let's examine two hypothetical candidates to show how the scorecard plays out in practice.

Mike Jones This candidate scored well in many of the soft skills with particularly high marks in work ethic, accountability, and intelligence. Regarding hard skills, Mike scored well in general sales ability as well as time management and note taking but below average in industry knowledge. He sees himself as Analytical, but his company assessment indicates that he is more expressive. Both his and the company's social style assessments grade him as level 1, meaning he's near the center of the spectrum and not extreme in his personality traits.

This candidate would likely be hired, particularly for a junior-level role. Strong soft skill scores indicate Mike would be willing to put in the work and has the aptitude to make up ground in the areas where he didn't score well, particularly in industry knowledge and experience working in the company's sales motion. Because he scored near the social style center, he would likely show strong versatility and openness to training and coaching up these skills.

Candidate	Work Ethic/Grit	Curiosity	Coachability	Intelligence	Performance-driven	Accountability	Grit	Purpose	Emotional Intelligence	Communication Skills	Active Listening	Industry Knowledge	Customer Experience	Sales Motion Experience	Time Management Skills	Note Taking Ability	Weighted Average	Max Weighted Score	Social Style (Self Assessment)	Social Style (Company Assessment)
Weight	0.7	0.8	1	1	0.6	0.7	0.8	0.5	0.8	0.6	0.8	0.5	0.5	0.7	0.5	0.7				
Mike Jones	5	4	4	5	3	4	5	3	3	4	4	2	3	2	5	5	43.6	56	Analytic 1	Expressive 1
Johnny Closer	3	2	2	4	3	2	3	3	2	4	1	5	5	5	3	1	32.3	56	Expressive 3	Expressive 3
Peter Perfect	5	5	5	5	5	5	5	5	5	5	5	5	5	5	5	5	56	56	Driver 1	Driver 1
																		56		
																		56		
																		56		

Skills Scoring Logic	Social Styles	Social Styles Scoring Logic
1 = Poor	Driver - Tell/Task	1 = Centered
2 = Below Average	Expressive - Tell/People	2 = Moderate
3 = Average	Amiable - Ask/People	3 = Extreme
4 = Above Average	Analytic - Ask/Task	
5 = Superior		

Figure 4.1 Sales Hiring Scorecard

Johnny Closer This is an all-too-common candidate in sales. Johnny is an industry veteran with a résumé of experience working with your customer in a similar sales motion. Maybe he worked at, or is currently working at, a competitor. Johnny scores low on a number of key soft skills like coachability, accountability, and emotional intelligence and is a poor note-taker. Johnny is highly expressive and knows it.

Johnny gets hired by most sales teams. He's charismatic and can talk a good game about signing the very customers you want. But as far as collaboration goes, Johnny is a nightmare. Low scores on coachability, accountability, and active listening combined with an extreme social style score show that he is inflexible, will not grow, and will be very hard to lead.

His poor notetaking only makes the cross-team collaboration worse as the customers he does bring are passed along to other areas of the business blind, with no context or detail to maintain expectations. At Rock, we learned early that Johnny is not a good hire.

The Peter Perfect profile is a hypothetical data set, there to remind all interviewers what ICP looks like when grading attributes. Just having the numbers associated there with an ICP image helps to give balance and prevent unwarranted five scores.

At Rock, we ran a challenger-style, consultative sales process with a brand and product offer that was not established in the market. Driver social styles tended to perform best in this environment, as they sold with confidence, maintained control of the conversations with clients, and were willing to challenge the prospect's worldview. Like all healthy social styles (at least healthy for sales roles) the top performers were close to the middle of the spectrum and could adjust to Analytics, Amiables, and Expressives fluidly.

The long-term magic of the scorecard is borne out with regression analysis. Over time it becomes the predictive index for the future success of the candidates moving through your interview process. It also helps those whom you hire to understand better why they fit in the role and what attributes they need to lean into in order to maximize results.

To squeeze the most value out of the scorecard, share the results with new hires on day 1 with the company. Let them know exactly what you saw in them that indicated fit. Also, review where they fell short regarding ICP attribute scores and have an open conversation about the impact of social style awareness. This early conversation sets the tone of open feedback on the team and frames up the first action plan for the new hire to step toward self-improvement.

The Role-Play Scorecard

A key step in many sales interview processes is live role play. Rock was no exception. A role play is a great way to test drive the candidate's current hard skills (rapport-building, discovery process, business acumen, etc.), but also their soft skills.

One of the key steps to the role-play screening is the second take. At Rock, we separated the first and second role plays by at least one day, allowing the interviewer to provide not only verbal, but also written feedback by email and the candidate to reflect on performance and prepare for round 2. This allowed us to test, not only sales acumen, but also active listening, intelligence, and coachability. Did they take feedback well and show the willingness to change their approach and the aptitude to execute better from one call to the next?

Given all the moving parts to grading on a role play, we created a scorecard just for this step of the process. Like the Sales Hiring Scorecard, the Sales Role-Play Scorecard catalogs key criteria for grading and applies weight to the criteria based on how essential it is for rep performance at the time of the interview.

Elements like how the candidate opened the call or conducted a "placement test" to qualify for a prospect's buyer journey stage were scored lower as they were skills shown to be easier to teach post-hire. Other skills like "follow-on questioning" or the overall "communication skill" were weighted as essential for candidates to have when role-playing.

Let's drill into how Mike Jones performed according to the scorecard in Figure 4.2.

On role play 1, Mike demonstrated clear skill strength in building rapport, first-level discovery questioning, summarizing learnings, and setting next steps. His overall communication ability was above average. Areas the interviewer deemed he needed to improve on were the

Candidate	Opening	Rapport Building	Setting Agenda	First-Level Questioning	Follow-on Questioning	Summary	Placement Test	Communication Skill	Qualifying the Buyer	Next Steps	Weighted Average	Max Weighted Score	Role Play (Self Assessment)	Role Play (Manager Assessment)	
Weight	0.06	0.7	0.8	1	1	0.7	0.5	1	0.8	1					
Mike Jones (RP 1)	3	4	1	4	2	5	1	4	3	5	25	40.5	50%	61.73%	Quality of Performance (1-5)
Mike Jones (RP 2)	5	4	4	4	4	5	3	4	3	5	30.4	40.5	70%	75.06%	Coachability (1-5)
												40.5			
												40.5			

Scoring Logic
1 = Poor
2 = Below Average
3 = Average
4 = Above Average
5 = Superior

Figure 4.2 Role Play Scorecard, Mike Jones

opening of the call (usually marked by the energy or overall greeting), setting a call agenda, asking follow-on discovery questions to drill deeper into the prospect's situation, qualifying the prospect's current level of solution knowledge (placement test), and qualifying the buyer for end-of-call interest, authority, and budget.

On role play 2, Mike showed measurable improvement. On a second pass, he took the feedback and upped his game in the call opening, asking follow-on questions, and installed a placement test in his process. Though his other skill scores didn't improve from the first role play, they didn't decline. This shows Mike's ability to improve his process with new feedback without losing any of what's already working. As such his overall score rose more than five points from role play 1 to role play 2.

One additional area to note is the self-assessment vs. manager assessment section on the right side of the scorecard. At the close of each role play, the interviewing manager would ask the candidate to grade his/her performance. Here we were testing for self-awareness and humility, two bedrock qualities of an open-minded, coachable rep.

In both instances, Mike graded himself lower than the manager assessment, but not by much. This showed that he has a decent perspective on his own level of ability and is humble enough to admit he has things to improve. Based on his level of self-awareness, the skills where Mike already showed strength, and the measured improvement he made from the first role play to the second, Mike would likely have been qualified for the next step in the interview process.

Triple Session for Candidate Screening

We took this scorecard process from Roberge and the Sales Acceleration Formula and modified it for our own use case inside Rock's sales team. It provided a solid foundation for our candidate-screening process for years. It was our database for coordinating candidate evaluation and documenting how interview performance correlated to sales performance. There were, however, areas we did find needed an upgrade.

The biggest being the overall subjectivity of the process. The scores we attributed to candidates all came from the interviewer's personal opinions, given a very limited data set, usually a single conversation or role play. The scorecard was an effort to become more data-driven, but there was room to improve. We wanted to bring a larger data set to the decision and have a more objective means of assessing candidate fit.

We started using free, online certifications as part of the pre-screening process. These helped prove some level of engagement (candidates who returned their certifications faster showed a greater level of seriousness for earning the role). But they failed to show any real level of technical knowledge. It left us wondering: "How well did they do on the cert test? Did they ace it or just barely pass? Did they pass the first time or did it take them 2, 3, 10 attempts?" We wanted more data for an accurate measure of the breadth and depth of a candidate's current knowledge before investing time in the live-interview process.

The gap in the screening process was even more evident in determining a candidate's soft skills. The way we were running our screening process was the same way our parents and grandparents had done it. Candidate provides a résumé. A live-interview Q&A is performed where the hiring manager plays detective, trying to squeeze the truth out of the witness. Judgment call is made (subjectively) by the interviewer on whether or not to move the candidate forward. It was "résumé, Q&A, have your say, hope, and pray." We thought this needed an upgrade.

We knew what we wanted to learn about candidates. Are they curious, coachable, dedicated, results-oriented, and competitive? These were the core ingredients for success in our sales system. The Q&A

with the role-play process left us with little confidence that we knew the character of the candidate. There had to be a better way.

In 2020 we developed an in-house tool to help our salespeople continue to learn, measure, and stay sharp with hundreds of core skills essential for success in their roles. We called the tool Triple Session as it systemized a three-step practice methodology of standardized testing, associated quizzes, and immediate feedback on test results and benchmarks. Sales reps put a number to their knowledge and measured how consistently they practiced as part of a daily routine of self-improvement.

Triple Session was originally designed to help improve and advance sales hard skills – prospecting, discovery, presenting, negotiating, and so on. What unexpectedly emerged was a perfect measure of the sales soft skills we championed as part of our culture and core competencies. The power users of the tool were the reps who were the most curious, most coachable, most hard-working and performance-driven. And it was no surprise that it was these reps who were also most of our top revenue performers as well.

We replaced the use of third-party certifications in our candidate screening process with Triple Session. This opened up a much clearer, data-driven assessment of:

- **Specific Technical Skills** – We could see clearly which skills the candidate tested on, how well they scored, and what they still had yet to train.

- **Active Listening and Comprehension** – The quizzes weren't hard if you paid close attention to the content. Lower scores on easy tests we flagged as risks of poor active listening skills or low course comprehension.

- **A Measure of Curiosity and Dedication to Learning** – Did the candidate train consistently or just take a couple of sessions and quit? Did they wait until the day before the first interview and try to jam everything in to make it look good, or did they start training right when we opened up Triple Session access and stick with it?

- **A Measure of Performance Drive** – Did they visit the in-app leaderboard to monitor their scores and rankings? Did they maintain streaks and show a drive toward measurable consistency, or were they inconsistent? If they scored poorly on a quiz, did they go back and retake it to cover the knowledge gap and improve their score?

A candidate's performance readout from Triple Session offered a layer of objective analysis for both hard and soft skills. It became another pillar in the process of evaluating candidate quality and helped inform us when making hiring decisions.

The Interview Process

With ideal candidate profiles documented, scorecards defined, and Triple Session ready, it's important to define the step-by-step process for screening talent. Who will do what at which point in the conversation with job applicants to ensure accurate and comprehensive evaluations are done while maintaining efficiency within the team.? Time is the greatest expense when interviewing at scale. Investing the time to plan interview-stage ownership and exit criteria early pays back in higher time-saving multiples later.

The key questions to ask and answer are:

- What are the disqualifiers that remove bad-fit candidates from the process at each step?
- What are the qualifiers that signal a high-quality candidate warranting prioritization or extra attention (bring out the Queen) at each step?
- What are the process steps best used to qualify/disqualify at each step?
- Which members of the HR and sales team are best to run each of the agreed-upon steps defined?

The process we matured over the years and ultimately got the best results with at Rock was:

1. Send formal job description and culture deck before any live interactions.
   a. Owner – HR.
   b. Exit Criteria – Candidate agrees to live phone screening within three business days. (The timeframe qualifies for the level of priority by the candidate.)

2. Initial phone screen.
   a. Owner – HR.
   b. Exit Criteria – Candidate qualified for communication skills, demonstrated preparation, asked tactful questions, interest in moving toward the new role vs. away from the current position/company.

3. Assigned homework in triplesession.com and schedule manager interview.
   a. Owner – HR.
   b. Exit Criteria – Candidate engaged in Triple Session sales training, and scores well. Came back to the platform repeatedly, showing engagement, openness to learn, and effort.

4. Initial Manager Interview.
   a. Owner – Hiring Manager.
   b. Exit Criteria – Completed sales hiring scorecard.

5. Role Play 1. Send a case study of a typical lead scenario, early sales process and test for current sales process maturity. (See Role Play Rubric.)
   a. Owner – Senior-level Sales Rep (future manager in training).
   b. Exit Criteria – Completes role-play scorecard. Qualifies for minimum sales-skill ability. Verbal and written feedback was provided to the candidate.

6. Role Play 2. Rerun of the same role play after feedback is provided.
   a. Owner – Sales Rep (future manager in training).
   b. Exit Criteria – Completes role-play scorecard. Qualified for improvement over role play 1 signaling coachability and intelligence.

7. Inverted Interview – Candidate interviews a member of the team doing that same job.
   a. Owner – Senior-level sales rep (future manager in training).
   b. Exit Criteria – Documents questions asked by the candidate to qualify for engagement and insight.
8. Second Manager Interview.
   a. Owner – Non-hiring manager or senior-level sales rep (future manager in training).
   b. Exit Criteria – Completed second sales hiring scorecard.
9. Committee Roundtable to Make Hire/No Hire Decision.
   a. Owner – Hiring manager.
   b. Exit Criteria – Decision to move forward with offer or pass.
10. Final Interview with the Hiring Manager.
    a. Owner – Hiring Manager.
    b. Exit Criteria – Final Q&A. Alignment on role expectations and verbal agreement regarding the offer.

At each of the 10 steps, the conversation with the candidate is recorded in the HR CRM records with scorecards and notes taken for reference. The first three steps are owned by HR with the goal of sending only qualified candidates over to the sales manager for further review. The hiring manager has first-look at a candidate when forwarded from HR, given that she will be the best judge as to whether the candidate is worth investing more time from the sales hiring committee on screening. The screening steps that happen after that become more time-intensive, so efficiency upfront is key.

By the time a candidate has run the gauntlet of the 10-step process, there was high confidence that he was committed to the role (he would have bailed earlier otherwise). There's also high convenience that an objectively positive decision to invite the person to join the team can be made. Four to six people have met with and screened the candidate, recording scores and notes and approving the next step in the process based on pre-set criteria.

A ten-step process like this elapses over a 10- to 15-day timespan. All these steps and time investments from several key members of the HR and sales teams and from the candidate may seem like overkill. They're not. Superficial interview processes yield superficial hiring decisions. Superficial hiring decisions yield expensive mis-hires that could have been avoided. The cost of poor hiring is wasted training, wasted leads, frustrated co-workers, and a misaligned new hire who exits the company with a bad taste in his mouth. Investing in intense candidate screening pays off in high returns downstream.

Recruiting

Staffing your sales team with qualified players is not unlike bringing on great-fit customers. After defining your ICP and screening process, you need a demand-generation strategy. And whether the focus is on customer acquisition or talent acquisition, a relentless effort across multiple channels will often yield high-quality outcomes.

Inbound, outbound, and partner channels all play a role. Referrals and high-value old ops turn talent-acquisition funnels into talent-acquisition flywheels. Effective execution means coordination with literally everyone in your company.

Design-Building a Recruiting System

To organize a talent demand-gen engine across multiple, independent channels over an extended period, HR, Marketing, Sales Leadership, Operations, and the CEO all need to work in lockstep. Each plays a key role in effective recruiting, and talent acquisition, so all need to weigh in on the system design. Talent-acquisition channels each take on a life of their own, with a unique set of actions needed to success-fully recruit candidates.

Inbound Talent Acquisition

Inbound is the "always keep the lights on" effort, which involves a small, continuous drip of activity across all talent-acquisition stakeholders. In addition to regularly promoting open spots on the careers page of the company site, HR collaborates with marketing to post "life in the company" content. (Publishing and regular references to the culture deck fit perfectly here.) Updates on company milestones, team outings, incentives, benefits, employee sentiment, and third-party "great place to work" achievements help ongoing brand recognition in the job market.

Sales personnel extend the reach of inbound by reposting content on their social pages. Win an incentive? Tell the world. Earn a promotion? Update LinkedIn and celebrate the accomplishment. Current team members are often connected to future team members. Make it easy for them to keep up brand visibility within their networks. Offering moments of promotion from company events and career growth (more on this later in this chapter) will create a steady stream of positive employee energy out into the jobs market.

There's no voice louder and more impactful than that of the CEO (see the case of Cate Castillo, Neivor CEO – First Principles of Demand Generation). Part of the CEO's primary function is to get on the microphone and tell the world about the great team you are to work with.

For smaller companies, the CEO should be posting company-touting content several times per month and hands-on in the process of signing key talent. For larger businesses, this may be a tall order, so work to carve out at least a monthly communication from the desk of the chief executive to hit the market and be shared by the team.

Outbound Talent Acquisition

The best people you can bring into your organization aren't typically sitting on the couch. They are active members of another team and doing quite well. No different than outbound customer acquisition, you need to zero in on where your ICP is and get their attention, interest, and curiosity. A-players change the trajectory of your entire team and company, so even though the outbound win rate may be small, the payoff is huge.

Casual LinkedIn messages are not enough. Think of the complete outbound motion here. In a role reversal, front-line, outbound sales-people assume the design-side of the conversation, assisting HR with mapping the end-to-end outbound cadence. Databases are used to mine work, personal, and phone info of ideal candidates. Talent acquisition takes on the role of Business Development with their prospects being ICPs.

Contacts, opportunities, and signed or lost candidates are all tracked in an HR CRM (there are a number of solid options in this space). ICP selling is team selling, so with outbound candidate prospecting it's wise for the talent-acquisition team to get hiring managers or even the C-suite involved early. When we did this in key deals at Rock, we referred to it as bringing out the Queen, a reference to the chess strategy of getting your most powerful player involved in the game early. Few things are a better time investment than winning key talent to your team, so put everything on the field in these efforts.

Channel Talent Acquisition

Traditional staffing agencies typically work on a success basis, keeping the risk low for their clients. There is a time factor to take into account as the total cost of these partnerships. At Rock, the best staffing agencies I worked with specialized in a specific market and level of professional (entry-level, experienced, C-suite, etc.), which improved the efficiency of time spent on their candidates.

In addition to job boards, a new channel of sales communities has emerged in recent years as a new venue to gain visibility and connect with candidates. Pavilion, RevGenius, Bravado, and others all open up venues for directly interacting with sales professionals across various industries, geographies, and levels of experience. Get to know the landscape and participate accordingly, to generate candidate interest.

Referral Talent Acquisition

The highest hit rate you'll have in attracting ICPs to your team will come through your current teammates. High-caliber professionals tend to swim in the same circles. Those who are on your team are the perfect ambassadors to bring in the next generation. Create the incentive for motivation and the habit of messaging.

One thing I never understood was why companies are willing to compensate a staffing agency three months of an employee's salary when they fill a role, but only a fraction of that to their own employees who help fill roles, usually with better-fit candidates. We should pay our own people more than agencies, not less.

If an enterprise sales exec earns a $100,000 base and an agency makes $25,000 on the placement, comp your own employees the same $25,000 for bringing in the top-notch teammate. The higher cost has a positive side-effect on keeping everyone disciplined to only hire the best. If you pay handsomely for talent, you'll think twice about hiring B players.

As with any referral program, marketing matters. It's important to keep the incentive top of mind with the team so they keep their eyes and ears open to ICP opportunities as they connect and reconnect with their networks. One of the best sales leaders I ever worked for messaged the referral incentive and high-priority open positions at every team meeting. This was something I thankfully ripped off and used from day 1 at Rock. It paid huge dividends.

Triple Session for Talent Acquisition

Eventually, word got out that we had developed an open-access tool for learning sales skills and keeping them sharp. People started sharing the tool with their friends in sales, and those friends shared it with theirs, and the member base in Triple Session started to grow organically. We loved it.

Without any additional effort, we had a base of potential candidates to go to when spots on the team opened up. Because all Triple Session accounts were synced with LinkedIn, we knew who the person was, what their resume looked like, and where to find them. From the Triple Session scoring and activity reports, we could see which of these external members were most engaged and putting the work into sales skill-building. We had inadvertently created our own channel for sales talent.

Old Ops Talent Acquisition

The very best teammate opportunities are like the very best customer opportunities. You never close the door completely, just put the conversation on ice for a while, waiting to revisit it later. Whichever CRM the HR team is using to track ICP contacts, a future task system should be employed and revisited with leadership on an agreed-upon cadence to keep working on bringing in the big fish.

One sales manager I hired, whom I met in December, declined the first offer I made him in January, revisited the conversation in March, paused until May, and delayed until June. The second offer was made in July and accepted. The guy was worth it. The hard-to-gets usually are. He helped reengineer our sales playbook, upgraded our messaging and onboarding, breathed new life into sales training and coaching, and helped attract and sign new talent. If I had given up after the first declined offer, we never would have seen those great benefits.

Great companies with great products and a high-value proposition will undoubtedly suffer if they hire poorly. Companies who are diligent and thoughtful about hiring well – even immature products and teams that need a lot of work – can make it through with the contribution of a great team. Steve Jobs once said, "The secret of my success is that we have gone to exceptional lengths to hire the best people in the world."

Selling Your Vision

When interviewing the highest-value candidates, you are selling them as much as they are selling you. One strange phenomenon I've witnessed throughout my career is that even the best salespeople fail to apply sales best practices when interviewing. Selling yourself well enough to get a job can result in millions of dollars in earnings, career growth, new connections, and an overall higher quality of life.

It's without a doubt the single most important sale of a sales professional's career. And yet they don't qualify their buyer (the hiring manager) to control the conversation with questions and present themselves in light of the learnings from discovery. The context throws them off their game.

Hiring managers are equally culpable. The same manager who would help a rep run a great customer-needs analysis and only present solutions based on those needs will commonly violate this principle when trying to sell high-value candidates on taking a spot on their team.

All too often sales managers run through what *they* deem as value to the role and the company – the comp package, benefits, ping pong tables, and snacks in the break room. They fail to listen, learn, and understand what *the candidate* deems as valuable and to link where the role and the company fit to that value. It's basic consultative selling, and it's seldom used when hiring.

"Prescribing without diagnosing is malpractice" is a phrase commonly trotted out by consultative sales teams. The same applies when interviewing. Data indicates what is often important to a candidate goes far beyond the paycheck. Things like:

- Work/life balance
- Learning/training and skill development opportunities
- Positive culture/sense of purpose
- Career growth opportunities
- Flexible working arrangement/work from home or hybrid model

High-value candidates are sold to a lot by staffing agencies, HR teams, and hiring managers. You've got to put the work in to stand out from the crowd. If work/life balance is valued, have the candidate speak with current team members exercising that in their routines. When learning and skill development is top of mind, give real examples of how your company invests in employees vs. the hypothetical explanation.

Like any sale, the deal is won piece by piece, aligning needs and goals with what the company delivers. And just as the career move may be the best sale in the candidate's career, for the company, there's no greater gain within a manager's control than signing great talent onto the team.

Compensating Salespeople

As discussed previously in the Demand-Generation System, the costs associated with paying a salesperson's base salary and commission are combined with demand-gen costs and weighed against the value of the revenue they bring in. The value of revenue is driven by two key factors, the profit margins of the revenue and the lifetime value of revenue receivables from that customer. All this is represented clearly in the Skok sheet.

When these key numbers are plotted out on a sheet, a compensation plan for the salesperson is now able to take shape. Numbers paid in base salary, commission rate, or payment frequency can be adjusted based on determining factors like:

- What is a healthy, full-ramp efficiency balance role?
- How much of a loss is the business willing to take when adding a new salesperson?
- How long is the company willing to take losses when adding a new salesperson?
- What type of sales behavior is the company looking to motivate with the comp plan?
- What is the going market rate for the role you are hiring?

Adjusting numbers based on the answers to these questions is a collaborative effort by a team made up of HR/compensation specialist, sales ops, sales leadership, finance, and (depending on the size of the business) the C-suite. Striking the right balance between individual, team, and company benefits is key. Ideally, all are represented in the final outcome so that when one wins, all win. Let's dissect a few examples.

Example 1: Enterprise Account Executive (SaaS)

In this example, an enterprise SaaS company sells a platform with an average annual contract value of $100,000 at 80% gross margins and a new hire ramp of two quarters (67% quota target in quarter 3 and full quota by quarter 4).

- A healthy full-ramp efficiency is 5× revenue vs. on-target earnings.
- Max loss during the lifetime of a rep is $300,000.
- Target payback period (breakeven) for a new sales hire is 24 months.

- The company aims to optimize net dollar retention to maintain healthy unit economics.
- Market research shows the going rate for comparable roles is $240,000 base+ variable.

Fixed parameters are set for the ACV ($100,000), margins, ramp timeline, target compensation ($240,000 ata 120,000/120,000 base/variable split), target full quota at $1.2 million, and net dollar retention at 100%. The key variable to adjust to make the payback number work is minimum quota attainment. What is the worst performance an account executive (AE) would be allowed to post and still keep his job? In this scenario the math when Skoked proves out to be 80%.

In this scenario (see Figure 4.3), the rep efficiency bottoms out in actual cash position at month 7, having sold nothing and incurring base salary and demand-gen costs totaling $188,883. This is the cash position logic, given that the customers in this scenario are booked as payment up-front and the AE's first sale in month 8 will actually bring in about $64,000 in net profit ($100,000 80% margins × 80% attainment).

When we extrapolate the numbers through year 2, we find that at the 80% attainment minimum the max loss is breached for 1 month before pulling back under the $300,000 threshold. The breakeven is hit on month 25, right at the deadline.

Income	Month 1	Month 2	Month 3	Month 4	Month 5	Month 6	Month 7	Month 8	Month 9	Month 10	Month 11	Month 12
Ramp Schedule	0%	0%	0%	0%	0%	0%	0%	100%	100%	100%	100%	100%
Bookings (ACV)	$ -	$ -	$ -	$ -	$ -	$ -	$ -	$ 80,000	$ 80,000	$ 80,000	$ 80,000	$ 80,000
New MRR added this month (billed)	$ -	$ -	$ -	$ -	$ -	$ -	$ -	$ 6,667	$ 6,667	$ 6,667	$ 6,667	$ 6,667
MRR from prior months bookings	$ -	$ -	$ -	$ -	$ -	$ -	$ -	$ -	$ 6,667	$ 13,333	$ 20,000	$ 26,667
Churn	$ -	$ -	$ -	$ -	$ -	$ -	$ -	$ -	$ -	$ -	$ -	$ -
Total MRR (billings)	$ -	$ -	$ -	$ -	$ -	$ -	$ -	$ 6,667	$ 13,333	$ 20,000	$ 26,667	$ 33,333
Cumulative Billings	$ -	$ -	$ -	$ -	$ -	$ -	$ -	$ 6,667	$ 20,000	$ 40,000	$ 66,667	$ 100,000
Cumulative Gross Profit	$ -	$ -	$ -	$ -	$ -	$ -	$ -	$ 5,333	$ 16,000	$ 32,000	$ 53,333	$ 80,000

Expenses	Month 1	Month 2	Month 3	Month 4	Month 5	Month 6	Month 7	Month 8	Month 9	Month 10	Month 11	Month 12
Base Salary	$ 10,000	$ 10,000	$ 10,000	$ 10,000	$ 10,000	$ 10,000	$ 10,000	$ 10,000	$ 10,000	$ 10,000	$ 10,000	$ 10,000
Variable Compensation	$ -	$ -	$ -	$ -	$ -	$ -	$ -	$ 10,000	$ 10,000	$ 10,000	$ 10,000	$ 10,000
Overhead	$ 3,333	$ 3,333	$ 3,333	$ 3,333	$ 3,333	$ 3,333	$ 3,333	$ 3,333	$ 3,333	$ 3,333	$ 3,333	$ 3,333
Cost of leads required	$ 13,650	$ 13,650	$ 13,650	$ 13,650	$ 13,650	$ 13,650	$ 13,650	$ 13,650	$ 14,400	$ 14,400	$ 14,400	$ 14,400
Total Expenses	$ 26,983	$ 26,983	$ 26,983	$ 26,983	$ 26,983	$ 26,983	$ 26,983	$ 36,983	$ 37,733	$ 37,733	$ 37,733	$ 37,733
Cumulative expenses	$ 26,983	$ 53,967	$ 80,950	$ 107,933	$ 134,917	$ 161,900	$ 188,883	$ 225,867	$ 263,600	$ 301,333	$ 339,067	$ 376,800

Breakeven Analysis	Month 1	Month 2	Month 3	Month 4	Month 5	Month 6	Month 7	Month 8	Month 9	Month 10	Month 11	Month 12
Net profit	$ (26,983)	$ (26,983)	$ (26,983)	$ (26,983)	$ (26,983)	$ (26,983)	$ (26,983)	$ (31,650)	$ (27,067)	$ (21,733)	$ (16,400)	$ (11,067)
Cumulative Net Profit	$ (26,983)	$ (53,967)	$ (80,950)	$ (107,933)	$ (134,917)	$ (161,900)	$ (188,883)	$ (220,533)	$ (247,600)	$ (269,333)	$ (285,733)	$ (296,800)

Figure 4.3   Skok Analysis, Enterprise AE

The numbers all look better at higher attainment rates. (See Figure 4.4.) At 90%, 100%, and 110% quota attainment, the AE is more productive, meaning the losses don't run as deep, revenues mount, payback occurs faster, and growth accelerates. This comp plan with a minimum performance of 80% productivity, by quarter 5 in the AE's tenure is healthy for the company, the AE manager, and the AE who has a clear sense of what he needs to do and by when to keep his spot on the team.

With sales compensation plans, simplicity is key. Simplicity allows front-line personnel to focus on just the one or two things that matter most to their performance. Simplicity helps managers drive behavior in targeted directions. Simplicity allows for clear, easy-to-understand commissioning and payouts, which removes stress from salespeople and from the finance team.

The example of a simple commission plan for the enterprise SaaS account exec described here could be:

- 10% commission on all new SaaS revenue
- 12% commission on all expansion SaaS revenue within the first year of the contract
- +2% add-on for revenue collected in advance for at least one year

Figure 4.4 Skok Analysis, Enterprise AE #2

The mandate to the AE here is clear.

1. Sell.
2. Set up deals with great expectations and stick with your customers to win expansion revenue.
3. Structure contract terms to collect cash up front.

The above is just one, very specific enterprise SaaS AE comp plan. This commission used a simple, flat rate on booked revenue. Depending on the behaviors you aim to motivate from the sales team or safeguards you need to put on payouts, some alternatives to consider when creating or iterating on a variable comp plan are:

- **Tiered Commissioning** – Setting lower rates on commission below a target threshold and high rates above, providing a stick for underperformance and carrot for overperformance. It's also a great way to retain top performers, as they are compensated according to their superior results.

- **Gross Margin Commissioning** – If your company has a wide range of possible profit margins, then the value of top-line revenue can vary greatly. One means to de-risk overpaying for low-margin revenue is to compensate on the gross margins on the deal sold. This is also a safeguard against sales reps offering aggressive discounts as it greatly impacts their commissions.

- **Percent-to-Plan Commissioning** – When customer totals or revenue numbers vary within a team, it's often the simplest choice to attach a commission payout to percentages of goal attainment. This allows individual goals to be customized while the core commission plan is simple and universally applied to all.

Regardless of whether you are designing a commission plan for high-touch or low-touch sales, B2B or B2C, recurring revenue or transaction, there are a few core elements to help guide you through the process:

- Know the long-term impact of your commission plan.
- Set the floor of performance based on maximum acceptable losses.

- Keep the commission plan simple and communicate it openly so that the AE understands the logic behind how and why he gets paid.

Example 2: SDR/BDR

Creating comp plans for sales development reps (SDRs) trips up many sales leaders and business owners. They don't directly bring in the revenue so having a clear ROI can be hard to track and thus determine an appropriate compensation plan.

The answer is to not look at sales development as sales costs, but more like you would marketing costs. Their function is demand gen, not customer acquisition. Pay them according to the demand. "But how do I justify paying someone if their deals may never convert and bring in revenue?" Businesses do that every day. It's called marketing expense.

That's not to say that revenue never enters the conversation of SDR compensation. It just typically takes the form of pipeline vs. signed or collected dollars. Waiting for the deal to close takes too long and is too disconnected from the actual work done by the SDR to motivate behaviors.

The balance needed is a healthy incentive for the quantity and quality of deals. If too many low-quality deals flood the pipeline, valuable AE time is wasted, conversion rates suffer, and in the long term the cost of the SDR is not recouped by a sufficient amount of revenue. Not enough volume leaves the AE unproductive and leads to the same long-term inefficiency.

After years of research, experimentation, and interviewing a number of experienced SDR leaders, I landed on a hybrid model of SDR variable compensation. The commission plans for SDRs at Rock were part volume and part quality measure. A $30,000 on-target commission would be split 50/50; $15,000 was paid for hitting the meetings-generated target (quantity control), and the other $15,000 was paid for hitting the S4 pipeline stage target, the point where the AE presents the proposal to the prospect (quality control).

Once again, the plan is simple to measure. There are two components of performance, both easily measured in a deal-tracking dashboard. How to determine the economics of how much to pay and the target of how many opportunities the SDR needs to generate? Once again, the design-build committee of HR, Sales Leadership, Ops, and Finance need to answer the cost-benefit and market salary competitiveness questions. And as always, Skok it.

Key takeaways here:

- Look at SDR/BDR comp as demand gen, not sales performance.
- Balance quantity and quality for performance measures,
- Set the floor of performance based on maximum acceptable losses.
- Keep the commission plan simple and communicate it openly so the AE understands the logic behind how and why he gets paid.

Example 3: Sales Manager

Much like SDR comp, creating an effective sales manager commission plan can throw you for a loop, as they are not directly tied to revenue acquisition, but rather influencers of it. In the Skok sheet manager costs are listed in the simple box of "Additional Overhead." Let's unpack this and detail the manager-comp structures available.

First, much like with the AE comp plan described earlier, there are a few base questions that need answering to set guardrails.

- How much additional cost/dollar sold is logical for the revenue attributed to the manager's team?
- What type of sales behavior is the company looking to motivate with the comp plan?
- What is the going market rate for the role you are hiring?

The answers to these questions can often help set the parameters to a manager's comp plan.

Where many front-line salespeople will have an at or near 50/50 split for base/variable, it's common for managers to work with 60/40 or 70/30 splits. The higher base salary proportional to the total on-target earnings is due in part to managers having less control over their variable comp. It's harder to move the needle on a team-wide bonus plan, so manager comp is offset with bigger base salaries to cover them.

Also, much of the manager's job is administrative (creating play-books, running, reviewing and analyzing reports, interviewing and hiring, etc.) and not directly tied to revenue acquisition. For that reason, it's common to use a percent-to-plan commission structure, rather than a direct payment on revenue. The floor to start commissioning sales managers in a percent-to-plan payout structure is often near where a minimum performance percentage may be for an individual rep (say 80%). If a manager is earning a heavy base salary and the team performs below the threshold, it's hard to justify a variable bonus payout.

At Rock, we used two factors (simple) for calculating manager bonuses.

1. Percent-to-plan on revenue – scaling up at 80%, 90%, 100%, 110%, 120%+

2. Percent-to-plan on team members achieving a goal – scaling up at 50%, 60%, 70%, 80%, 90%, 100%

The second payout factor was key. Many teams can ride the performance of one or two superstar reps to hit the revenue target. This is an unhealthy measure of manager performance for a number of reasons. The superstars are usually plug-and-play-play reps who will post a solid number with or without the manager. Having too much revenue in the hands of too few people runs a high risk of future performance if the superstars are promoted or quit.

Also, if a few reps are performing in a fair system, it means all can perform and the manager has work to do, so they stop losing winnable opportunities. If a few are performing due to an unfair system, the manager needs to fix it. The solution? Measure and comp managers on how many of their team cross the finish line.

This second measure has another positive effect. Managers can sometimes avoid having tough conversations with underperforming reps and let them languish on the team while they focus on the reps who perform. If there are reps who consistently miss their goals on the team, the percent-to-plan on team goals motivates managers to move low performers out.

Fairness and motivation to earn a competitive salary are key in any comp plan. In sales, the variable commission rules set the stage for the behaviors you want to see from your team, aligning company, team, and individuals to all work in the same direction.

The Key Design-Build Element to Sales Compensation

As we've hit upon throughout this book, design-build modeling puts system architects in the room with the people who will take the blueprint plans and make them a reality. In sales compensation, the designers are often finance, ops, HR, and sales management. The builders are the salespeople whose performance will be steered by the compensation rules. All too often, the builders are left out of compensation planning.

When management designs and launches a variable-compensation plan without front-line sales involvement, they invite downstream friction. In the worst-case scenario, the design team working alone creates a confusing, misaligned, and demotivating comp plan that fails to get sales buy-in and eventually ends up hurting performance.

But even in the best case, when management does not invite salespeople to review and provide feedback on the compensation plan, they feel unheard. When a plan is designed and implemented without me, it's your plan; with me, it's our plan. The latter scenario helps in better communicating the logic of the plan, working out any bugs pre-launch, and creating a greater sense of accountability by build-side. When everybody signs off before a plan is launched, a greater sense of "we're all in this together" is created.

Compensation Beyond On-Target Earnings (OTE)

There's more to compensation than money. A lot more. And especially today, when Millennials and Gen Z are much more attuned to non-financial rewards, it's essential to consider compensation from a more holistic view. As mentioned previously, it's critical to match what your company offers to what candidates value in making a career choice. According to The Deloitte Global 2020 Gen Z and Millennial Survey[21] there's much to consider.

What are you learning from candidates during the interview regarding what they value? How are you matching those values, not just with words, but actions and examples? Does your vacation down-time policy check the box for good work/life balance? Do you have a formal reimbursement for learning and development that will excite candidates? Does the company have a social-impact program fostering a greater sense of meaning from work and healthy company culture?

How you answer these questions often makes the difference between winning or losing candidates. Aligning with HR and Finance to create a holistic comp plan is key. If you want to hire the best, you have to be prepared to offer the best, and that goes well beyond salary.

Career Paths

Nearly a quarter of Millennials and Gen Z rank career growth at the top of the list of reasons why they work where they work. Having clear, easy-to-understand promotion and career path criteria go a long way to signing key players onto your team and boosting morale. Having pre-set criteria for how team members earn promotions adds value by

- Getting candidates excited about a clearly defined career path awaiting them.
- Removing subjectivity out of the promotion conversation.
- Building urgency around performance from day 1.
- Matching sales' goal-attainment mindset to the benefit of career growth.
- Creating memorable moments within the team for culture-building and promotion.

This last element was particularly helpful. When the team at Rock scaled up to 50+ reps, we were announcing promotions virtually every month. The promoted rep would have a delicate slide in the monthly kickoff deck, get called up in front of the team, be handed a gift, and celebrate unanimously. It was fantastic for team morale, retention, and performance. The best month in the rep's year was always when a promotion was at stake.

Newly promoted reps would invariably update their LinkedIn profiles with their new titles, write up celebratory posts, and thank their teams and leaders. This created the best PR material in the job market. It was free, unsolicited, widely promoted, and came directly from our top reps who became models for the next generation of great new hires.

It's also an accretive retention tool. Who's worth more to your business and worth paying more? Reps who perform the very best. Designing a plan for where top reps command a higher pay scale and team status through performance versus qualitative review cycles (or even worse, by asking for a raise) creates a performance meritocracy. The question that needs to be answered when creating the promotion criteria is "What constitutes top performance?"

Promotion paths are a great tool for building motivational triggers into the comp plan beyond the core set of performance payout. One example we used at Rock was the net dollar retention criteria for sales promotion. We wanted to motivate salespeople to sell good deals, have a vested interest in customer alignment and adoption, and work with the customer-success team to help deliver value, re-engage, and even upsell customers when needed.

Paying out commissions to sales for net dollar retention would get messy. We were already comping customer-success managers on that revenue and didn't want to take sales' eye off the primary objective of selling to new customers. So, we added it as a promotion criterion at each level.

A trailing six-month new revenue quota attainment of 110% AND a net dollar retention of 100% on a rep's active customer base earned a promotion to the next level. The next level came with a new title, higher salary, and corresponding higher quota target. How to determine the new salary and quota? Skok it!

The results were game-changing. Sales and Customer Success collaborated on the mutual objective of customer satisfaction and revenue retention. Reps filled out better notes in CSM to set up CS with critical information to nail a great customer experience and often attended the first few onboarding calls to pitch in. When customers fell into risk, sales reps helped CSMs right the ship. When customers canceled, sales reps helped strategize upsell opportunities in the existing base to help get the lost revenue back.

Setting up this part of the promotion system takes careful tracking and reporting. Reps need a window into the health of their numbers toward a promotion at any given moment. This is where Business of One tracking comes in, as described in the Sales Process System. When you start collecting end-to-end performance data on reps for the entire lifecycle of a customer's journey with the company, you can track and report top performance from a business standpoint, not from just a new business standpoint.

Minimum Performance Thresholds

Just as high-performance players need clarity on career-growth criteria, low performance needs a line drawn in the sand for when to call it quits. Minimum performance criteria act as the immune system of the sales team. The floor is set and clearly communicated in advance, ideally explained during the offer call and stated in the offer itself, or at the very latest in week 1 of onboarding. From there, reps know clearly what the danger zone is that will put them at risk.

Most minimum performance thresholds are preempted with a performance improvement plan or PIP. At Rock, we called it "rehab." For shorter sales cycle teams, it was one month; for longer it was a quarter. As stated earlier, the best months reps ever had was when a promotion was at stake. The second best was rehab. It often acted as the exact smelling salts a rep would need to focus on for success, get mad, keep their head in the game, and come through the other side.

When it didn't work out and the rep failed to recover during rehab, the conversations were very rarely awkward and never unexpected. We tried. We fought hard. It didn't happen. Let's move on as professionals. Every sales manager who works long enough will eventually have to fire reps for poor performance. It's best to align when and how that happens from day zero to remove surprise from the equation and keep the team motivated not only with the carrot of promotion, but with the stick of termination.

Expectation and Communication

I once heard somebody say – I can't remember who – "The two things that can destroy any relationship are unrealistic expectations and poor communication." In my opinion, that pretty much covers all work relationships, too. Far too many times, I allowed assumptions on what I thought was common understanding to undermine generally healthy work relationships.

This is a symptom of build-side upbringing. Salespeople have a tendency to just go and let the chips fall where they may. Figure things out when we get there. In a leadership role, this type of work philosophy comes back at you in the form of misaligned teams, undefined goals, and murky processes. Better to think about the long game when it comes to the relationships in your sales org and design for future contingencies.

At Rock, we used an expectation-and-communication checklist, initially used in the first rep-manager 1-on-1 meeting and later moved up to the final interview call where the formal offer was made. This was done to let the candidate know very clearly what he was signing up for and give him one last chance to jump ship before signing and committing to the mission.

The conversation covered:

- The reason why we are making an offer is . . . (review of where the candidate scored well).
- There were some gaps in the evaluation, however, such as . . . (review of where the candidate scored lower).
- What you can expect from me as your direct manager is . . . (explanation of leadership and communication style).
- What should I expect working with you . . . (allows the new hire to set the tone of the relationship and make a commitment to the road ahead).
- How do you prefer I approach a conversation with you when I believe a problem needs to be addressed or constructive criticism is warranted? (Sensitive conversations will invariably come up. It's better to set the ground rules on how to handle them before they arise.)
- Walk me through your understanding of the compensation plan, so we are clear on how you get paid and why. (Comp plans are meant to set a clear motivation on what is valued. Too many times this is not clear for a new hire.)

- Walk me through your career path and how you get promoted. (Sets the table for top performers who are out to get out of the gates fast.)
- Walk me through your minimum performance threshold and the floor performance you are required to put in to stay in good standing in this role. (This makes it clear what the floor is and communicates that min performance is real.)

This conversation is best run face to face with the new hire, then followed up immediately after with written confirmation. Sales leadership is one of the least prepared for roles in the professional world. Nobody tells you that part of your job is to lawyer your way through conversations. But unless you do just that, future issues pop up months or years later, which could have been avoided with just a little more preparation and documentation.

Setting the Table for Long-Term Success

Part of the rationale behind early communication and expectation-setting is to prime the pump for long-term success. Sharing a common language and a common vision for the work to be done is key for maximizing outcomes. In the design-build model, this is like meeting with your construction supervisor for a final walkthrough of the blueprint before construction starts.

In the "Selling Your Vision" section of the interview process we covered how value is determined by the candidate looking at the position, company, and the "what" they will get out of working with you. Defining success is no different. For the company, success is very easily defined by revenue and customer-satisfaction performance. For a person, success can take on any number of forms and interpretations.

What does each person on the sales team define as success? What personal satisfaction do each BDR, Rep, and Manager get from the work they do? Moreover, what drives them, excites them, motivates them to give their absolute best every day beyond the performance and the paycheck? What we really need to align on early is the person's intrinsic versus extrinsic motivators.

Extrinsic vs. Intrinsic Motivation

Extrinsic motivators are driven by external rewards. A commission payout, incentive win, and earning a promotion are forms of extrinsic rewards. Sales has historically been built on the concept that salespeople are "coin operated" and structuring the right payout system is all you need to motivate strong performance and maximize output.

Intrinsic motivation comes from within. If a commission check is an external motivator for strong performance, the satisfaction of getting the job done at a high level is its intrinsic counterpart. When the motivation for earning a promotion is higher pay, more authority, and team recognition it's extrinsic; when it's the feeling of accomplishment and personal growth, intrinsic.

The nuts and bolts of a comp plan, career path, and minimum-performance criteria are all structural extrinsic motivators. These can and should be done at the macro level. Entire teams, and often entire companies have the same rules governing their pay and performance measures to keep the systems fair and objective. The work needed to effectively design-build an intrinsic model of motivation, however, is done at the micro level, person by person, customized and tailored to the individual.

Design-Building Intrinsic Motivators – Core Needs

When applying design-build to the construction of intrinsic motivation alignment, the team manager is the designer, and the individual rep or BDR is the builder. As the goal with intrinsic motivation is to tap into the personal drivers of the individual, there's simply no other way but to have each team member define their own understanding of what success looks like. The manager is just there to guide and help structure the process.

The best coach I ever had, Jeb Bates, CEO of ThoughtAction, refers to this process of identifying core needs as defining the "gas tanks." What are the aspects of your work that you find fulfilling and keep you fueled to work hard and overcome adversity? Each of these, Bates describes, is a tank of motivation, important to keep filling and refilling. Should too many of these tanks run low, work becomes meaningless or even demotivating. Performance suffers, low morale sets in, and negative outcomes are almost certain.

To help define my gas tanks, Jeb had me first write out my top 10 life highlights. A highlight was whatever I deemed it to be, which is key. In order to help me understand my own drivers, Jeb didn't ask me to talk about motivation in the abstract or hypothetical, but rather had me describe actual times of great personal motivation. Winning a boxing title, earning President's Club as a rep and manager, meeting my wife – each made my top 10 highlights list.

Next Jeb worked with me to drill into what it was about each of these highlights that gave them highlight status. Why did I deem them so personally fulfilling? Which aspects of the experience did I associate with the most personal value? The boxing title and the President's Club awards mattered because I valued the objective accomplishment that not everyone could earn. Meeting my wife mattered because I valued connection, trust, and companionship with those closest to me.

Other highlight attributes emerged, like broadening lived experiences, feeling a sense of freedom and autonomy, and deep sentiment for my connection to personal history. Each of these was a foundational point for what made a highlight a highlight. They were the root causes of my intrinsic motivators. They were my gas tanks.

The final (an ongoing step) was to identify which areas of my job could be associated with my gas tanks. In order for me to feel fulfilled by the work, the gas tanks would need to be regularly refilled by my work. As long as there were hard-fought battles that could objectively be won and not everyone could win them, I was good. As long as there were personal connections of trust and companionship at the company, I was good. The motivators for my performance were in place. Should these core attributes of work start to evaporate, so too would my drive to perform.

We used this process and baked it into the first 1-on-1 meetings between reps and managers. This helped customize the intrinsic framework each person needed as their personal identifiers of value from the work. Some ranked helping those around them as high on their intrinsic motivator list. Others valued social impact as a highlight attribute, needing to see how their work was having a positive impact on the world at large.

The gas tanks were documented on a 1-on-1 tracking sheet to maintain their visibility as the person's first principles of intrinsic value. Combined with written-out short, mid-, and long-term goals, the framework acted as a North Star to come back to in times of realignment. It also helped managers speak their team members' individual language of motivation. If ongoing self-improvement was a gas tank, the manager had the freedom not to throw a cash incentive at a rep, but rather offer to pay for a class the person wanted to take. Same cost, completely different value.

Health Check Reporting Inside the People System

The People System is the most powerful of all the six subsystems for influencing results in a sales organization. And because of its weight, quantifying and reporting on the trends to iterate and optimize processes where needed is supremely necessary. The People System is arguably the most subject to change and evolution inside high-growth companies, as there are new faces and new challenges constantly showing up as the team continues to grow.

Talent Channel of Acquisition Tracking

Much like in the Demand-Generation System, the People System needs to watch closely the channels of talent acquisition. Especially at scale, it's crucial to know where to invest time to find ideal candidates. Referrals from existing team members often offer the highest quality, but with the least consistency. To maintain staffing levels and quota capacity it's best to know where to go to get the best ROI during surges in hiring.

As channel-tracking data builds, more clearly defined talent pools emerge that inform acquisition strategy. In the early days of growing Rock's team, we noticed a disproportionate number of our top performers had graduated from IBMEC, a local business school. We highlighted this in both referral and outbound channel strategies, asking current team members to search their IBMEC connections for referrals. HR searched LinkedIn for IBMEC graduate profiles from cold outreach, and we arranged career day presentations for the graduating class there. Essentially, we took many of the tactics used in account-based marketing and applied them to talent acquisition, surrounding IBMEC. It worked, and we staffed a whole generation of top-performing sales reps from the strategy.

Scorecard Regression Analysis

The scorecards used during the hiring process are valuable for maintaining a structured, common language for candidate evaluation. But they also provide the key dataset for attribute-to-success tracking. Running regression analysis where interview performance is cross-referenced with actual sales performance assigns true value and weights to the attributes screened for during candidate evaluation. As a company and team evolve, often too will the attributes that are needed to get sales results. Refreshing how you look at the skills needed to perform often helps maintain alignment.

Triple Session Training Reports

Skills dry out over time. Triple Session helps keep them hydrated with the dashboards, itemized skill tracking, and activity reports for each rep. This puts data behind what each member of the team knows, how well they know it, how recently they measured on it, and how dedicated they are to learning new stuff.

Over time, practice patterns can be cross-referenced with performance patterns, and skill strength-to-success correlations emerge. Just as powerful as knowing who is working to keep skills strong is knowing who isn't. Seeing the absence of effort in self-improvement through organized practice can help add other key data for decision making.

Business-of-One Reporting

As discussed previously, true performance tracking must be done holistically from a lead's earliest interactions with sales, through each touch -point of a conversation, through purchase and long-term status. Having each member of the team able to easily access their individual business-of-one report is powerful. This allows them to stay on top of positive or negative trends. It provides an early warning system for when performance dips persist and they're in danger of falling below minimum performance criteria. It keeps the stats board visible for those reps who are working toward a promotion, allowing them to track exactly what they need to do by when to jump up to the next position.

The Record Book

Recognition is a powerful motivator not only extrinsically but also helps reinforce the internal drive many people have for feeling they're making a difference. A sales rep wants to be able to write his name on the wall and say, "I was here! I did this!" Give it to them. Week 1 on the job, I set up the Rock Record Book: a simple Google doc recording things like best month by a rep, biggest deals, most consecutive months at quota, and fastest to make the first sale – zero cost, a little time to update at the start of each month, huge value for our sales team culture, and creating another ongoing performance incentive.

After implementing Triple Session, we took the same record-book logic used for sales performance and applied it to sales practice: top all-time score, top score for the month, for the week. Most consecutive days of training streaks. All were recorded and published to the team to build pride and excitement into the actions for both performing today and preparing to perform better tomorrow.

eNPS Surveys

Employee Net Promoter Score (eNPS) surveys have become common practice for companies seeking to take the temperature of customer sentiment regarding products, services, and brand perception. The surveys are short, easy-to-follow questions with a simple grading logic. Questions are asked on a 10-point scale: Scores from 0 to 6 are detractors, 7 and 8 passives, and 9 and 10 promoters. Once a survey is complete, passives are removed, leaving the final score calculated as % promoters – % detractors. The highest possible score is 100 (100% – 0%), and the lowest possible score is –100 (0% – 100%).

Forward-thinking companies started using this same methodology to gauge employee sentiment, hence the employee Net Promoter Score. According to Gallup,[22] businesses with a highly engaged workforce have 81% lower absenteeism and are 23% more profitable. It pays to keep employees engaged . . . literally.

Sample questions for eNPS surveys look like:

- How helpful is your manager when you need help solving a problem?
- How confident are you that you will still be working here in 12 months?
- How exciting or interesting do you find your work?
- How close did the company meet or exceed expectations you had from when you first started working here?
- How likely are you to recommend working here to friends and associates?

Questions like these are easily graded on a 10-point scale. Follow-on open text boxes or Yes/No questions can add color to the scoring, but the quantifiable data allows for objective reporting and tracking trends over time. It's recommended to run eNPS surveys quarterly to allow previous remedies to take effect, but also stay on top of detractor sentiment.

Key to employee engagement is giving the team a voice, allowing them to air grievances or shortcomings they see in the business and treating the problem before it metastasizes. After surveys are administered and weak points in employee sentiment are identified it's critical to let the team know they were heard and take action.

The People System Rituals

Rituals of the People System underscore the cultural norms of your team and company. Consistency in this system specifically is so important and often relies not only on managerial muscle, but also on strong leadership skills. To effectively operate the People System means to take into account both how people think and how they feel.

Shout-Outs

Recognition is the most scalable ingredient you have for building team engagement. Slather it on liberally. There are countless numbers of opportunities for celebrating individual accomplishments. Among them are:

- A rep puts up a huge activity number in a day.
- A rep opens a huge number of new opportunities feeding their pipeline.
- A huge deal gets signed, significantly moving the revenue attainment.
- A huge deal gets signed, adding a significant logo to the customer base.
- Two reps collaborate to sign a deal, each adding value to one another and the customer experience.
- Sales collaborates with another team (Marketing, Customer Success, Services, Product, etc.) to solve an issue for a customer.
- A rep hits a significant training score or streak milestone in Triple Session.
- A rep earns a promotion.
- A group of reps earn an incentive.
- A team crushes their monthly or quarterly performance.
- A customer gives praise to the people they worked with in sales or service delivery.
- Anything that makes it into the record book.

To quote Maya Angelou, "People will forget what you said, they'll forget what you did, but people will never forget how you made them feel." Shout-outs can be a powerful tool for making people feel appreciated, that their work matters, and that they are having a positive impact beyond themselves. You don't need to wait until the next company-wide meeting, quarterly kickoff, or team get-together. A simple email celebrating someone's accomplishment goes a long way.

Marketing the People System

The People System requires its own marketing engine. And like any well-run marketing motion, it needs to consider all stages of the employee journey: awareness, consideration, action, and evangelism. When executed at the highest level, the virtuous cycle of a team-building flywheel sets into motion.

Awareness – Future employees become familiar with your brand and your great place to work. They see you winning awards and employees in their network raving about you. Regular victories in growth, customer satisfaction, or social impact land in their social feeds. Pulling this off takes a company-wide effort, spearheaded by Marketing and HR to get great content out there and in the hands of every employee to help maximize reach.

Consideration – New candidates engage in the interview process when new positions open up that fit their skills and interests. The best candidates are hard to get, so the light always has to be on welcoming them in. Former outbound prospected candidates should be re-approached by HR or when referred internally, by the referring team member, applying the same old ops deal nurturing used in the Demand-Generation System to the hiring flywheel.

Decision – Candidates sign with the company when offered. Sales enablement content is needed here. HR should promote the company's benefits plans prominently on the website, and all job descriptions. Interviewing managers should reinforce the benefits they uncover as most valuable throughout the interview process. Great storytelling from the team should weave in the "great place to work" message, especially during inverted interviews. The hiring manager should qualify the candidate at the end of the interview process, asking what aspects of the company resonate most positively with them.

Evangelism – Employees feel positive about their roles, teams, and the company at large. The eNPS scores consistently register a high number of promoters, employees regularly advocate for the company publicly and refer friends and former colleagues to apply when new positions open up.

Social media, especially LinkedIn, is the most scalable venue for running the People System's marketing engine as a team. Opportunities abound for nurturing each stage of the employee's journey. And just as with any other type of marketing, content is king in the People System. Regular publishing on company culture from HR, Marketing, the C-suite, and sales team members. Pictures tell a thousand words, and so creating memorable moments for teammates to capture on camera and share with the world helps fuel the marketing engine.

Business-of-One Review

Salespeople tend to follow a monthly cadence. Even for those who work on quarterly revenue cycles or longer, it is optimal to check performance in monthly spurts. Monthly reviews strike the balance between offering a statistically significant sample size of data (activity numbers, worked deals, pipeline movement, etc.), and timely agility. Monthly checks keep bad habits at bay and open up opportunities to take corrective action with time on the clock.

Business-of-one tracking provides the most complete data set for this conversation. It allows the rep and manager to check in on how all phases of the game are performing in order to isolate areas of strength to reinforce and area opportunities to realign.

Gas Tanks Review

Having the "gas tanks" conversation with team members and documenting what drives them is only the first step in building intrinsic motivation. You've got to check in. Knowing what a person needs to feel fulfilled by their work is pointless if you don't come back to check if they're actually being fulfilled by their work. A monthly check-in is likely overkill, especially when running monthly eNPS surveys, but a look, every quarter or semester, at the fuel gauges during a 1-on-1 can help reduce emotional drag on teammates.

Mistakes I've Made When Constructing the Salespeople System

If you believe as I do that the People System is the most influential to the results of the sales organization, you'll also agree that the mistakes you make in this system are the most costly. Wrong moves with the team linger, impacting numbers for months, quarters, or even years; they can also multiply, spreading from one person to another like a virus. Thoughtful planning regarding the people on your team, combined with careful execution, can help minimize risks but never eliminate them. Here are a few to watch out for which I've already made for you.

Making Exceptions to ICP or Hiring Process

The ideal candidate profile and step-by-step hiring process are only as effective as far as they are used. Deviate and pay the price. I learned this the hard way. Several times I fell in love with a résumé, and "clicked" with a candidate seducing me into overlooking gaps in the ICP profile when hiring. I can't recall a single case where it worked out well.

Even worse, I on occasion fast-tracked the hiring process, either bypassing the role-plays or skipping the interviews other members of the team were assigned to hold. Usually, this was triggered either by the candidate being referred from a trusted source, or the urgency to get an offer letter out and the candidate signed to hit a near-term start date. Not only does skipping steps allow for substandard hires to slip onto the team, it undermines the value of the other people involved in the hiring process, sending a signal that their input is not really that important. It is!

Stepping Out of the Interview Process Too Early

Just as the team's contribution to the interview process is critical, I realized too late that mine was, too. I remember reading *Lean In* by Sheryl Sandberg early on in Rock's scale-up. She wrote about how she stayed hands-on in the hiring process for too long and became a bottleneck in the team. I took that idea and ran with it, and in the third year with the company, I delegated the entire hiring process to each team's hiring manager, not having any interaction with candidates until after they were hired. New-hire quality suffered.

Rock was not Facebook or Google. We didn't have enough depth or interviewing experience in the ranks to cover the gap. I had been hiring salespeople for more than 15 years by that point and had developed enough fluency in interviewing and pattern recognition to ID good and bad fit candidates more accurately.

Also, in these early days, I owned the sales budget and forecasts, not the team managers. They were much more apt to take a chance on a questionable candidate as it wasn't their name next to the cost or long-term capacity of the seat we were filling. They didn't have enough skin in the game to be true guardians of the team.

Closing Rep Positions

Easily, the biggest mistake I made in the People System (and I made it repeatedly) was to close rep positions, shutting off applications and interviews. We would have surges in hiring demand, fill the open spots and when the team was staffed, I would call off HR, stop reaching out to ICP in the market, and go quiet on asking the team to refer their network.

While for some positions this is okay, you'll always make room for a great rep. And the best only become available at certain moments in their career. You need to be ready to catch them in transition or you'll miss the opportunity. Moreover, as teams scale up to 15, 20, and 30 reps, there needs to be a default mindset that someone will be leaving their seat soon. People take new jobs, quit, get fired, go out on long-term leave, and get promoted. Having a steady stream of candidates moving through the interview process at all times gives you optionality. You'll know if you lose someone or even several people at once, you have backup coming.

Constant interviewing also sends a strong message to the market and to your team. People see open spots promoted on the site and on LinkedIn and infer the company is growing. When the team sees or is involved in interviewing and frequently not hiring candidates, it sends the positive message that the company is picky and I am fortunate to have made it onto the team.

Inconsistent Team-Building Activities

Office work can be monotonous. Long spans of time, without a break in the action, can fray nerves and make people grow wary. Most people, especially most salespeople, like a good party. It builds connections, helps to humanize the people you work with, and offers something to look forward to with excitement and back on with nostalgia. A company that creates memorable moments is more enjoyable.

This was another area where I dropped the ball. In the pre–Covid-19 era, this was easily covered through in-office gatherings. Every Friday the company would roll in cases of beer, and we'd start the weekend together at 5:00. But once the pandemic hit, no one was getting together. It was demotivating, and the impacts were visible on team morale and measured clearly in the eNPS. The message was that an in-person all-hands meeting gets people excited, builds camaraderie, sends the message that the company cares, and allows people to build essential relationships that help them work better together.

Checkpoint – System 3

The layers of the Six Systems of a Sales Organization are now starting to stack. System 1 set the foundation of the process firmly in place. Ideal customer profiles were established and documented, a customer journey path defined, and sales process and methodology created to meet it. The CRM was set up as a framework for following protocol and as a guardrail for process adoption and data collection.

In the Demand-Generation System, the formula for finding and initiating conversations with prospective clients was constructed. A clear go-to-market strategy was established to meet potential buyers where they can be found, and proper efficiencies measured to determine how deals would be created and by whom.

With the Process and Demand Systems in place, the face of your team now comes to light. Different sales motions and prospecting strategies require different skills and levels of sales aptitude. Systems 1 and 2 govern the System 3 keystone of an ideal teammate (the ideal candidate profile). Having these first two systems set allows for clear expectation-setting with the road ahead for anyone brought into the team.

And once on the team, a well-thought-out People System provides team members with a reliable map of where to go and how to get there. The use of a design-build model invites them to be active participants in the construction of the business. They feel heard. Their ideas and input enrich the dialogue of the team and positive outcomes are felt both extrinsically as well as bottom line.

With the process in place, prospects ready to be approached, and people ready to sell, it's time to flip the switch on the revenue flywheel. The people just hired have been brought into a ready-made machine with a playbook manual for operation. It's now time to get them up to speed on the essentials of the playbook and upload the knowledge of how best to perform with the shortest learning curve possible. It's now time for the New-Hire Onboarding System.

Notes

1. "Lowell, Massachusetts Population History | 1840–2022," biggestuscities .com.
2. "American Community Survey 5-Year Data (2009–2021), census.gov.
3. Daniel Korschun and Grant Welker, *We Are Market Basket* (Harper Collins Leadership, 2015), 47.
4. "Avoidable Turnover Costing Employers Big," *Employee Benefit News*, August 9, 2017, https://www.benefitnews.com/news/avoidable-turnover-costing-employers-big.
5. Korschun and Welker, *We Are Market Basket*, 63.
6. Ibid., 77.
7. Casey Ross, "Judge OK's $300m Market Basket Payout to Shareholders," *Boston Globe*, September 26, 2013, https://www.wcvb.com/article/judge-approves-300m-market-basket-shareholder-payout/8188710.
8. Jeremy C. Fox, "Market Basket Workers Seek to Rally Customers," *Boston Globe*, https://www.bostonglobe.com/metro/2014/07/13/market-basket-employees-demand-return-ousted-ceo/u1cDqVjwNg148SQcTPx2aI/story.html.
9. Adam Vaccaro, "Workers Demand Reinstatement of Ousted Market Basket Leader, *Boston Globe*, July 17, 2014, https://www.boston.com/news/business/2014/07/17/market-basket-employees-demand-reinstatement-of-ousted-ceo/.

10. "Reinstate Fired Market Basket Workers, Ex CEO Says," Associated Press, July 22, 2014, https://www.wbur.org/news/2014/07/22/market-basket-ex-ceo-protesters.

11. Jack Newsham, "Market Basket Workers Rally in Tewksbury for 'Artie T.,'" *Boston Globe*, July 25, 2014, https://www.bostonglobe.com/business/2014/07/25/market-basket-workers-rallying-tewksbury/wgy7ixVE88fKXbYG1E0ouK/story.html.

12. Robert Gates, "Market Basket CEOs Tell Employees Return to Work or Be Replaced," *Patch*, Beverly, MA, https://patch.com/massachusetts/beverly/market-basket-ceos-tell-employees-return-work-or-be-replaced.

13. Grant Welker, "Eight Fired Market Basket Managers Sue the Company," *Lowell Sun*, August 1, 2014, https://www.lowellsun.com/2014/08/01/eight-fired-market-basket-managers-sue-the-company/.

14. Donna Goodison, "Market Basket to Advertise for New Workers, Schedules Job Fairs," *Boston Herald*, July 30, 2014, https://www.bostonherald.com/2014/07/30/market-basket-to-advertise-for-new-workers-schedules-job-fairs/.

15. Ibid.

16. Keiko Zoll, "Pictures from Tuesday's Massive Market Basket Protest," *Consumer Press*, August 5, 2014, https://consumer.press/scenes-from-tuesdays-massive-market-basket-rally-photos/.

17 "Artie T. Rejects Proposal to Return to Market Basket on Interim Basis," CBS Boston, August 8, 2014, https://www.cbsnews.com/boston/news/proposed-deal-could-end-market-basket-battle-and-return-artie-t-to-company/.

18. Noah R. Bombard, "Market Basket Deal Is Done; Arthur T. Buys Company for $1.5 Billion," MassLive, August 28, 2014, https://www.masslive.com/news/worcester/2014/08/market_basket_deal_is_done_art.html.

19. "Culture," Reed Hastings, https://www.slideshare.net/reed2001/culture-1798664.

20. "The SOCIAL STYLE Model," TRACOM Group, https://tracom.com/social-style-training/model.

21. "The Deloitte Global Millennial Survey 2020," https://www2.deloitte.com/content/dam/Deloitte/global/Documents/About-Deloitte/deloitte-2020-millennial-survey.pdf.

22. "What Is Employee Engagement and How Do You Improve It," Gallup, https://www.gallup.com/workplace/285674/improve-employee-engagement-workplace.aspx.

5

The New-Hire Onboarding System

The Case of Andy Stumpf – Navy SEAL Training

The United States Navy Sea, Air, and Land Teams, commonly known as Navy SEALs, is by all accounts the most elite special operations force in any military, anywhere in the world. SEAL units are built to conduct high-priority operations with tactical, small-unit teams. If an American POW is being held behind enemy lines, it's the SEALs who are asked to go in and get the prisoner out. If terrorists capture an oil tanker or seize control of a key port, it's the SEALs who are sent in to defuse the situation and regain command.

To give a sense of the kind of work SEALs are asked to do on a "business as usual" basis, we can look at the example of the Al Basrah Oil Terminal (ABOT) operation in March 2003. Just before the U.S. invasion of Iraq in the Second Gulf War, SEALs were asked to conduct raids on high-value targets, intended to cripple the Iraqi regime. One such target was ABOT. Along with one other platform, ABOT controlled 80% of Iraq's oil export to the world. Taking control meant shutting off the key source of funding to Saddam Hussein's war machine and securing a vital supply line of world energy.

Under the cover of darkness and underwater, SEALs swam beneath the oil platform to first gather intelligence. They measured submerged structures and access points, monitored Iraqi personnel and spent hours photographing the platforms and documenting the activity. This was just the preparation.

When they returned on March 20, the first day of the invasion, they had designed the operation so meticulously that ABOT was captured without a single casualty.[1]

SEALs are asked to jump out of planes and rappel from helicopters. They conduct underwater raids as well as urban assaults. SEALs are sent into deserts and densely packed cities, to jungles, and to the Arctic. To prove someone has the mental and physical ability for such extreme work, the navy requires all SEALs to successfully complete BUD/s – Basic Underwater Demolition SEAL Training.

From an outsider's perspective, BUD/s looks like a science experiment for the superhuman – a class of Olympic athletes pushed to the brink of mental exhaustion through rigorous training and sleep deprivation, while at the same time training for an iron man competition. Tests of strength, tests of endurance, tests of teamwork, tests of attention to detail, and the ability to follow instructions are all fired at BUD/s students in rapid succession.

BUD/s is a six-month training course, broken down into three key phases – physical conditioning, combat diving, and land warfare training, each taking about eight weeks to complete. On average, for every 100 recruits who enter a BUD/s training class, 70 don't graduate. More than half fail to complete phase 1 physical conditioning. The top reason is D.O.R. – Drop on request. They ask to leave. Many on the first day.

"You'll have 200 people sitting in a classroom saying that becoming a SEAL has been their life-long goal and by the end of the day there will be 30 helmets under the bell," says Andy Stumpf, when describing day 1 at BUD/s.

Stumpf is as familiar with what it takes to complete Navy SEAL onboarding as anybody. He's a graduate of BUD/s Class 212 and spent 17 years with the SEALs, including 18 months as a BUD/s instructor. He's seen SEAL life first-hand as a student, active-duty operator, and as an instructor.

At 45, Stumpf still looks like he could be rotated back into active duty tomorrow if needed. He's built like a division 1 fullback. His neck looks like it could hold a thousand-pound head if it had to. Andy Stumpf speaks with a measured consistency, not fast or slow. There are never any "ums" or "uhs" filling the cracks in sentences like when most of us talk. There are no cracks. He knows what he wants to say.

"As a student," Stumpf explains, "it looks like chaos. A behavior can be rewarded on Monday and punished on Tuesday." Returning as an instructor it became clear that every element of BUD/s is part of a carefully planned onboarding. "There's a three-ring binder for every single day of training," Stumpf says. "Creativity is not there for the instructors. We have to follow the curriculum."

Over the first three weeks of BUD/s training, students are put through test after test of physical endurance. Running, swimming, obstacle courses, sit-ups, pull-ups, seemingly endless requests to drop down and pump out dozens of push-ups on command. SEAL trainees are pushed to their limits and then past their limits. A four–mile run in wet, sandy gear is one measure of physical durability – tired, uncomfortable, feet slipping in the sand again and again. A four-mile run in the surf while carrying a boat over your head, in lockstep with six other students, is another matter altogether.

Each BUD/s class is split up into boat crews of six or seven men. The men are grouped by height as one of the routine tasks they'll be asked to perform is "land portage": timed runs where teams carry 200-pound inflatable boats on their heads. At the start, there can be as many as two dozen boat crews entering phase 1, all competing to win races. The prize for winning is a few minutes of rest while the other teams are pushed to work exhausted. At BUD/s there is only one winner. There are no prizes for finishing second.

Rewards drive behavior and motivate teams to work hard and work together. Punishment is used to elicit the same response. One study describes the compound value of both positive and negative reinforcement. Results indicate that behavior is more influenced by the use of both rewards and punishment together, versus either one exclusively. "One possible explanation for these results is that the combination of both contingencies increased the individual value of each reinforcer."[2]

Simply put, the value of a rest (reward) is greater when compared side-by-side with the punishment of seeing other teams re-run a torturous exercise (punishment). The same is true for what some refer to as "surf torture." A common and simple reward/punishment practice in BUD/s is feeling relatively warm on land versus excruciatingly cold lying in frigid ocean water. When students fail to follow directions properly, don't work effectively as a team, or fail an exercise test, the order to follow is often "hit the surf." Students sprint into the icy cold water repeatedly as a form of negative reinforcement.

Hypothermia breaks over the body in waves of increasing discomfort. After jumping into frigid ocean water, the body's first response immediately kicks in. Heart rate and blood pressure jump, increasing the metabolism. The hypothalamus, the brain's temperature control center, orders blood vessels to contract, moving blood away from the skin, preserving heat for more vital organs. Reduced blood flow brings on painful numbness to the hands and feet faster and faster. Cold water strips body heat away much faster than cold air, accelerating hypothermia.

When heat loss persists, and body temperature continues to drop, metabolism kicks into overdrive, spiking heart rate two to five times the resting beats/minute. Signals are sent to skeletal muscles ordering them to rapidly contract and release, visible in uncontrollable shivering and teeth chattering. Even when trainees are just lying in the water, their bodies are being worked to the extreme. These are all symptoms of just mild hypothermia.

Should the body temperature drop below 90 degrees Fahrenheit, moderate hypothermia sets in. Cognitive function becomes impaired, showing up in erratic speech and inability to follow simple commands. Should body temperature fall below 80 degrees Fahrenheit, people typically fall unconscious. The brain, unable to keep up with the effects of cold, simply shuts off. Body temperatures below 75 degrees typically result in death. The average winter ocean temperature in Coronado, CA, where BUD/s students surf train, is 58 degrees.[3]

Doctors are ever-present throughout Navy SEAL training. The idea is not to hurt the students, but to evaluate them down to the lowest common denominator of character. It's essential to see exactly who a student is when under extreme duress, as that is precisely the environment he may be in when sent into combat.

"It's a physical test, but we're using the body to test the mind," Stumpf explains. "We're stressing the body, we're going to make you tired, hungry, hypothermic. We're going to get you so exhausted to the point where you're going to hallucinate. And then we're going to take a look at how you behave. Do you value *we* over *me*?"[4]

In week 1 of BUD/s, each member of the class is paired up with a swim buddy. They are ordered to never be more than six feet away from their partner at any time during the training. When one student is faster during a run, he moves behind his swim buddy to help push him along. During a swim, the pair are side by side, never leaving one another. They're together during meals, and together when they use the bathroom. It's a lesson in both teamwork, trust, and the consequence of action. When a trainee fails an inspection or forgets to follow any detail of a command, that student does not drop down for push-ups alone. His swim buddy is punished as well.

The most extreme test for BUD/s students occurs in the middle of phase 1 physical conditioning, aptly referred to as "hell week." Hell week starts on a Sunday night and lasts a grueling five days. It's during these five days when the greatest number of SEAL candidates will quit.

Except for a two-hour respite on day 3, there is no sleep permitted during hell week. Students are in constant motion. Surf runs, push-ups, obstacle course runs, more push-ups, land portages, pull-ups, open ocean swims, more pull-ups. One of the most daunting tasks involves "Old Misery," a 400-pound telephone pole that an unfortunate boat crew needs to lift in unison for over-the-head shoulder presses. The exercise can last 30 seconds, a minute, or three minutes, hands slipping, shoulders burning under the strain. Drop the pole, and you do it again. Drop it again. Do it again. Drop it again, go sit in the icy surf.

More students drop on request in hell week than during any other stretch at BUD/s. Having completed the program as a student and trained hundreds of others as a BUD/s instructor, Andy Stumpf has a uniquely intimate understanding of why people quit. "What I arrived at as an instructor," Stumpf says, "is it's how you actually approach your goals and talk to yourself that are far more important than how disciplined or motivated you are."

A student's mental approach to adversity is core to BUD/s, given that it's a mission-critical character trait to working as a SEAL. "People will ask me, are you born mentally tough, or can it be taught? The answer is yes," according to Stumpf. "The question is how much can you build on top of what's already there?

"The muscle that fails in BUD/s is between the ears and it's not something you can measure with a tape measure or a timed run." From Stumpf's experience, if Vegas handicappers came to a BUD/s class on day 1 looking to lay bets on who would likely make it through to graduation, they would lose their shirts. As he puts it, the ones who make it through are generally "the very average, typical looking person. The gray man."

For the students who get past the eight–week crucible of physical conditioning, they enter phase 2 – combat diving. This is where Stumpf spent a year and a half instructing SEAL students across six different classes. As much as BUD/s is a physical challenge, SEAL candidates have an array of tactical information to absorb as well. The first two weeks of phase 2 are spent in the classroom. Students must first learn the theory of TTPs – tactics, techniques, and procedures. In phase 2 that means dive physics, dive medicine, and learning about the equipment.

"Everything is based on tactics and standard operating procedures," Stumpf says. "And everybody is trained to those procedures, so you know what to expect from somebody. It's not complicated. Actually, the way to make us less effective and efficient would be to make it complicated. The simpler that you can make it, the better you're going to be."[5]

After information is uploaded into students' brains, it's pressure tested, first in a pool, and later in open ocean dives. Describing pool competency training, Stumpf says it's "actually about your ability to deal with stress. Can you follow procedure regardless of the amount of stress that's on you?" Instructors accompany students underwater, systematically ripping off their masks, tying knots in their air hoses, pulling apart gear, anything to increase the stress level. They need to see how students will respond in light of unexpected challenges.

BUD/s is a constant series of tests, but all are given with extensive preparation. "There's no day at BUD/s that instructors would test you on something you haven't been taught in practice multiple times," says Stumpf. The tests are not just academic. There are clear standards of minimum performance. Not everyone leaves BUD/s by way of DOR. Performance drops are the second leading cause of failure in Navy SEAL training.

"If you deviate from procedure under stress," Stumpf says, "I don't care how good your run time is or any of that stuff. You are not tooled to do the job."

On Fridays, Stumpf would open up time for students to ask him anything about the job. Conversations would often turn toward life as a SEAL. Salary, relationships, how to balance personal life with the overwhelming requirements of a career. It was an opportunity for BUD/s students to zoom out and get context on the complete picture of what they were training for and what to expect next, should they graduate. Preparing students meant setting accurate expectations beyond the day-to-day technical requirements of the job.

By the time they complete BUD/s, newly minted SEALs are equipped not just with the physical strength to earn the job, but the emotional intelligence needed to execute under pressure. Physical fitness is at its peak when students graduate, but most were top-tier athletes before they started anyway. The real change that takes place during Navy SEAL training is at the cerebral level.

Neuroplasticity, put simply, is the brain's ability to change its structure in order to adapt how it operates in order to meet new requirements. Learning a new job flexes neuroplasticity. Deep learning means that new neural pathways are constructed, and new wiring is created in the brain for sending clear messages to other parts of the brain and body. When athletes talk about "muscle memory" this is what they're referring to. Muscles don't have memory themselves. Well-developed neural pathways fire signals to muscles faster and faster as learning advances. How to build strong neural pathways? Repetition.[6]

Stumpf says that "80–85% of the SEAL career is spent on training. It's just repetition after repetition after repetition, and it's based on fundamental principles. At the end of it, you're able to do really high-speed stuff with large groups, but we always go back to the minimum size maneuver element."[7]

Stumpf's advice for successfully completing BUD/s? Keep your world small and focus on what you can control. "Circle of influence and circle of concern," as he puts it. Circle of influence pulls attention to the controllable. Uncontrollable, environmental influencers or what other people may or may not do should be acknowledged and observed, but not the focus. Circle of concern determines to which tasks should influence be applied.

"What I arrived at as an instructor," Stumpf explains, "is how you actually approach your goals and talk to yourself is far more important than how disciplined or motivated you are."

In Navy SEAL onboarding the first and most important battle students are taught to fight is within.

First Principles of the New-Hire Onboarding System

In BUD/s we find the most extreme example of a New-Hire Onboarding System. And from it and the experience of Andy Stumpf as a student and instructor, clear first principles emerge for how to prepare people for success regardless of how hard the job may be.

Standard Operating Procedures

As we learned from Stumpf's description of a "three-ring binder for every single day of training," learning must be made simple and have clear documentation. Without a single source of procedural truth, chaos reigns. In order to achieve the eventual outcome of getting a team "able to do really high-speed stuff" together, they need a playbook. Without a documented standard for every detail of a job, there can be no system of learning.

Standards of Performance

You cannot improve what you do not measure. Documented operating procedures allow for the clear uploading of information into people's brains, but the essence of the New-Hire Onboarding System is proving comprehension and execution. Rapid teaching is done through simplicity and documentation and engagement. Rapid learning is proven through testing.

"Having endurance" is subjective. Completing a four-mile run in 30 minutes is an objective measure of endurance. "Staying calm under pressure," subjective. "I'm going to rip off your dive gear and you have 60 seconds to collect yourself and stabilize the situation," objective. The only way to effectively measure training effectiveness is to set a clear bar for executing the use of that training and holding the learner accountable for hitting it.

Repetition Is the Rule

One-time training results in superficial learning. For a New-Hire Onboarding System to deliver on its full promise of transformational long-term knowledge-building, the information needs to be grounded. Holding information in short-term memory is not enough. World-class onboarding builds new connections in the brain for long-lasting recall.

To go deep into learning, onboarding must go deep into recall. Train, perform, and measure. Then do it again. Then again. Then again. Over time, the language of the work needed is hard coded, and the new hire is not so new anymore.

Sticks and Carrots

The psychology of positive and negative reinforcement is a vital setting foundational to the process of retaining knowledge. The most-developed area of the brain, the neocortex is great at processing information, but not nearly as strong with hard-coding information. For that, you need to tap into the brain's emotional center, the limbic system. Learning is best when the process can be felt, not just considered.

In BUD/s the rewards of rest and recognition for winning a race offer strong memory-building value connected to the emotional centers of the brain. For a salesperson, successfully completing onboarding or winning a new hire incentive prize can offer that same limbic effect.

While subjecting new hires to hypothermic conditions is a valuable reinforcement technique in SEAL training, the frigid feeling left in the minds of sales trainees who fail to meet early milestones can have a similar impact on their motivation to perform.

"The Gray Man"

Whether in SEALs or sales, the old adage to not judge a book by its cover holds true. Both jobs are more cerebral than physical. Buying into how someone looks as an indication of their ability to do the work is a red herring.

The experience of Andy Stumpf teaches us that even in the most extreme physical environments, it is the mind and mindset of a new hire that drives success, not the body. And it is that mental ability that needs to be surfaced, tested, and built upon to run an effective New-Hire Onboarding System.

Swim Buddies

Sales teams and SEAL teams are just collections of individual contributors. Learning, recalling, and executing alone is not enough. Unified teams are a force multiplier, delivering the promise of a whole being greater than the sum of its parts.

The process of onboarding needs to be delivered in this context. Collaboration is critical. From the onset the values of trust and dependability are key ingredients. To build a team, the New-Hire Onboarding System must take upon itself the responsibility of forging the bonds of teammates.

Elements of the New-Hire Onboarding System

Mapping the Essentials

If you don't know where you're going, you might not get there.

– Yogi Berra

Onboarding is like charting the course for a new hire's early travel with your team. The first step is not to define the path, provisions, or personnel needed, but rather to determine the destination. Where do you want the new member of your team to be by the time they complete the first leg of the journey with you?

The first order of business is to craft the list of what a new hire needs to know, by the end of the formal onboarding period. What are the core elements of the day-to-day work being asked that the newest members of the team need to have uploaded in their brains to stand on their own feet for 80% of the job?

Here is where systems order pays dividends. Having already done the work of defining and documenting the elements of the Process, Demand-Generation, and People Systems, much of the work needed for new-hire onboarding has already been done. It now comes down to content selection, organization, delivery, and measurement.

The design-build model impacts the New-Hire Onboarding System from its inception. Here sales leadership (not HR) must take the lead in the project committee. Those who are the most responsible for the results of the new hire, and will live with the finished product long after onboarding is complete, should be accountable for its execution. HR and Operations also play key roles on the design-build team helping to structure the content and organize measures and cross-collaboration from other functional areas.

Each design-build stakeholder team member should compose their own list of what they see as vital knowledge for a sales new hire to know at the conclusion of onboarding. Sales, HR, and Ops can and should have very different lists. It's the responsibility of the sales leader in the design-build committee to empower and encourage HR and Ops to weigh in confidently on what they believe is of key value. The context and alternative views help in the construction of the most well-rounded onboarding.

A completed list of necessary training could include subjects like:

- Company mission, vision, culture
- Customer persona, ICP, journey
- Customer success process overview

- Product-services delivery overview
- Deep dives into each core product/service
- Sales process overview
- Deep dives into each sales process step
- Pricing and package-building
- CRM training
- Marketing service-level agreements and lead ownership
- Sales enablement material overview
- Deep dives in key enablement material (competitors, case studies, etc.)
- Learning platform training (Where can you go to get answers on your own?)
- Sales readiness scores – Triple Session

With each stakeholder having submitted their list of sales onboarding essentials, the sales leader should then work to refine the onboarding set list. The list should not be time or training constrained. Depending on how elaborate your process and product are, onboarding can span anywhere from a couple of weeks to several months.

If it takes several months and a cast of collaborators from around the company to onboard effectively, then so be it. Play fast and loose with your onboarding and you'll have underprepared reps sent into battle. Explain this concept when recruiting internally for training assistance.

- **Marketing** – "How well prepared to sell do you want the new salespeople who will be receiving the leads you generate?"
- **Customer Onboarding/Support** – "How proficient do you want new salespeople to be when they educate and set expectations with the clients they sell and hand over to you?"
- **Product/Services** – "How knowledgeable would you like to see our new class of salespeople on the stuff you build and deliver to clients every day?"

- **Ops** – "How familiar with the systems, rules, and operating procedures do you want new salespeople to be as they start to impact the performance of the team?"
- **HR** – "How confident in the company and their own readiness do you want new salespeople to be at the conclusion of their onboarding?"

It takes a village to raise a sales rep. When getting the team involved don't forget to sell it. That means educating and gaining agreement from your internal customer, based on what they define as value.

With the set list complete and the contributing team assembled, the beginnings of an onboarding calendar can start to take shape. What should be taught to the new hire class, by when, and by whom? Also, key to determining is the training delivery system. How will the ongoing content be delivered to maximize the value of knowledge transfer while minimizing inefficiencies and drag on the team – both teachers and students?

At Rock, we employed five types of training formats for onboarding – Live Group, On-demand, Live 1-on-1, Simulation, and Active Practice.

Live Group Training. This is what most people think of when they envision onboarding – groups of new hires sitting together, learning at once as a team. This format is key for standard lecture-style training. Some information just needs to be uploaded into the brains of new team members. It makes sense to make it a batch upload. Added value comes from this format when team members ask questions in front of the group. If one person has a question regarding the content, it is often the case that others are thinking the same thing. Encourage interaction.

On-Demand. Live trainings are great for engagement interaction but can be a drag on speed to train. Coordinating schedules can be tough, and every minute a trainer is live, in front of a group, they are not doing more scalable work. For subject matter that is standardized and repeated for every hiring class, on-demand is often the way to go. Open time blocks can be used for new hires to work on their own, read blogs and case studies, watch video training, use the product, and build mock presentations. If onboarding is going back to school to learn your business, on-demand training is the homework. TripleSession was essential for us during this process, as it allowed for assigning, measuring, and validating the learning across the team.

Live 1-on-1. Many teams delay manager 1-on-1 meetings until after onboarding is complete. I fundamentally disagree with this approach; 1-on-1s are not just for pipe reviews or follow-on training. (More on this in the Ongoing Improvement System.) Beginning the weekly cadence of manager-rep 1-on-1s during onboarding starts the trust and familiarity-building in this key work relationship and allows for knowledge reinforcement. New hires can ask follow-on questions from their manager regarding onboarding content to get their perspective or further clarity. Managers can start to validate content comprehension and add clarity and context.

Simulation. As boxers have sparring sessions, salespeople have role plays. Better to get beat up in practice than in the live show. With so much of the job being live, human interaction, getting as much simulation time in during onboarding can help with practicing messaging, refining presentation skills, and testing readiness to handle objections. Light simulation is worthless. There's no value in preparing for easy conversations. The best managers don't pull punches during role plays. The best players don't want them to.

Active Practice. There's no better training than the real thing. Get on the phone and get the uniform dirty early. Matching the theoretical learning of a process step to live practice helps new hires get through their awkward phase of a new job faster and builds confidence. Never wanting to burn high-value leads, this is typically where outbound, old inbound, and low-grade closed-lost deals can be recycled and used as cannon fodder for new hires to try out messaging.

Blending these five training formats throughout onboarding helps to maximize time-to-learn and new-hire engagement, keeping the info-sharing fresh. Sales leaders should look at a new-hire class more like customers than employees. How do you maximize retention and learning so the time-to-value is short and life-time-value of the training is long?

One additional element we used at Rock to help new hires get the most out of their first month was theme weeks. It's common knowledge by now that people learn more from a story than they do from raw data. Creating an onboarding narrative uses the power of storytelling with your new hire class.

The week-over-week themes were Week 1 – The Customer; Week 2 – Sales Process; Week 3 – The Product; and Week 4 – The System. The first month's calendar looked something like Figure 5.1.

Notice the new-hire onboarding starts with the customer. It's surprising how many companies who claim to be "customer-focused" do not prioritize the customer in their new-hire onboarding. This is fundamentally flawed. Your new people will value what you show them you value, not what you tell them you value. Leading with everything customer (persona, problem, industry intel, case studies, etc.) will imprint on the new class that the customer comes first in everything you do.

Much as the steps of a sales process have exit criteria, so too do the steps of an onboarding process: items that need to have been accomplished and checked off the list as "done" before confidently moving on to the next step in the process.

Taking Onboarding Live

Onboarding doesn't start on the new hire's first day. It begins when they sign the job offer. Athletes never start a game cold; they warm up before the whistle blows or the bell rings. Your new hire class shows up warm and ready to play.

On-demand learning allows for training to take place anytime, anywhere. Take full advantage of this by sending out a pre-work syllabus for new hires to get going on. At Rock, we had a base curriculum of marketing (the customer), sales (the process), company (the product), and professional skill-building (the system). This gave new hires a foundation of knowledge for each of the four theme weeks they would work on during onboarding.

Legend: On-Demand | Live Group | Live 1-1 | Simulation | Active Practice

Month - 1 Onboarding Calendar

Week - 1 — The Customer

	Monday	Tuesday	Wednesday	Thursday	Friday
09:00	HR General Orientation	Onboarding Overview	Customer Case Study Review	Case Study Roundtable	Good Fit/Bad Fit Identification
10:00		General Sales Team Overview	CS Overview	Preds/Svcs Overview	Ride Along (F/f)
11:00			CSM 1-1		CRM Training
12:00	Lunch	Lunch	Lunch	Lunch	Lunch
01:00		Tools/Tech Set-Up	CSM Ride Along	Buyer Jrny - Gen / Buyer Jrny - Spc	Building Good Fit / Fit Lead Lists
02:00	HR General Orientation	Comp. Promo, Mkt Perf	Indst Overview / ICP Training	Sales Process Overview	Build First Lead List
03:00					
04:00					
05:00	Case Stdy Prep		Product Prep	Fit Criteria Docs	Weekly Review

Week - 2 — Sales Process

	Monday	Tuesday	Wednesday	Thursday	Friday
09:00	Week 1 Review	Prev Day Review	Prev Day Review	Prev Day Review	Prev Day Review
10:00	Lead List Review	Discovery General	Discovery Review	Discovery Review	Discovery
11:00	Connect		Discovery Tape	Discovery	Lunch
12:00	Lunch	Lunch	Lunch	Lunch	Lunch
01:00	Connecting	Discovery Spcfc	Discovery Ride Along	Discovery	Discovery
02:00	Connecting	Connecting			
03:00	Connecting	Connecting	Connecting	Connecting	Connecting
04:00					
05:00	Connect Tape	Discovery Tape	Discovery Tape	Discovery Tape	Weekly Review

Week - 3 — The Product

	Monday	Tuesday	Wednesday	Thursday	Friday
09:00	Week 2 Review	Prev Day Review	Prev Day Review	Prev Day Review	Prev Day Review
10:00	Product Training	Demo Training	Demo	Pricing & Packaging	Preso
11:00					
12:00	Lunch	Lunch	Lunch	Lunch	Lunch
01:00	Sales Engineer	Demo	Demo	Preso Tape	Preso
02:00					
03:00	Phone Time	Phone Time	Phone Time	Phone Time	Phone Time
04:00					
05:00	Demo Prep	Demo Tape	Preso Prep	Built a Package	Weekly Review

Week - 4 — The System

	Monday	Tuesday	Wednesday	Thursday	Friday
09:00	Week 3 Review	Prev Day Review	Prev Day Review	Prev Day Review	OB Exam Review
10:00	Meeting-Sales Alignment	CS-Synch-Sales Alignment	Time MGT	Emotional Intel	Review Session
11:00			Build Daily Cal	Sales Coaching	OB Exam
12:00	Lunch	Lunch	Lunch	Lunch	Lunch
01:00	Competitive Landscape	Sales Enablement			Phone Time
02:00					
03:00	Phone Time	Phone Time	Phone Time	Phone Time	
04:00					
05:00	Objections	Negotiating			OB Feedback Session

Figure 5.1 New-Hire Month 1 Calendar

Triple Session for Sales Onboarding

With Triple Session already in use, first as our ongoing practice system and later as a key talent prospecting channel, it made sense for us to arrange our on-demand training there. After a new hire signed their offer letter, they received a welcome email with a pre-work track of training sessions to have completed by day 1. For new hires already active in the platform, it was merely a continuation of their current practice.

Throughout a new hire's first month of onboarding, on-demand learning sessions at Rock were delivered inside Triple Session. We wanted content that was both original and curated. We wanted our people to have the most well-rounded learning experience possible. It was our view that the team should receive the benefit of not just role-specific content like prospecting and presenting, but also professional skill-building. We added sessions on topics like time management and financial planning.

Thinking even broader, we knew that people were more than their careers, and we saw value in enriching their Triple Session experience beyond the technical and professional. We added sessions on topics like emotional intelligence, growth mindset, and the power of deliberate practice.

We knew that this "outer ring" of sessions would positively impact the technical and professional performance, but it went beyond that. The goal was to positively impact the new team member's experience with the company as much as we could. We saw significant gaps in the professional and personal readiness programs universities and other companies offered and aimed to fill the void.

New-Hire Onboarding – Day 1

As mentioned previously in the People System, so much of building a healthy, productive relationship is based on two key elements – aligned expectations and clear communication. Day 1 allows for the opportunity to build this solid foundation. What should they expect during month 1? What do you expect of them? Any questions on what the next four weeks will look like?

A common mistake many companies make is under-communicating to their new hires. When we stop to see the world through the new team member's perspective, the situation is pretty overwhelming. A new company, new people to meet and work with, new products and services to learn about, and new policies and procedures to follow.

That's a lot coming at someone all at once when they sign on to a new job. If the objective is to offer a high-value experience that maximizes learning and the speed to deliver results, it's best to be deliberately attentive to the new hire class early and reduce as much stress and insecurity as possible. A few of the items we learned over time to clarify and set as expectations on day 1 at Rock were:

- What success looks like at the end of onboarding
- Encouraged behaviors – punctuality, participation, note-taking, etc.
- Wrong answers and thin ideas are better than silence
- A growth mindset is highly valued
- Onboarding is month 1 of ramp, and there are KPIs to hit
- There will be a final exam at the conclusion of onboarding

Merely stating what you may see as obvious can have worlds of value. Don't assume people, especially new people, come pre-loaded, seeing things the same way you do. Make it easy and make it obvious. Tell them.

The Onboarding Final Exam

A key day 1 communication is letting the new hire class know there will be a final exam. You are taking a class of new hires through basic training. You need to know if they achieved the required learning and if you got the job done by effectively teaching. You've got to test for it. This may seem obvious, but most companies skip this and release their new hires out into full-time work without a measurable standard of basic knowledge proficiency.

Letting the new hires know about the final on day 1 is key. The idea of the exam is not to catch people sleeping through class. It's to promote engagement, preparation, and comprehension. When new hires know they will be graded on how well they have absorbed the onboarding content, they are much more keyed into doing just that.

A few tips on crafting the best new hire exam.

- The more open text boxes the better. Standardized multiple-choice style quizzes like in Triple Session have their place, but with so much attention given to new hires during onboarding, make them work their brains in writing out thoughtful answers.
- Follow the story. If you roll out your onboarding in the recommended narrative format, follow that same order in the final exam flow. It will help reinforce the message of what the company prioritizes.
- Make it hard. The goal of the final isn't to make the new hire feel good. It's to verify that they're truly prepared for the job ahead. Test them for the hard cases to make sure they are battle ready.

Remember that the results of the final exam are as much a report on how well the trainer taught as they are on how well the new hire learned. Keep an eye out for questions that all or most of the class gets wrong. The issue is more likely with how the item was taught or the question phrased than it was with how the class performed.

Calculating New Hire Ramp

The time it takes for a salesperson to reach full productivity in your sales system (ramp) can be a bit of a black box in the early days. Onboarding is clearly the beginning of the ramp period, but how long is long enough, but not too long to require that a new person be running at full speed?

The goal is to give the new hire enough time to learn and get good at the job, but not so long that weak performers or bad-fit hires linger, burning leads, and poisoning the winning culture of the team. The key is finding that sweet spot in the middle, then optimizing for speed. The faster reps start delivering the better it is for them and the company. Everybody starts making money, and everybody knows rep-company fit has been validated with results.

Teams at scale have historical data on which to base ramp performance and timelines. A simple analysis of the past performance of the team reveals how quickly new hires achieved first revenue and full ramp. The only decision to be made is to go by average past performance or minimum efficiency performance.

For teams with little historical data to look back on, following an industry-standard formula can help cover the data gap and provide the team productivity guidance in the early days. Two of the more commonly used are Sales Cycle + 90 Days and Activities Expectation. Let's look at both.

Sales Cycle + 90 Days Ramp

As it sounds, the Sales Cycle + 90 Days Ramp is a simple, two-factor ramp formula. Either by using historical sales cycle data (days from the opportunity created to closed won) or an educated hypothesis, set the standard sales cycle. It's common here to round up in order to be more generous than the average to new people, so if the typical deal cycles through in 72 days, consider rounding up to 90, giving the rep a full 3 months. Then simply add another 90 days for onboarding, learning the job, building the pipeline, and so on.

Sales Cycle + 90 Days is a common formula for teams with extended sales motions who run on a quarterly performance cadence. The first quarter is set aside for learning and building pipe. On day 91 the cycle clock begins, and the expectation is that opportunities generated in month 4 will be the first to cross the finish line after the expected process time elapses. Many teams using this formula will offer sales a commission draw during this time, covering the shortfall from the anticipated lack of commissions.

Activities Expectation Ramp

More commonly used by teams with shorter sales cycles, the Activities Expectation Ramp is also a calculus of the sales cycle. This form of ramp focuses more on how process stage inputs are used to determine new hire outputs month-over-month. Here the defining factors are localized on reps hitting deal-stage targets for a graduated revenue ramp delivery. The productivity by channel waterfall used in the Demand-Generation System is an example of an Activities Expectation Ramp. (See Figure 5.2.)

	Month-1	Month-2	Month-3	Month-4	Month-5	Month-6	Month-7	Month-8	Month-9	Month-10
Inbound New	0	6	8	10	10	10	10	10	10	10
Inbound Old	4	4	4	4	4	4	2	2	2	2
Outbound	1	2	2	0	0	0	0	0	0	0
Referrals/Old Ops	0	0	0	0	0	0	2	2	2	2
S1 Live Connects	5	12	14	14	14	14	14	14	14	14
S2 Qualified Ops	0	3	6	7	7	7	7	7	7	7
S3 Presented Package	0	0	2	3	5	5	5	5	5	5
Deals Won	0	0	0	1	2	2	2	2	2	2
Total Revenue	–	–	–	$25,000	$50,000	$50,000	$50,000	$50,000	$50,000	$50,000

Figure 5.2 Demand-Gen Productivity by Channel

Here the new hire is tasked with achieving monthly deal-stage activities goals right away. In month 1, the goals focus entirely on early-stage deal production. The new rep is still spending most of her time in onboarding, so the productivity asks are small.

As the months progress, the expectations for achieving later-stage pipeline measures increase. By month 4 the first revenue is assessed during a ramp, but it is half of the full quota correlation to the reduced volume of activity (and quality of process) the new hire executes in her early days on the job. By month 5 in this example, the rep is now expected to deliver a full revenue quota – correlation to month 4 at full pipeline quota and a 30-day sales cycle.

The Positive Power of Ramp Productivity Tracking

Antoine de Saint-Exupéry is credited as saying, "If you want to build a ship, don't drum up the men to gather wood, divide the work, and give orders. Instead, teach them to yearn for the vast and endless sea."[8] He was wrong.

The point is clear, that people need a broader motivation for their work and a clear picture as to how sometimes menial tasks are connected to bigger, more meaningful outcomes. Hence all the teaching them to yearn stuff. But Saint-Exupéry uses an "either/or logic" where an "and" formula is needed. Teach them to yearn and gather wood, divide orders, and so on.

Ramp is best when it is simple and spelled out clearly. Teaching and then tracking productivity inputs whether using Sales Cycle + 90, Activities Expectation, or some other ramp formula has a high value, especially for the new hire. Tracking provides measured focus, a sense of early accomplishment, and an objective assessment of where some-one is on track and where they need to focus attention.

All too often sales teams set the long-term revenue target and are so fearful of being seen as micromanagers that they neglect the short-term inputs. Avoid this. Cover both long-term vision and short-term insight into your team.

Shortening the Time to Ramp

Having a detailed plan for ramp accelerates a new hire's time to full production. A detailed, step-by-step action plan reveals areas of the onboarding where the learning curve can be shortened. Approaching sales onboarding with a *laissez-faire* attitude is lazy and negligent. Maximize the rep's chances of success and minimize ramp time through focused action. Early time investment saves future work as you're able to engrain good habits and build rep confidence before they leave the nest of onboarding.

- Communicate the minimum performance and promotion path criteria on day 1 to build urgency around hitting performance milestones.

- Track and report onboarding team performance to reinforce the message that ramp production is meaningful and needs to be taken seriously.

- Create a mentor program for new hires with senior reps to build an underlying support system and learn from various sources.

- Make training interactive and participatory. "Tell me and I forget, teach me and I might remember, involve me and I learn."

- Encourage open conversations around anxiety and failures. Problems are addressed and resolved faster when they are talked about freely among the team.

- Start 1-on-1 coaching sessions during onboarding to build the cadence of documented, weekly objectives, action plans, and results (more on this in the Ongoing Improvement System).

- Run an Onboarding Incentive, motivating the new-hire class to run after a short-term performance goal.

Onboarding is the first opportunity for management to lead by example. If you want a team that shows attention to detail, you must show attention to detail. If you want a team who collaborate and work together, you must collaborate and work with them. If you want a team that is measured and performance-driven, you must show that you measure and are driven by performance early. Absentee managers during onboarding create the culture that breeds absentee reps later.

Onboarding Documentation

One of my former bosses once told me, "Documentation is like sex. When it's good it's very good. When it's bad, it's still better than nothing." The corporate world today may frown on explicit analogies, but the sentiment is still valid. Writing things down builds intellectual equity.

Stuff to consider having documented before, during, and upon concluding the New-Hire Onboarding System are:

- **The Onboarding Calendar/Syllabus** – New hires should have readily available the upcoming course material. Trainers should be able to see what the class has already studied easily. This is especially valuable when training by committee.
- **The Sales Playbook** – As covered in the Process System, the sales playbook is your team's operating manual. They should know where it is and how to use it early in the onboarding process.
- **Call Recordings Archive** – Not all documentation is text-based. In recent years, technology has given us the gift of live sales call archives. These add the most value when cataloged and able to be filtered by specific highlighted items like individual stages in the sales process or examples of working through specific objections.
- **Individual Notes** – New hires should be encouraged, if not required, to take detailed notes throughout their onboarding. Encourage them to use a digital note-taking app like Evernote or Notion. It's hard to catalog paper notes. Apps can be tagged and filtered for search.

- **1-on-1 Trackers** – Short-term goals, long-term goals, social styles, and gas tanks were covered in the People System; 1-on-1 trackers should be created during onboarding and worked on throughout the salesperson's career. More on this in the Ongoing Improvement System.

Comprehensive documentation like this not only underpins the clarity of new teaching, it builds autonomy and accountability. When information is cataloged and easy to access, the team takes ownership of doing the research to answer its own questions. When assets like playbooks and call archives are introduced early, they set a formal standard for what good looks like and clear examples of what the road ahead entails.

Mentor-Mentee Pairings

Being the new kid is tough. There are new products to learn about, people to meet, processes to adopt, and all the while performance measures to achieve. The pressure is on from day 1. It helps to have a trusted advisor whose shoulder you can tap when needed.

A direct manager is A leader on the team not THE leader of the team. Senior reps and BDRs provide a supplemental source of leadership to new hires. Because they are doing the same job the new hire is actively learning, they offer a unique context and perspective from the manager on how to achieve results.

Oftentimes the rep-manager relationship is loaded with unwanted anxiety. Even when you promote learning through failure, new people don't like to look bad in front of the boss. Having a peer they can rely on to ask for help and guidance opens up the lines of learning communication.

The benefits to these pairings also benefit the mentor. Being asked to mentor a new hire is a powerful acknowledgment of a rep's value to the team. The learning they get from helping new hires onboard and ramp makes them better reps. Maybe the most obvious benefit is manager training. Being a mentor allows a senior player on the team to test out the manager's life on a small scale, learn if they want to pursue that as a career path, and show an aptitude for the role with real-world examples.

A few items to consider when setting-up mentor-mentee pairings are:

- **Compatibility** – Collecting data throughout the interview process allows you to mentor-mentee match beyond demographics. People with similar starting points and social styles tend to be more compatible. Overlaying the mentor's hiring scorecard with the mentee's and aligning similar profiles offers an objective matching formula.

- **Cadence** – Calendars fill up fast. Especially for mentors who are busy focusing on hitting numbers. To assure the value of the pairing is being delivered, lay some ground rules over how and how often mentors and mentees should meet.

- **Documentation** – New hires are already primed for constant note-taking. The same expectation should be set for mentors. The learning in this relationship occurs in both directions. Mentors should be prepared to share mentoring notes with their managers as an opportunity to learn and improve teaching skills.

Health Check Reporting Inside the New-Hire Onboarding System

Measuring performance during onboarding has a dual effect. Not only does it enhance the learning experience of the new-hire class and hold them accountable to an early standard of excellence, it also informs long-term improvement. Knowing what to measure and report on is key. Here are a few critical KPIs that helped us optimize the New-Hire Onboarding System at Rock.

Triple Session Readiness Score

Certifications are limited in a number of ways. Most are blanket, pass-fail formatted. They do not give you a granular report on the specific knowledge points the certified person has down and which are still weak. Also, based on how recently the certification was taken, the information held in the person's short-term memory may have since evaporated. The certification doesn't reveal what the person currently knows and how ready they are to perform right now.

We answered this gap with the Triple Session Readiness Score. By selecting and organizing key sets of skills a specific position needs to have strong at any given moment for max results, Triple Session allowed us to build and maintain role-specific readiness scores. Skill sets for BDRs leaned heavily into prospecting, connect calling, social selling, and objection handling. Account exec tracks incorporated more discovery, presentation, and negotiating skills. All needed to maintain base scores in business acumen, professional-skills time management, and personal improvements like emotional intelligence and growth mindset.

Final Exam

As discussed previously, the final exam has tons of value: from aligning expectations around measuring new-hire aptitude to the effectiveness of training and clarity of test questions. Reporting the final exam results back to each new hire is a key step in their evolution. Correct answers help reinforce learning and give reps some early wins and wind at their backs.

An incorrect answer review session is even more beneficial. Going over the areas of onboarding the rep was not able to effectively absorb in the first pass allows for a final tightening of screws before graduation. It also sets the tone that direct, negative feedback is encouraged, and humility is a valuable trait in a profession not easy to learn and achieve mastery.

Time to KPI Attainment

Much of the onboarding experience is focused on inputs – learning the customer, the sales process, the CRM protocol, scoring in Triple Session and during role plays. There are, however, plenty of opportunities to score sales outputs.

Earlier we detailed the positive power of productivity tracking. This is valuable not only for the new hires, but also for the overall health tracking of the New-Hire Onboarding System. Watching how quickly reps perform against KPI goals allows for the creation of an onboarding retrospective. Each onboarding class should have its performance documented and compared to previous classes. Trends can indicate where training and processes need to improve. Attainment rates of KPIs over time help modulate whether goals need to be increased or decreased accordingly.

Percent and Time to Ramp Attainment

There's no better indication of the health of the New-Hire Onboarding System than how many new hires ramp and how quickly they ramp. A design-built People System will deliver great-fit new hires with high-quality raw materials. Onboarding is the factory they need to smelt them into sales machines. It's only working when a high percentage of new hires ramp and ramp fast.

At Rock, before design building our People and New-Hire Onboarding Systems, we would lose roughly one in four new hires due to performance failure. Afterward, the ratio dropped to fewer than 1 in 10. We didn't make the goals any easier; we just got much better at identifying ideal candidates and more effective at uploading the information they needed to succeed.

Onboarding eNPS

A unique employee net promoter score survey post-onboarding provides key insights directly from end customers (the new hires) on how your initial training was received. One of the fastest ways to learn where and how to optimize the New-Hire Onboarding System is from user feedback. The simplest form of this is to ask them what they would recommend that the company start doing, stop doing, and continue doing to enhance the effectiveness of your onboarding.

Companies can learn a lot from how high-volume apps onboard their new users. Onboarding workflows are launched, user behavior tracked throughout, interviews performed to gauge sentiment, and the process refined to remove friction. And the cycle repeats. The work of launching, measuring, and improving onboarding is never done.

Once again, this perspective is enriched by design-build modeling. It looks at the onboarding experience less like an employee-employer relationship and more like a customer-company relationship. The new hire is viewed more like a new customer and takes on the build role. The company (sales leadership, HR, and ops) is less an employer and more a service provider, taking the design side of structuring the best, most-valuable onboarding experience.

New-Hire Onboarding System Rituals

Onboarding rituals go well beyond recognition and system optimization. They allow for the setting of standards at the critical moment when people are joining your team and are most impressionable. Rituals that inlay positive behaviors have a high lifetime value. Failure to capitalize on this opportunity for priming healthy routines squanders an opportunity to set up your team for scalable success.

Daily/Weekly Checkpoints

Being hands-on early allows you to be hands-free later. A second look at the sample month 1 onboarding calendar reveals that each day starts with a review of the previous day's learnings. Each week concludes with a weekly onboarding review. This is standard operating procedure in a design-built New-Hire Onboarding System.

The routine of starting today with a recap of yesterday carries a few advantages. The team is reminded every day that they will be expected to show what they've learned in front of the group. Social pressure can be a positive force for good. The refresh also allows for an early indicator of new-hire quality. The best will engage often and have accurate answers and insightful questions. Finally, it's a means for new trainers (when onboarding by committee) to get a sense of what the class knows or doesn't know, before launching into the next section of content.

Weekly team review sessions allow new hires to share their knowledge and experience. They have an opportunity to ask questions after having time to reflect on learnings to date. They can also provide the trainer with valuable feedback, especially when a section of the training was not clearly taught or moved through too quickly. The meeting, when done as a new-hire class, builds valuable team relationships that can last for the lifetime of the new hire's tenure with the company.

Daily Incentives

It pays to be a winner. This is nowhere more true in the professional world than in sales. Onboarding provides a great opportunity to engrain this as part of the sales culture of the team. Incentives based on Triple Session scores, morning live quiz performance, role-play performance, or early achievements in building pipeline help to set good habits. A reward can be as simple as lunch on the company credit card, getting to sit out of a live team role play, or simply just the status recognition of daily champ.

New Hire Slack Group

Technology now allows us to easily create environments for team building and info-sharing. Creating a Slack group for each hiring cohort starts to build a collaborative environment where new reps can learn together. The questions asked and answers given for one new hire have their value multiplied when done in front of a group. Each rep benefits from those around him, and the shared experience of going through the same process at the same time enhances the enjoyment of the work.

Shout-Outs

Just like in the People and Demand-Generation Systems, recognition of superior achievement helps reinforce positive behaviors and breeds a culture of winning. Onboarding is where the recognition rewards system should begin. Celebrating daily incentive winners, early performance measures or overall engagement in the learning process underscores the culture that strong performance will be noticed and rewarded.

Recognizing Failures as Learning Moments

The opposite of winning is not losing. It's failure to try. Making this clear early and emphasizing failure as part of the new hire process is key. New hires should be encouraged to put the effort in above all else while striving for success, not to fear failure.

Failure from sales new hires comes in many forms, from superficial discovery to choppy presentation delivery to not knowing key information when needed to an inability to handle objections. Public displays of accountability for these missteps offer value in building self-awareness, coachability, and group learning.

Using morning review sessions, new-hire weekly meetups, or Slack groups as a forum for showcasing failures as much as successes was a valuable tool at Rock. We put new hires on display and used their rookie mistakes as learning opportunities for the group. This not only multiplied the value of the learning, but it also removed the stigma of failure and celebrated accountability – one of our core cultural values.

Graduation Day

Onboarding is like going through the internal university at your company. A closing ceremony helps to formalize the process for the new hires, offers another opportunity for recognition, and sets a clear standard for what success looks like in phase 1, and rapid growth. Celebrating the accomplishment of overcoming the first milestone helps build morale and confidence for the next step in the sales rep's journey.

Mistakes I've Made When Constructing the New-Hire Onboarding System

Unforced errors in the New-Hire Onboarding System are painful, given the sunk costs of the investments already made. You and your team have labored to create a process and demand-generation system that works. Go to the market to find great-fit talent and get them to sign. A flawed onboarding can destroy the value of all that work and result in avoidable failures to ramp, increase productivity, and build team morale.

Unstructured Scheduling

Onboarding throws a lot at new hires. The best results come when the system is streamlined to have them focus on the essentials and nothing else. For years, I left my team's onboarding with open time blocks of "free" time. What can look like freedom is actually friction. It invites unproductive time into the new hire's onboarding.

Take the thought process out of any nonessential work and schedule everything. Removing the stress of having to figure out "What do I do now, whom should I talk to next," and so forth allows people to get hyper-focused on the task at hand and stay present in the learning moment. Not only does that help yield a faster learning path, but it's also a better overall experience for the new hire. They expect you to have them in a structured environment in the early days. When you don't, it destroys morale and can deteriorate company credibility in the mind's eye of the new member to the team.

Late Start to Onboarding

For years I started the onboarding process on the new hire's first day with the company. It seemed logical only to ask for them to start learning once they were on the payroll. It was a missed opportunity.

As soon as someone signs the offer letter, they're part of the team. Don't wait to get them involved. Today new hires receive a pre-work list of materials to read up on and Triple Session tracks to complete before their start date. The preparation increases the success rate, speeds up ramp, and helps build confidence in the new hire. Everyone wins.

Late Start to Documentation

Along with early onboarding, early documentation is key to maximizing efficiency and shortening the time to results. I was late to deliver formal docs or require new hires and trainers to log specific info into performance trackers. This oftentimes led to unclear directions and misaligned work. Things like incomplete playbooks (eventually filled out), unstructured on-demand content (eventually solved by Triple Session), and no objective analysis of role plays (eventually solved by scorecards).

Lack of measurement early breeds informality. Informality leads to a lack of attention to detail. And lack of attention to detail yields sloppy work with no standard expectations and no structure around the process. I learned the hard (slow) way that the devil is in the details with the New-Hire Onboarding System. You can't over-explain something to a new member of your team. Getting the formalized documentation and standard operating procedures set early provides a foundation for detailed training and early-stage work.

Superficial KPI Measurement

What you do not measure, you cannot improve. And onboarding is all about improvement. Daily improvement. Micro-skill improvement. For too long, I was lax about what can and should be measured during onboarding, only tracking some basic performance measures. Consequently, new hires were not always kept on pace, and performance suffered.

Onboarding measurement should be broad and deep. It should cover not only the early KPI production of sales activity (the only thing I tracked in the early days), but also the learning, effort, learning scores, role-play performance, and improvement over time. Performance measurement, like onboarding in general, should begin with the pre-work assignments delivered immediately after the new hire signs the offer.

Superficial Mentor-Mentee Matching

"Senior rep, please help junior rep. Okay? Okay." That was the extent of our mentor-mentee pairing in the early days. My lack of detailed work here oftentimes led to mismatching rather than matching. A poorly matched mentor hurts a new hire's onboarding more than if there was no mentor at all. Later, we looked at personality traits, background, and common goals and set a structure around expectations for both mentor and mentee. A more positive and profitable experience was shared by both parties.

Solo Hiring

Hiring in groups brings a number of benefits. Learning as a group offers a shared experience for the new hires. They feel less isolated going through the trial by fire. It also multiplies the value of learning. When one person asks a question, everyone benefits from hearing it, as well as the answer that follows.

From a company perspective, hiring in groups helps to better determine if later performance was more influenced by the trainee or the training. With a sample size of one, it's much harder to isolate contributing factors of success or failure. On many occasions, in a rush to fill a single open seat, I hired one person who went through onboarding alone, stripping away all these benefits.

Checkpoint – System 4

Reverting back to design-build and looking at the revenue organization like a construction project, the architecture is starting to take shape. The process blueprint was drafted, and construction started in the form of CRM governance and playbook design. The raw material of customer demand has been localized and is ready to bring on site. The build team of reps, SDRs, and managers have been identified, hired, and now trained to operate the heavy machinery.

The construction of a business is not unlike the building of a skyscraper or tunnel. The work is done one brick at a time, one shovel load at a time, and one employee at a time. The integrity of the structure depends not only on the quality of the plan, the products, or the people but also on the performance of the crew.

Execution is an ongoing cycle. Great performance is not just repeated but enhanced. Processes are reengineered, channels of customer acquisition reevaluated, and team profiles enriched and evolved. New tactics and technologies need to be learned and put into action as they come available. Previously learned skills need to be relearned again and again, bad habits worked out, and best practices realigned.

A formula for continuous optimization and re-optimization takes shape when a process to improve the process is design-built – the Ongoing Improvement System.

Notes

1. James Dao, "A Nation at War: The Commandos; Navy Seals Easily Seize 2 Oil Sites," *New York Times*, March 22, 2003, https://www.nytimes.com/2003/03/22/world/a-nation-at-war-the-commandos-navy-seals-easily-seize-2-oil-sites.html.

2. Kelly J. Bouxsein, Henry S. Roane, and Tara Harper, "Evaluating the Separate and Combined Effects of Positive and Negative Reinforcement on Task Compliance," *Journal of Applied Behavior Analysis* 44, no. 1 (Spring 2011): 175–179.

3. "Coronado Water Temperature (CA)," SeaTemperature.org, https://www.seatemperature.org/north-america/united-states/coronado.htm.

4. "Andy Stumpf Gets Honest About Navy Seal Training," Joe Rogan, YouTube, https://www.youtube.com/watch?v=4S-6d99n2h4.

5. Ibid.

6. Sean H. K. Kang, "Spaced Repetition Promotes Efficient and Effective Learning: Policy Implications for Instruction," *Policy Insights from the Behavioral and Brain Sciences* 3, no. 1 (January 2016).

7. "Andy Stumpf Gets Honest About Navy Seal Training."

8. https://www.bookbrowse.com/quotes/detail/index.cfm/quote_number/401/if-you-want-to-build-a-ship-dont-drum-up-people-but-rather-teach-them-to-long-for-the-endless-immensity-of-the-sea.

6

The Ongoing Improvement System

The Case of Tom Brady and the TB12 Method

By all accounts, Tom Brady wasn't all that special. At the University of Michigan, his four-year career stats finished with a 61.9 completion percentage, 4,773 yards, and just 30 touchdowns versus throwing 17 interceptions, a mediocre 2-to-1 ratio.[1] The University of Florida's Tim Tebow by comparison finished his college career with a 66.4 completion percentage, 9,285 yards, and a staggering 88 touchdowns to just 16 interceptions.[2] Tebow also ran for 58 touchdowns in his career. Brady, 8. Tebow beats Brady handily in every category. But that was college.

As many of you reading this already know, Tom Brady went on to assemble the most prolific professional football career of any quarterback ever. He finished his 23-year career with records in literally dozens of categories. A few of the most notable: most championships, most passing yards, most touchdowns, and most wins.

What's most interesting about Brady's career is not that he improved from college to the pros, but that he improved throughout his professional career. Pro football is hard. It's hard on the body and the mind. Most players break down both physically and mentally over time, and performance eventually drops. Tom Brady's performance, however, continued to improve over the span of his career, long after the age when most players decline or retire. He Benjamin-Buttoned the story of playing quarterback.

When breaking down the first 20 years of his career in half, it's easy to see the progression: more yards, more first or second team all pro team appearances.

This consistent improvement as he aged did not start by accident, but rather by injury. As his long-time trainer, Alex Guerrero, put it, "Tom and I, we got together around 2004. He had sustained an injury and wasn't really responding to traditional therapy he was receiving."[3]

Guerrero's résumé looks one part nutritionist, one part physical therapist, and one part shaman. He has a degree in traditional Chinese medicine and works through a process of prehab, rehab, and nutrition. His approach appears to zoom out on an athlete's performance, looking at as wide a spectrum of data as possible to match plans to outcomes.

When working with athletes, Guerrero wants to know what they eat and how much they sleep. He watches how they perform and how they prepare to perform. He seems concerned as much about the mind as he is about the body. He talks to his athletes about exercise and nutrition, but also about mindfulness and meditation.[4]

That injury and subsequent introduction to Guerrero was an inflection point for Brady. The trajectory of his career took a new direction leading to "a holistic approach to health and wellness."[5] This has since been formalized as "The TB12 method."

According to their website, the TB12 method consists of five pillars – pliability, nutrition, hydration, movement, and mental fitness. This covers a lot of ground and goes well beyond – and even contrary to – the traditional "lift more and guzzle protein shake" approach to physical fitness. Pliability promotes softer muscle tissue to help with flexibility and increased resilience.

The pliability approach to muscle preparation as a means of improved performance has bucked much of the conventional stereotypes of how an athlete should maximize performance. When asked in one interview about the typical call for bigger, harder muscle mass, Brady seemed ready to push back: "I think that's what we've been educated on. Well, I may argue something differently. I've seen really strong, physically-fit guys that, you know, would be the definition of health, that are the ones that are injured the most."[6]

Beyond the physical, the mental preparation has proved a key ingredient to Brady's improvement throughout his career. By his own admission, he did not set his sights on beating his opponents through pure athleticism. "I was never going to be as good as those other guys were physically," he said in his Facebook docuseries *Tom vs. Time.* "Making good decisions and leadership ability and all those mental aspects of the game" is where Brady spent most time optimizing his performance.[7]

In this documentary, Brady is filmed working with quarterback coach Tom House. House is shown critiquing the throwing motion, making adjustments, at one time shaking his head in disapproval. Brady at this point is entering his eighteenth year as a professional football player, holds most of the records for playing quarterback, including five Super Bowl titles. He's just coming off the season where he led the New England Patriots to the biggest Super Bowl comeback of all time and he's paying a guy to needle him on where he needs to improve.

The process by which experts achieve mastery is referred to as deliberate practice. The critical elements of deliberate practice are clear – specific goals, intense focus, immediate feedback, frequent discomfort, and expert coaching. The process is a cycle, not a line. Set a goal that pushes just beyond the previous performance highpoint, practice with complete concentration, analyze results with the feedback from a trusted advisor. Tom Brady has been deliberately practicing for decades.

Brady appears to examine game tapes with a forensic eye. Watch the play, rewind, slow motion, rewind again, watch in slow motion again, and again. He reportedly has spent four to five hours at a time reviewing game films. "If you want to perform at the highest level, then you've got to prepare at the highest level mentally," Brady says. "I think I process a lot of information really quickly."[8]

In *Peak: Secrets from the New Science of Expertise*, Anders Ericsson and Robert Pool describe how chess grandmasters are able to win expert-level tournaments blindfolded. "The ability to recognize and remember meaningful patterns arises from the way chess players develop their abilities."

Grandmasters create visual models, known as "mental representations," which "make it possible for chess players to recognize patterns of chess pieces – not just their positions." Ericsson and Pool go on to explain: "Anyone who is serious about developing skills on the chessboard will do it mainly by spending countless hours studying games played."[9] Rather than the playing of the game itself, it is the analysis of the game that leads to mastery.

"I have the answers to the test now," Brady said in one interview late in the back half of his career. "You can't surprise me on defense. I've seen it all. I've processed 261 games."[10] Notice the word choice here. He didn't just play the games, he "processed" them. What Brady is describing as the answers to the test are mental representations. He was able to recognize patterns of chess pieces, not just their positions.

Simon Sinek once described an infinite game as having "known and unknown players, the rules are changeable, and the goal is to keep the game in play to perpetuate the game."[11] When you set the goal of being at your very best, you are playing an infinite game. The player is known, given that you know what you are capable of and unknown as you don't know the limits of your capabilities at the moment. The rules are changeable as the definition of what "very best" means can vary. And the goal is to perpetuate the game. Tomorrow always resets the scoreboard on being at the best of your current abilities.

In the final analysis, the infinite game mindset takes into account the Stoic virtue of progress over perfection. The business of self-improvement is never done, the game is never over. Winning is not a possibility, as the end game is never realized. And losing only occurs when the effort to improve ceases to exist. In that respect, Tom Brady is still undefeated.

First Principles of the Ongoing Improvement System

Holistic Outputs

When goal setting, Guerrero and Brady talked more about the long-term view. The outcomes sought after are not faster run times, or hours of game film matched. The goals talked about were far-reaching. At 40 Brady talked a lot about playing until 45. And he did.

Outputs yielded from the Ongoing Improvement System go far beyond hitting the monthly or quarterly number. The rigors and often frustrations of constant scrutiny and the picking apart of weak points can be exhausting. The motivation to keep coming back to the process day after day must be rooted deep in the foundation of the team's psyche in order to have lasting strength. The most substantive motivators aren't professional achievements, but personal and intrinsic.

Holistic Inputs

With the help of Alex Guerrero, Tom Brady looked well past the practice field and weight room in his quest to achieve mastery. He broadened his sphere of influence out to its widest reaches, considering everything within his control that would influence his performance. Every exercise, part of his diet, sleep, order of scheduling, and recovery processes. Nothing was left out that would impact how he played on Sunday.

If we consider a holistic view of what influences sales performance, the order of magnitude goes far beyond pipeline reviews and lead funnels. Beyond just the technical, what is the professional and personal support salespeople need to optimize performance? What are not only the things salespeople should do, but what should they not do? What are the counter intuitive habits that could be hurting performance? What does downtime look like, and how can we optimize the counterweight effect of time away from selling? Are we considering the full person when crafting the Ongoing Improvement System or just who they are from 9 to 5?

Deliberate Practice

Science has delivered us the formula for how to optimize training to achieve mastery. Its name is deliberate practice. Tom Brady recycled the formula of deliberate practice for decades and built the mental models that afforded him the answers to the football test every week. The process is there and readily available for all of us to use.

Through the perpetual loop of deliberate practice, we are able to help salespeople build the mental models for sales mastery. Ongoing improvement is an infinite game, but the milestones of progress in sales should readily be measured, boundaries pushed, feedback analyzed, and coaching omnipresent.

Brush Your Teeth

There are no big, one-time events in the TB12 methodology. No silver-bullet growth hacks or magic potions for achieving superior performance. Eat better. Drink more water. Mentally prepare for your work. Stay flexible. It's far less a major medical procedure and much more like brushing your teeth. A series of small, consistent, daily habits that over time result in maintaining health and more positive long-term outcomes.

The Ongoing Improvement System for sales is no different. Our results don't suddenly appear one day, but are matured and fine-tuned over the course of daily mindful improvement. Sales training delivered in big batches is wholly ineffective. Maximum output in self-improvement is only achieved when a maximum input of small, daily practice habits is maintained consistently over a long stretch of time.

Mindset

Brady once said, "I'm always in competition with myself." When your competition is you, the next level of achievement is always within reach, but the work is never done. It's the quintessential infinite game.

Setting up your team with the expectation that the work of improvement is never done is key from pre-hire. It's not a work requirement, it's a culture requirement. The right type of salesperson to fit into the Ongoing Improvement System knows that their work is never done before they sign with the team.

Elements of the Ongoing Improvement System

A Culture of Ongoing Improvement

Each of the previous four systems started with very technical foundations. The Process System focused on the customer with the research and creation of a detailed persona. The Demand-Generation System began with the Skoking out of sales economics to refine go-to-market. The People System is your ideal candidate profile, and the Onboarding is the map of what new hires need to learn. At its core, the Ongoing Improvement System is more philosophical than physical. It's a mindset more than a map of the process.

For ongoing improvement to truly take root as an integral system in your sales organization, it needs to be part of the ethos of the team. Constantly working to get better can't just be what you do, it must be who you are at all levels. New hires finish onboarding and move right into continuous coaching cycles. Senior reps seek out help at getting better in the weakest part of their game. Managers pull feedback from eNPS reports, their teams, colleagues, and leaders, and construct personal-improvement action plans for themselves.

The idea is simple: Maintain a constant momentum toward better performance with a consistent effort at input influencers. In her groundbreaking book *Mindset: The New Psychology of Success*, Carol Dweck describes a growth mindset as the belief that "with the right strategy and enough effort" improvement is possible in any field. Strategy and effort. Design and build.

Design-Building a Culture of Ongoing Improvement

A well-built Ongoing Improvement System has the desire for continuous learning poured into the mix of its foundation. As there is a logical order to the six systems sales org building, the Ongoing Improvement System stands on the bedrock of previously constructed pillars. The benefit of design-built systems taking a holistic view prior to construction immediately bears fruit at the onset of System 5.

In the Process System, sales leadership and sales ops collaborated to define KPIs and measurement systems built into CRM. Reporting was set, and business-of-one metrics were crafted and put into place, allowing for the capture of company, team, and individual performance. The sales team playbook clearly documents the standards for excellence in detail for all tasks asked of the team.

In the People System, a company-wide community of collaborators contributed to the creation of team culture. The documentation of these norms codifies that ongoing improvement is part of the team's identity. Before candidates are even invited to the interview process, sending the culture deck communicates the expectations loud and clear. Work here only if you see constant self-improvement as essential to how you work and who you are.

Within these essential actions, the culture of ongoing improvement has already been laid down. New hires join the team, primed for and expecting continuous learning and growth. Leaders have in their mandate the responsibility of exemplifying routine self-improvement in action. To hold others accountable, they too must be accountable. To expect coachability, they too must be coached.

Measuring for Improvement

What you do not measure you cannot improve. In the previous four systems, we closed the conversation by assessing performance tracking. Here we open with it. Improvement requires a baseline, a starting point from which to do better. Let the data lead you to the point of focus.

One way (not the only way) is to analyze individual vs. team average performance and pick out the lowest-performing measure to isolate for improvement. Figure 6.1 shows the side-by-side comparisons of one rep (Mike Jones) and the average monthly performance of all members of Mike's team. This gives us an objective analysis of where specifically Mike needs to focus his efforts in order to improve his overall performance.

Here you can see Mike's early-stage performance is only about 90% of what an average member of the team is doing. This is adversely

	Mike Jones		Team Average	
Leads Worked	676		737	
Ops Created	30	4.4%	34	4.6%
S1	25	83.3%	28	82.4%
S2	16	64%	10	36%
Won	4	25%	5	50%
Revenue	49000		72500	
ASP	$12.250		$14.500	
Net Retention	98%		108%	
Referral Ops	0		2	

Figure 6.1 Individual Rep vs. Team Performance

impacting the number of ops he creates in a month. His stick rate from op to stage 2 is comparable to the teams.

Here's where it gets interesting. His stage 2 pipeline (discovery/qualification) to stage 3 (presentation) is almost double the team's average, but his stage 3 to won deals is half. He's presenting more but winning less. And the deals he does win are coming in at a 15% smaller average ticket price. Post-sale, they don't retain as well, and Mike is not getting referrals from them to help bolster his pipeline and build a demand-gen flywheel.

> **Assessment –** Mike is under-qualifying his opportunities at stage 2. He's allowing too many weak deals to progress to stage 3, where they convert at a lower percentage. The ones that do convert are not buying big enough (possibly given discounts to get in the door) and are either not followed up with for referrals or not willing to give them.

> **Point of Focus –** Mike needs to work on better qualifying, disqualifying, and building value at the S1 (discovery) stage of the process. The time he saves weeding out weak deals should be reinvested in doing higher-quality work in the remaining, stronger deals, increasing win rate and average ticket. Also, some of the time saved presenting to just 10 prospects versus 16 should be reinvested in creating new ops, both from working more leads and mining customers for referrals.

Design-Building a Sales Coaching Model

Sales coaching is a staple in any well-run sales organization. Managers will routinely hold 1-on-1 meetings with everyone on their team. From skill-building to pipe reviews to career-building sessions, coaching yields a positive impact on several fronts.

Most sales coaching programs are build-heavy. Sales managers create the format and run with it. As the build-side is focused more on immediate action, the coaching results tend to move the needle in the short term, without the lasting impact of a design-built model. The costs of this approach are immense, as it erodes the compounding value of coaching over time and diminishes the accountability to both reps and managers to put up results from the invested time in 1-on-1s.

A design-build model of coaching, however, has a number of hallmarks that insulate the 1-on-1 process, capturing and harnessing the value over time.

1. **Aligned with individual goals.** A sales rep's personal goals drive their engagement and execution of effective sales coaching. The immediate goal is to win more deals but understanding the bigger-picture "whys" that influence a rep's behavior providing more substantive change. Connecting individual goals to short-term gains wins rep buy-in for behavioral change. Positive behavioral change creates longer-term results.

2. **Documented process.** A design-build model of sales coaching comes with an operating manual. What preparation needs to be done before a 1-on-1? How will the time be spent? What are the responsibilities of the managers and rep? How will the coaching session work be documented?

3. **Documented session work.** Tracking the work done, commitments agreed to, and progress made from one coaching session to the next is critical to design-build coaching. It acts as an accountability measure for the progress sought after and builds a track of learning knowledge to build on from one meeting to the next.

How Rock Content Aligned Coaching with Individual Goals

Much of the Ongoing Improvement System is built on the foundational brick of the previously constructed four systems. Goals alignment in a design-build sales model is first identified and recorded in the People System. When new hires first join the team, the initial 1-on-1 with their direct leader focuses on defining their "gas tanks," the intrinsic motivators that determine what drives each person. Common drivers tend to hold emotional value like feelings of accomplishment or security or a sense of belonging.

In addition to the gas tanks, Rock's initial 1-on-1 process involved the definition of short-, mid-, and long-term goals. The guidance we offered for how to think of the timelines was that short is within the next 12 months, mid is 2–3 years out, and long is 20 years. Most people didn't come to the first conversation with their goals fully formed, so it became common practice for them to take some time to think seriously about what they want for themselves. It's interesting to learn how little most people consider their personal goals and the value they get from this step of the coaching process.

Once gas tanks were defined and goals documented we had the core value elements down on paper – the stuff they really care about that will drive their performance. Value is why we do what we do. Each of us is different, and understanding individual motivators is essential to maintaining alignment. One rep I coached had a very career-minded goal structure – promoted in a year, manager in 2–3, and running his own successful business in 20. Another rep brought more personal goals to the conversation, superior performance in a year, the ability to buy a vacation home in 2–3, and financial security to travel internationally twice/year in 20.

The goal of alignment is simple. Know your people and what they care about. Alignment happens when what they care about on a personal level is connected to what they can achieve professionally.

How Rock Content Documented the Coaching Process

Coaching is a process, and just like other processes in the sales organization, it requires a playbook. Writing a detailed guide to why coaching matters, and how a coaching session should be conducted, sets the stage for productive, well-aligned 1-on-1. Much of the first 1-on-1 with a new member of the team is setting up how the subsequent 1-on-1s will run.

At Rock, we developed a few guiding principles for how a 1-on-1 coaching session should run.

- **Rep-led.** Coaching should be fueled by the player and guided by the coach. This helps build ongoing self-awareness and accountability, making the rep the owner of his own self-improvement.

Important to note, rep-led does not also mean rep-determined. If a rep suggests spending valuable 1-on-1 time talking about what kind of snacks should be in the breakroom, or their plans for the weekend, it's the coach's responsibility to bring them back to focus on a higher-value topic.

- **Prepared.** Time is our most valuable investment. Showing up for a 1-on-1 unprepared burns valuable minutes that should be spent in collaborating. Doing research on a deal, pulling data, looking for a call, or any back-office work should be done prior to the coaching session. This is true for both stakeholders, that is, the reps and managers.

- **Focused.** Coaching time moves fast. Stuffing too much into a single conversation results in superficial, low-value work. Ideally, a single coaching session focuses on a single topic and goes deep. One skill to work on improving, one deal to pull apart and strategize on how to win. Progress doesn't happen by spreading attention thinly across several different topics, but when going all in on just one.

- **Documented.** Not to get too meta, but the coaching playbook should document how to document the ongoing coaching. Logging the topics discussed, commitments made, and the next steps agreed upon serves to retain the value created during the coaching session. Keeping notes on session after session builds a track record of work done and progress made over time. Reps and coaches change all the time. A detailed coaching doc provides the same value as a medical record for a doctor. When a new coach steps in to work with a rep, she can quickly get caught up with the rep's full history.

How Rock Content Documented Coaching Session Work

Over time we developed a progress tracker that served to pull together all the essential ingredients of ongoing coaching in one place. Rep goals at the top as a definition of the deeper value of work. Social style so communication by the manager was delivered in the most-valuable format. Personality traits (determined through a formal test) to document the rep's mental operating system. Gas tanks to keep present the intrinsic motivators the person needs to stay energized. A three-step format for structuring the conversation around singular focus and measurable progress.

This format guides reps and managers through a focused, repeatable coaching process. The holy trinity of sales coaching – point of focus, action plan, results associated with progress. (See Figure 6.2.) Each session is treated as a small project aimed at moving the needle with one skill or one deal with one rep at a time.

Point of Focus

By definition, priority is singular. If you have more than one, then you have none. As the name suggests, point of focus is meant to set the work to be done in each coaching session squarely in a singular direction. To go all in on one thing at a time and put all attention and effort on improving in a single area. This helps maximize the progress of a micro-skill or single, high-value deal while at the same time building accountability to execute. If you have just one thing you have agreed to get done, your name is now on its success or its failure.

A point of focus is often either a micro-skill (building rapport on a first call, second-level discovery questions, dealing with price objections) or a single deal in the pipeline to be worked on. Coaching sessions are great forums for using small skill-building or single-deal strategies and recording the progress to apply learnings to other skills

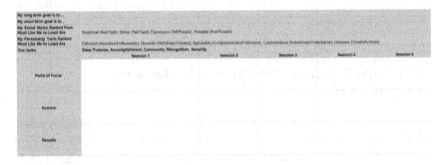

Figure 6.2 Coaching Tracker Template

and deals. Using business-of-one metrics and other data sources is valuable for localizing where to best find a point of focus worthy of the time investment.

Actions

What changes need to be made to improve performance in the point-of-focus area? To improve is to change. If both the coach and player have come to the coaching session prepared, it's in this phase of the conversation where they will spend most of their time. As with all areas of coaching, it should be the rep who is driving this conversation and the coach who is guiding it with questions and provocations.

It is in this section of the tracker that the rep will write out the details of what she will do differently when executing the specifics of the point-of-focus tasks. Even a list of bulleted action items helps to build muscle memory and ownership of execution. Think of it like a mini-playbook, written by the rep, which rep and manager will refer to during the next coaching session to check execution.

Results

The micro-project of a coaching session should have a micro-goal, and the best goals are SMART – Specific, Measurable, Attainable, Relevant, and Timebound. Nailing an objective removes any doubt from the conversation that the process is purely academic. We don't invest time in coaching just to know more about the job. We aim to improve results.

The broader gains of sales coaching are, of course, increased sales. If it's working, sales go up. But revenue itself is seldom the selected output of a coaching session. Coaching results aim to measure the effects of the action plan centered on a targeted point of focus.

All results should be measured objectively, that is, quantitatively. For some results that's easy. If a rep needs to better confirm budget qualification, simply measure over time what percentage of deals at an agreed-upon stage have budget intel logged in CRM. Other results are trickier. How do you measure objectively that a rep has improved rapport-building skills? One word: compliance. Pull a random set of recorded calls from one coaching session to the next. If the rep is showing a measured improvement in complying with the details of the documented action plan, check the box and move on to the next point of focus.

Live Training

When a broader message, applicable to a larger group, needs to be sent, team trainings are often the best forum. Where coaching is repled and driven by a Socratic Q&A flow, trainings are better delivered by a leader, presented from a pre-set agenda of prepared information. Like most of the practices repeated in a sales organization, there's a formula for success inside a repeatable framework.

- **Mission.** As a group you all share common values and a common objective for the team. The coaching tracker has as its header the individual purpose for each member of the team. Use the first slide of any group presentation as an opportunity to set the tone with the team's *why*.

- **Agenda.** Let people know the subject matter and what to expect next. It helps provide context and gets them engaged and participating. Pro tip here – let people know how long the presentation will be. If they know their attention is only being sought after for a set period, they're more likely to stay engaged, versus if it's open-ended and unknown.

- **Why?** Getting together as a group to train on a specific topic comes at the expense of time and the opportunity cost of doing other essential tasks. Trainers should not leave the meaning of it open to interpretation. What is the value to everyone in the group and to the team at large? What if things don't improve? What if they do? Building value into the training material before it's delivered is another tool for increasing engagement as well as inviting greater personal context into the content for the audience.

- **Story.** The goal of group training is to have a team learn and take away new knowledge. People retain information longer and more clearly when it is delivered in narrative form versus a data dump. When training on a skill, try using actual sales call examples to highlight the good, the bad, and the ugly sides of execution. When updating the team on a new product or service, weave in the narrative of how the offer came to be, whom it was built for, why and how it will be used by the client.

- **Engagement.** Even though it is led by a presenter, team training shouldn't be completely devoid of audience participation. Polling the audience with a show of hands can help pull them into the conversation. Randomly asking someone a question not only can make the training more dynamic, it also gets the team to focus as they may be the next randomly selected involuntary participant you call on.

- **Marketing.** The team's collective attention also provides an opportunity to get some internal marketing done on key topics. If you're running a sprint incentive, a status update on performance and who is close to or has already qualified can help get the team's engines running. Looking to fill some vital positions on the team, a quick announcement on what those roles are, and a reminder of the company's employee referral bonus could help raise team awareness the team of potential good-fit candidates in their network.

- **Test.** Given the goal of group training is for the team to leave with more information than when they arrived; the results on whether the goal was achieved or not should be measured. Test the team. Too often training is delivered into an abyss. Just like the final exam at the end of onboarding is meant to test both student aptitude and teacher proficiency, so too is a training test. If a training message missed the mark, it's better to know early through testing than late by reading closed-lost notes in CRM. A 5- to 10-question test emailed to the group while they are all together provides the most immediate feedback.

Cross-Training

In sports, cross-training refers to practicing multiple skills or working out more than one muscle group to provide a greater balance of readiness. In the Ongoing Improvement System, it's when a rep takes on the lead role of running a training session. In both, the benefit is the same, multiplying the value of the workout to maximize its impact on performance.

When a rep is called upon to train her peers, everyone wins. The training she delivers is typically world-class, as she has been given a unique opportunity to put her skills on display and wants to present with value. The team wins as they receive skill-building from a fresh voice and unique perspective, and from a person currently doing the job. For the team's manager it's an opportunity to recognize and celebrate a key player on the team, use her knowledge for the benefit of all, and work-in an element of leadership training, should the rep be interested in pursuing a career path in leadership.

Cross-training can also serve as the greatest upskilling opportunity for the trainer. One time at Rock, a very capable young rep asked for some training on how to best structure the conversation when prospects had objections. I assigned her that topic for training, with her as the trainer, and gave her two weeks to prepare. The training was well-researched, rich, engaging, and delivered with detail and context. The rep from that point on became one of our best at overcoming objections and winning deals.

Live Call Review

There's nothing better than the real thing. Live call review is a valuable tactic used in both 1-on-1 coaching and group training sessions. The process of extracting valuable insights from a call recording, whether with a team or individual, is simple, but effective. Preparation pays in efficiency. The manager or rep presenting the recorded call should know exactly which points to highlight, when to pause and open for discussion, and when to fast-forward over less valuable spans of dialogue.

When a recording is paused and a section of a call is highlighted for discussion, there's a structured learning cadence that elicits the most value from the time investment. First, the group is asked to comment on the positive aspects of the call to that point, with the rep whose call it is being asked to speak last. Most calls are gray, with strong and weak performance mixed throughout.

Once everyone has commented on the positives, the group is then asked to critique on improvement areas, and once again the rep on the recording reserves the final word. The process of inviting everyone in allows for maximum engagement and a diverse set of perspectives and voices on the pros and cons of a call.

As a valuable by-product, reps begin a process of self-assessment, applying to their own performance what they are hearing in the recordings of others. In an era where work from home is on the rise, the osmosis of learning through listening to the calls around you is less and less an option for many reps. Structured, regular live call reviews can provide a much-needed replacement for this loss.

Triple Session for Ongoing Improvement

Ongoing improvement means continuous learning. If you're not acquiring new knowledge all the time, you don't just stay at a flat skill level. You'll fall behind. Current skills dull, and the world around you will evolve and pass you by.

This issue isn't just with learning and applying new skills, but also with maintaining the knowledge already acquired. For seldom-used skills, it's natural for people to forget details of what they may have learned weeks, months, or years ago. The same is true for the tactics applied with regularity. Bad habits form that take people away from best practices and erode performance. If you look at the skill of driving a car, you don't necessarily become a better driver as years go by. Often you become worse, sloppy, careless, and more accident-prone.

This is nowhere more true in sales, where there are a vast number of complex cognitive skills used on any given day. Best-in-class salespeople have advanced abilities and breadth of knowledge that they access from moment to moment to perform at the highest level. To name just a handful of sales-specific skills:

- Rapport-building
- Deal nurturing
- Prospecting
- Referral selling
- Social selling
- Objection-handling

- Negotiating
- Presenting
- Cold-calling
- Needs analysis
- Value messaging
- Closing

In addition to technical sales knowledge, top salespeople exhibit a host of general professional skills such as:

- Written communication
- Oral communication
- Time management
- Interpersonal alignment
- Working with a coach
- Business acumen

Beyond the technical and professional abilities, various life skills directly impact performance such as:

- Emotional intelligence
- Growth mindset
- Positive habits
- Mindfulness
- Human psychology
- Sleep
- Diet
- Exercise

We aimed to deliver to reps a tool that covered the full array of technical, professional, and personal skills they needed to perform at their very best. We had some of this covered by internal training material but found a treasure trove of value in publicly shared content from amazing thought leaders in these topic areas. We decided to blend together both curated and original content.

Further research led us to explore the science of mastery. As we took it upon ourselves to build our own application from the ground up, we wanted it to follow the most current information that the social sciences were reporting on how to achieve mastery. In short, mastery in highly cognitive processes requires rapid reaction and accurate responses. Over time, the result is pattern recognition. And pattern recognition abilities can be enhanced through practice and repetition. This applies to playing chess, most sports, flying a fighter jet, and (in our case) sales where accurate, timely responses based on rapidly changing environmental inputs is essential for top-tier success.

Studies have also shown that spaced learning in micro-sessions is the best delivery method for acquiring and retaining knowledge, essential ingredients to pattern recognition.[12] Furthermore, apps like DuoLingo have led the way, using gamification to maintain engagement and build a habit around continuous learning.

Putting the pieces together, it became clear that to optimize the ongoing improvement of sales skills we would need a tool which:

1. Collected a wide range of learning micro-sessions that covered the technical, professional, and personal skills reps needed to learn and maintain.

2. Graded the comprehension of micro-sessions with standardized tests, recording not only how well the rep scored, but also how recently they studied the content and when they would need to refresh on the knowledge.

3. Provided reps with immediate feedback on what they got right, where they missed, how they scored versus peers, where they ranked across all skill levels as a whole, and what sessions were aging in their learning portfolio and needed to be revisited.

We built a tool that covered these three key components of micro-learning, objective grading, and immediate feedback and benchmarking. The Triple Session methodology was born. We soon after added streaks, which tracked not only how much the reps studied, but how

consistently they studied. The goal was to build the habit of daily practice of small micro-courses, which science told us would yield the best
results for long-term learning and skill-building.

The key element to the Triple Session readiness score is the half-
life. Scores degrade over time. Every three months a rep would need to
re-take quizzes on previously taken sessions, to refresh the skill knowledge. Skills are perishable, and session scores reflect this. If the rep
failed to prove readiness by re-upping their skill strength on sessions
taken months ago, their score would degrade, and their overall strength
gauge would drop. The quiz provides a clear picture of what information is fresh in the rep's mind and what skills need retraining.

The results inside Rock's sales team exceeded expectations. Reps
took to the app right away and began building their personal profiles
of skill scores. We built an atmosphere not unlike a sports team's practice facility where our "players" competed with one another for who
was building the strongest muscles in the skills "strength training."
When we added daily streaks, they competed there as well, sometimes
logging into the app at 11:30 at night just to get their daily reps in.

Triple Session met the reps where they were (online), on their
schedules (on-demand), pulled them into engagement (gamified),
while delivering the results everyone wanted (sustained learning and
skill building). Onboarding new reps became faster and easier, maintaining best practice skills much more scalable, particularly in our
work-from-home environment.

Because we could easily invite new users into Triple Session and
track their usage, we eventually began using the app for talent recruit-
ment and candidate qualification. The seeds of the Ongoing Improvement System would begin even before some reps had their first
interview.

Health Check Reporting Inside the Ongoing Improvement System

Much of the health check reporting in the Ongoing Improvement
System rests on the foundation of data architecture of the first two
design-build systems. Business-of-one metrics, daily stack rankings,

and team retrospectives set up in the Process System set the benchmark KPIs from which to measure improvement over time.

Lead-conversion performance and channel-specific measurement from the Demand-Generation System inform on the health and diversity of pipeline creation. But just like the People and New-Hire Onboarding Systems, the Ongoing Improvement System has its own set of native measurements and feedback loops.

Training and Coaching eNPS Surveys

As detailed in the People System, employee net promotor scores can be a great way of fact-checking the system's health with direct feedback from the team. Within the Ongoing Improvement System, focused surveys are geared to measure the content, delivery, and value derived from team training and individual 1-on-1 coaching services to strengthen the improvement processes.

Triple Session Scores and Engagement

When practice is adopted as a habit, we start to measure training very differently. Much like how apps measure daily active use and weekly active use, those KPIs prove vital to gauge how the team is engaged in ongoing self-improvement. With the skill-specific scoring and user data inside the app, Triple Session offers a treasure trove of detailed metrics to follow the team's learning performance over time. Cross-referencing this data with business-of-one metrics offers a closed loop of how skill strength impacts performance and how performance should impact skill training.

Sales Performance

The most obvious health check on the Ongoing Improvement System in a sales organization is revenue growth. If your improvement efforts are having their desired effect, sales performance improves. There are a number of metrics to measure this impact, among them:

- Revenue/lead
- Revenue/opportunity

- Revenue/sales rep
- Quota attainment/rep
- Process step conversion rates
- Sales cycle
- Average sale price
- Average gross margins
- Customer lifetime value

Once again, design-build modeling is key. Sales leadership, operations, marketing, customer success, and finance each have a stake in the outcomes of the Ongoing Improvement System. The design-build team should include members from each of these functional areas.

Ongoing Improvement System Rituals

The Ongoing Improvement System by itself is a ritual – hence the "ongoing." Within the system there are routines that help shore up the habit of continuous self-improvement. Ongoing improvement is a mindset and a culture. The following are some actions that help communicate that culture is celebrated in the team.

Daily Readiness Rankings

As soon as we had Triple Session up and running and telling us who was scoring on which skill, we were able to report objectively on who had studied recently and mentally prepared for the work of the day. We called it the "Readiness Ranking." It was a simple way for us to document and celebrate the effort reps were making to stay as sharp as possible for the myriad skills needed to master their roles.

The skill-strength scores reps earned became a source of pride and healthy competition. When we added "streaks" to the app, reporting how many consecutive days a rep trained, the habit of daily practice was further reinforced. We treated it more like the consistency of going to the gym, working out your brain to stay strong, much like you would your body.

Practice Incentives

As detailed early in this system, incentives are of the greatest value when they drive input behaviors that influence output revenue. The entire Ongoing Improvement System is a controllable input aimed at increasing sales performance. As practice is left out of core compensation plans, using spot incentives to reward the effort helps reinforce the long-term impact ongoing improvement has on results.

Recognition of Practice Performance

As in the previous four systems, recognition can often get better engagement than remuneration in the Ongoing Improvement System. Time and energy to improve have delayed payouts in performance. It's easy for mental fatigue to erode the team's efforts in this capacity. A shout-out by leadership highlighting a rep's practice accomplishments helps reinforce the practice of practice and build in a short-term win for the rep. Team meetings, sales kickoffs, group emails, or LinkedIn posts are all great forums for practice recognition.

Mistakes I've Made When Constructing the Ongoing Improvement System

As mentioned earlier, mistakes in the People System are the costliest, as the residual effects of poor hiring, bad expectation-setting, and miscommunication are the hardest to undo. Conversely, missteps in the Ongoing Improvement System are the least painful. The system itself is born from the concept that the status quo is imperfect and in perpetual maintenance. As long as the culture of self-development is intact, mistakes in System 5 are expected as the team is constantly under construction. Nevertheless, there are a host of items I wish I had learned sooner.

Not Setting the Expectation of Ongoing Improvement Before Hiring

Conceptually, the idea of continuous self-development can sound appealing. The company is always working to help make everyone better. In reality, many people can get frustrated with the constant scrutiny of their weakest abilities. Regular recognition of the highlights and individual strengths can help give some balance to the messaging, but it's best to start the conversation from the firm understanding that never-ending, ongoing improvement is expected by all.

In the early days at Rock, I set this as part of the agenda during the onboarding process. It was too late. All the messages did at onboarding was preaching to the choir of believers or getting subtle eye rolls from those who were hired without the true buy-in of this aspect of team culture.

Onboarding is meant for learning new information or refreshing existing knowledge. Interviewing is where culture fit needs to happen. As ongoing improvement is less a skill and more a mindset and part of the team's character, we moved it, adding it as part of the pre-offer expectation-setting conversation. "Don't sign with this team unless you're open to having your weakest skills surfaced and talked about week after week, month after month, year after year."

Not Qualifying for Communication Style

If communication isn't clear, the knowledge transfer needed for ongoing improvement cannot happen. And clear communication relies on speaker-listener compatibility. One simple test for this was detailed in the social styles section of People System. Taking social style into account, and its impacts on how people give and receive information, is a key ingredient to communication compatibility.

As we get more comfortable with people, it's easy to fall back into our personal communication comfort zone. I personally test as a Driver/ Expressive. If I'm working with someone analytical or amiable, I can come across as too impatient, long-winded, or overly story-focused versus data focused. Even worse, they may shut down, not feeling comfortable enough to demand the data or thoughtfulness they need to maximize their learning from the interaction.

The simple act of educating the team on social styles by itself helped improve communication. The empathy and communication syncs became clearer with greater transparency. When people, particularly leaders, became more aware of their own social style and the adjustments needed to meet teammates where and how they best absorbed knowledge, overall communication improved.

Not Testing After Training

Ongoing improvement can be broken down into five components: identifying a point of improvement, crafting a plan to improve, training, confirming the training was absorbed, and executing the plan. For most of my leadership career, the fourth piece of confirming understanding of the plan was either done superficially or not at all. Team training frequently finished with a quick Q&A, and trust that the message was received. This often resulted in having to go back and retrain on the plan which slowed improvement outcomes. Better to trust but verify.

How can you confirm your understanding of a training? Test for it. Training should conclude with a formal quiz highlighting that the key elements of the content were absorbed and comprehended. As an added bonus, just like with the onboarding final exam, when people know they will be asked to answer questions on training, they tend to pay closer attention and work harder to learn the material.

Not Building a System of Retraining

For years, once someone was trained on a tactic or technique, it would only be revisited if it came up as a point of focus during coaching. Given the narrow focus of 1-on-1s, only focusing on one skill at a time, a lot of ground is left uncovered at any given time. Only when one of my best reps, Barbara Moreira, asked me again and again to re-run trainings I had previously delivered to the team, that I took seriously the need for re-training.

I started at Rock in 2015. In 2018 I started a regular Tuesday session, where I would rerun previous training. Given the hundreds of skills needed to keep sharp, it wasn't enough. The first version of Triple Session wasn't released until 2020, and we had fewer than 100 sessions until June 2022. Better late than never.

Not Documenting Coaching

Much like untested training, undocumented coaching sessions were the norm for most of my leadership career. Just as my former managers had met with me, I met with my reps, talked through strategies, and walked out without a word of anything noted. Too many conversations would end up in the coaching black hole.

For reps, tracking coaching builds accountability, reinforces the point of focus and action plan agreed upon, and provides compounding value from one coaching session to the next. For managers, the tracker allows for a refresher on where to pick up each conversation from one meeting to the next, and a reminder of the rep's social styles, goals, and gas tanks. Without a tracker, all that value can easily be lost in undocumented conversations.

Checkpoint – System 5

The first four systems, Process, Demand-Generation, People, and Onboarding, build upon one another, forming the core of a sales organization. The Ongoing Improvement System is the maintenance and fine-tuning of these four systems. Processes are measured, analyzed, and optimized for performance, all in an effort to better the results of each individual and the team as a whole.

But sales does not operate on an island. All other functional areas in a business impact sales and sales impacts them. For optimal performance of both sales and the business as a whole, we must zoom all the way out and look at the entire ecosystem. How teams should interact, measure one another's performance, and hold each other accountable are issues so vital to the health of the business, they warrant their own design-build project and set of governing principles: the Internal Alignment System.

Notes

1. Khadrice Rollins, "Where Did Tom Brady Go to College?" *Sports Illustrated*, February 4, 2018, https://www.si.com/nfl/2018/02/04/tom-brady-college-attended.

2. "Tim Tebow College Stats, School, Draft, Gamelog, Splits, College Football," https://www.sports-reference.com/cfb/players/tim-tebow-1.html.

3. Kevin Reilly and Graham Flanagan, "How Tom Brady Met His Controversial Personal Trainer Who Was Just Banned from the Patriots' Sideline," *Business Insider*, December 24, 2017, https://www.businessinsider.com/tom-brady-alex-guerrero-controversial-personal-trainer-interview-2017-12.

4. Mike Chambers, "The Fitness Secrets of Alex Guerrero, Tom Brady's Personal Trainer," *Men's Journal*, March 23, 2020, https://www.mens-journal.com/health-fitness/the-secrets-of-tom-bradys-personal-trainer-w479755.

5. "TB12 Method Explained," tb12sports.com.

6. "Tom Brady Promotes Muscle Pliability for Better Health," CBS News, January 1, 2018, https://www.cbsnews.com/news/tom-brady-promotes-muscle-pliability-for-better-health/.

7. "Tom vs. Time," series, Episode 2, 2018, https://www.google.com/search?q=tom+vs.+time&oq=Tom+vs.+Time&aqs=chrome.0.0i355i512j46i512j0i22i30l8.1401j0j4&sourceid=chrome&ie=UTF-8.

8. Ibid.

9. Anders Ericsson and Robert Pool, *Peak: Secrets from the New Science of Expertise* (Houghton Mifflin Harcourt, 2016), 19, 27, 57.

10. Peter King, "Tom Brady, in Montana, on Lifestyle, Legacy, NFL Future," *Sports Illustrated*, February 15, 2017, https://www.si.com/nfl/2017/02/15/themmqb-podcast-peter-king-tom-brady-talks-legacy-nutrition-injuries-future-super-bowl-51.

11. Simon Sinek, "The Infinite Game – ONE OF BEST SPEECHES EVER," YouTube, https://www.youtube.com/watch?v=cr6a8lz1NOg.

12. Sean H. K. Kang, "Spaced Repetition Promotes Efficient and Effective Learning: Policy Implications for Instruction," *Policy Insights from the Behavioral and Brain Sciences* 3, no. 1 (2016), https://www.researchgate.net/publication/290511665_Spaced_Repetition_Promotes_Efficient_and_Effective_Learning_Policy_Implications_for_Instruction.

7

The Internal Alignment System

The Case of Tyler Dvorak, Fifth Season Co-Op

> We got a snowstorm coming in tonight, so one of my trucks that usually comes in on Thursday is coming in today, he just called and said his ETA is like 10:15, or 10:30. Just letting you know the phone might ring. I'm gonna have to answer, talk to the driver and sort it out briefly. So, I apologize for that.

That's how my conversation with Tyler Dvorak started. Launched right into triaging a supply chain issue.

His title is Markets and Finance Manager, but that doesn't say much about his day-to-day. The sheer breadth of work Dvorak is pulled into at any moment calls on him to be a more general problem solver. Dvorak works at Fifth Season, a food cooperative in Viroqua, Wisconsin, close to where Iowa, Minnesota, and Wisconsin all converge on the banks of the Mississippi River.

Like many local food cooperatives, Fifth Season was created to build a marketplace where local farmers could sell their products and businesses and institutions could buy from area growers. A wholesale market and a go-between for small farmers and local buyers. Lettuce, cucumbers, maple syrup, and dozens of other products come into Fifth Season's warehouse, are screened for quality, stored, or sent out right away to fill waiting orders. It's Dvorak's responsibility to manage the flow from start to finish.

Fifth Season coordinates the purchase of the product, schedules deliveries, inspects for quality, and coordinates sales with local buyers in local schools, hospitals, and restaurants. In a cooperative, buyers, sellers, workers, and distributors all buy into a mutually beneficial system. When a potato farmer sells his harvest to Fifth Season for $10,000 and Fifth Season sells those potatoes to Viroqua High School for $12,000, the $2,000 profit goes back into the co-op to benefit them both or is distributed equitably as a dividend.

The concept of an equitable social contract in business can be traced back through generations of social and socioeconomic theory, from Kant to Rousseau to Locke to more recently John Rawls. In 1971 Rawls published *A Theory of Justice* where he advocates the need for what he calls the "veil of ignorance."[1] The idea was that in order to make fair decisions in a group, decision makers should create rules and make judgments as though they didn't know which role in the community they would assume.

"Because it's multi-stakeholder," Dvorak explains, "you're seeing the world from all those different perspectives, and you're just going to be more and more efficient at operating within that world." Dvorak approaches his work with a Rawlsian vantage point as he needs to create if not the most fair arrangements, the least unfair for all parties involved.

Dvorak looks like a young Jimmy Stewart. Wiry, strong from work outside. You get the sense when talking to him that he's instantly capable of handling himself in the conference room or the cattle farm. He grew up on his grandfather's lumber yard in northeastern Wisconsin, college-educated and farm savvy. A published research biologist and the former head of a sheep farm. If you had to reverse engineer the perfect résumé for managing a local food cooperative, it would likely look just like Tyler Dvorak's.

When he arrived at Fifth Season in early 2020, the cooperative was defaulting on payments and at risk of going under. On the supply side,

Fifth Season aims to provide local farmers with a source of fair and steady income for their products and produce. On the demand side, the value of buying fresh, locally sourced food, produced with high ecological and ethical standards. This means little or no pesticides, humane treatment of animals, and fair compensation for farmers.

In early 2020, Fifth Season was buying more than it could sell and paying more for products than it could sell them for in the market. This favored farmers in the short term with consistent income but threatened the long-term health of the co-op. The previous tenant of the warehouse where Fifth Season is located was a food services start-up. The start-up raised venture capital, spent it all, and went out of business, failing to achieve healthy growth. Dvorak aimed to keep Fifth Season from that same fate. He took action fast.

Immediately after taking the job, Dvorak dug into the books. Fresh produce was the riskiest business for Fifth Season, given that the products are perishable. If you buy 20 cases of lettuce, the clock starts ticking immediately on how long you have to sell them before the product is no longer edible. If not sold fast, about 10 days after it's harvested, the lettuce wilts and is only good for compost or hog feed.

One of the first actions Dvorak took at Fifth Season was to kill spec buys on fresh produce. If Fifth Season was going to buy 100 pounds of tomatoes or 12 cases of blackberries, he'd need to already have buyers ready to accept them at a set price. Pre-sold orders on produce only. No exceptions.

Securing the demand first is not without its risks. Oftentimes, farmers will only fill one-half or one-third of a promised order. Their farms are so small that they are unable to mitigate the risks of harvesting less of a crop than anticipated. If a larger farm's harvest from plots 39 and 40 is less than expected, they can make up the difference from plot 41. Small farms don't have a plot 41. They have plot 1, that's it. What you get is what you get.

Shorting orders burns "social capital," Dvorak says. This hurts his credibility and ultimately long-term demand with buyers and steers him toward doing more business with larger farms to keep the reputation of the co-op, and the demand it relies on, squarely intact.

After solving the immediate supply and demand imbalance, he took a deep dive into the economics of the goods sold. Before Dvorak,

Fifth Season kept P&Ls (profit and loss statements) on fresh produce, frozen goods, and dry goods. Dvorak started tracking profits and losses at the item level. If Granny Smith apples had more demand and sold better than Macintoshes, he wanted to know about it. He sorted out the winners and losers down to the product level, in order to favor the money makers and shore up the financial health of the business. This meant some products would just no longer be bought and sold at Fifth Season. Broccoli was the first on the chopping block.

"I don't want to get into the weeds with it," Dvorak explains, "but with black mold and the weather conditions that it's harvested in, and the conditions that it's transporting in. But basically, the long story short, broccoli is very difficult to maintain the primo quality and speed through the system to the end consumer and have it be in good shape. It's just a tough one."

Broccoli growers who previously sold their crops to Fifth Season had to be turned away. Dvorak lost no sleep over the decision. For as much as he wants to support every farmer, he knows without a healthy profit-and-loss balance, Fifth Season will fold, and won't be around to help any farmer. Where larger food distributors can move products faster and manage losses, the added risk to Fifth Season was too great.

With the co-op now focused on buying pre-ordered products and confidence that the shipped goods would arrive with integrity, financial stability was starting to take shape. And then Covid-19 hit.

In early 2020, most of Fifth Season's sales were done by local restaurants and the county school system. Overnight, both were shuttered due to Covid-19 restrictions, and purchase orders for the co-op's products evaporated. Dvorak once again had to work fast.

Tyler Dvorak is a pragmatist. As he explained when working through the Covid-19 crisis, "It can't be done away with . . . the amount of food people are eating. It's only transformed by type or location." What he soon realized was that the type and location shift caused by the pandemic displaced consumption back to consumers. The demand was showing up in Community Supported Agriculture groups (CSAs).

CSAs use a direct-to-consumer economic model pairing farmers with families. Individual buyers purchase a share of a farmer's future harvest, commonly paying for their shares in advance. The cash up front allows farmers to buy seed, soil, labor, and other expenses during the growing season. The community front-loads the costs of the farmers' business and shares the risk in the harvest. If a frost or mold or drought kills off some of the harvest, buyers may not receive everything they pre-ordered. The community and the growers are in it together.

During Covid-19, the popularity of CSAs exploded. Consumers weren't dining out. They recognized the supply chain issues in the global market and saw real value in supporting locally sourced foods. The demand Dvorak was looking for had moved to the CSAs. They had way more than they could supply. In stepped Fifth Season.

With the supply side of the food chain already in place, Dvorak set up orders with one CSA after another shoring-up demand. Having Fifth Season brokering the deal between farmers and CSAs was more costly than the direct farm-to-customer model, but there were no alternatives. The CSAs couldn't keep up with orders on their own, and Fifth Season presented a natural fit for the surplus.

Six months into Covid-19 the paradigm had completely shifted: 80–90% of Fifth Season's products were going to CSAs. It was the perfect puzzle piece for Dvorak. The CSAs already had the product sold and cash on hand. He just had to find the orders and fill them.

Eventually, the demand shifted back. CSAs, looking to rebalance their margins, developed relationships with new farmers or subsidized the growth of their existing farms to meet their supply needs on their own. At the same time, Covid-19 regulations relaxed, and Fifth Season rebuilt its distribution network with schools and restaurants. Once again, most of its produce is shipped to local institutions and restaurants.

Today Fifth Season is operating in the middle. The giant factory farms play in the global ecosystem. The smallest, single-acre planters, the ones Fifth Season originally set out to help, are better served by CSAs, farmers' markets, and local restaurants that promote farm-to-table dining experiences where the economics work.

Dvorak is on a mission to get the smaller farms back in the co-op's ecosystem and give them an opportunity for consistent, fair income through Fifth Season. If he can maintain enough consistent demand in his network, economies of scale will allow him to bring the relationship full circle and start spec-buying products without firm commitments of sales in hand once more. If he can pull it off, the small, local farmer would again have a home for selling their products. As it had done years ago, Fifth Season would be able to shoulder the risk in the supply chain with their farmers and producers. Some risk that is. Still . . . no broccoli.

First Principles of Internal Alignment

Tyler Dvorak and his constant balancing and rebalancing of stakeholder expectations and the different players in Fifth Season highlight several first principles from which any business can learn. These learnings create the bedrock upon which the Internal Alignment System should be built.

Detailed Tracking

When looking at the health of the Internal Alignment System, the devil is in the details. Healthy connections between teams and people aren't made in batches but in bites. Just like with root-cause analysis (see the Process System), determining where weak spots may exist means a deep dive into data.

The cracks in Fifth Season's alignment agreements weren't foundational. They lived in very specific areas (e.g., broccoli). Measuring the finer points of a pass-off including who is the agent, where did the customer come from, how were expectations set, was the timeline for delivery achieved, and so on are all key to understanding where the system is strong and where it isn't.

Veil of Ignorance

Tyler Dvorak doesn't play favorites. He knows his role is to make the best arrangements for all parties regardless of their position. When he creates a win that's best for the entire group, he digs in and explains the compromises some of the individual players need to make in order to see it through.

Like Fifth Season, companies need to create the best outcomes for all, as viewed by each of the parties involved. Agreements should be made, and compromises struck, only after considering the impact for each stakeholder and the best outcome for all. This oftentimes means the sacrifice of self-interest in favor of team gains. When the team wins, we all win.

Tough Calls Early

Fifth Season got into trouble when the balance of decision making tipped in favor of the growers and producers. It's hard to say no to people whose livelihood depends on you. Telling a farmer who's sweating in the field all season that his harvest needs to be sold somewhere else can't be easy. What Dvorak quickly came to realize after joining Fifth Season was that eventually having to tell all farmers that all of their products would have to be sold somewhere else was even worse.

Bad news early and to a few is better than bad news late and to the masses. Setting the right expectations, and making the tough calls early, helps maintain the healthiest system for all. It's an investment like any other. Paying a small amount today for bigger future gains tomorrow. Easier said than done, but a critical ingredient of the Internal Alignment System.

Realign as the Business Evolves

Few businesses operate in a vacuum. In just his first three years, Dvorak had to redesign the supply-side economics of Fifth Season, relocate demand, and rebuild distribution channels again and again. Perpetual plate spinning.

All businesses confront similar challenges. Markets shift, the economy rises and falls, competition builds and recedes, and employees come and go. As the landscape changes beneath your feet, it's necessary to reassess the ever-changing situation and realign internal relationships where, when, and with whom needed. In the game of Internal Alignment, only the paranoid survive.

Elements of the Internal Alignment System

Network versus Circuit

In electrical engineering, a network is considered any group of two or more electrical elements that are connected in any way. Paths are open, but it does not necessarily mean electricity is flowing to all elements in the network at all times. If your home is on the power grid, it is part of an electrical network.

An electrical circuit, on the other hand, is a closed system. Electricity flows through the circuit but at least one point does not leave the system. Your blender is part of a closed circuit. Current flows through the connected components of wiring, switches, and transistors to spin up your smoothie. There is no opening for electricity to flow back to the network.

All circuits are networks, but not all networks are circuits. The key differentiator is the closed loop. Circuits don't allow energy back into the network.

The Internal Alignment System is a network, not a circuit. For simplicity, we will detail the alignment between two teams at a time, sales and one other. But this should not be interpreted that these teams' alignment is a closed system. Every team and every team alignment impact all other teams in the network. There are just active and passive players in the relationships.

Passive players should be open and able to access the information, agreements, and especially performance data of the transfers between sales and other teams. At the very least, the information provides them with greater context to the company as a whole. At times, passive teams benefit from the insights into seeing how cross-functional alignment between sales and other teams operates. With a window into the alignment, they can also help by providing third-party perspective, improving the alignments with a unique point of view. Don't close-circuit your cross-functional alignments. Build a company-wide network.

SLAs

Service-level agreements, or SLAs, are a critical piece of documentation to help formalize team alignment. They also build transparency into the agreements, accountability to the deliverables, and a foundational piece of training material.

SLAs originated between companies and customers, and that is exactly how they should be looked at within the team. The SLA is a formal agreement between an internal provider and an internal customer. They not only document the terms of what is to be delivered but also by when and how. In a well-crafted SLA, there are clearly defined metrics governing the quality and quantity of work expected to be done, as well as the standard operating procedures to follow should the agreement be breached. The minimum performance and promotion path criteria detailed in the People System are examples of internal service level agreements.

Sales and Sales Alignment

"To know thyself is the beginning of wisdom." This Socratic principle is worth taking into account at the onset of the Internal Alignment System. As soon as you have any type of role specialization within the sales team, where hand-offs are made, alignment will be needed. Three interfunctional conversations should be considered within the sales organization, provided these roles exist in the company for clear communication and clean interaction.

Sales Reps and BDRs

A sales rep's performance is deeply impacted by her BDRs and vice versa. When these two don't match, the price is paid in friction and inefficiency, slowing down the flywheel. With great power over one another's performance comes great responsibility to perform.

BDRs need to clearly understand the ideal customer profile and not waste a rep's time setting up bad-fit opportunities. This will not only waste the rep's time but destroy the collaborative credibility that is key to making this relationship work. There also needs to be a clear alignment on qualification criteria. What is the "must-have" info the BDR needs to get to qualify for the opportunity? What should he stay away from and leave for the rep to explore? How will he get this info over to the rep? And finally, what is the clear expectation that should be set with the prospect? The rep needs to know what she's walking into.

Reps need to hold up their end of the bargain and prepare for each BDR call like they're gold (because if the BDR did his job, they are!). A review of the BDR's notes in CRM is table stakes to taking the call with the prospect. Preparation of the contract, company, and current state should be required time investments. Most BDRs' performance depends not only on the first meeting sticking, but also on the deal progressing to late-stage pipeline or even to revenue. When that's the case, an SLA on scheduled next steps and attempts and a deal-nurturing cadence should be installed and reps held accountable.

Sales Reps and Sales Engineers

Sales reps and sales engineers are some of the least aligned teammates in many sales organizations. When these two groups fail to collaborate, it not only hurts performance but can leave prospects with a very poor impression of the company. Poor planning and misalignment reek of unprofessionalism.

Sales engineers need to do their homework on the prospect before entering the call. Research should not be limited to notes in the CRM. The technical teaching usually required of sales engineers is best told through a customer-centric narrative. Prepare to tell the story. Customer success cases, industry references, and specific use cases help enrich the narrative.

Reps are the driving force in the conversation and need to set up their engineer for success. Make the research easy. Package the info gathered to date. Prepare the engineer on what points to hit, what to avoid, and how to best convey value through the presentation.

Sales and Sales Ops Alignment

Ops is involved in virtually every design-build project across the sales organization. They are almost always the key players on the design side. To set up the systems accordingly, there needs to be open communication at expectations in both directions.

Sales Ops needs to communicate clearly what needs to be executed and how in order to follow standard operating guidelines and capture the data needed for accurate performance measurement. Following process is not abstract art. It's paint-by-numbers. How to document processes should be written at a third-grade level. Screenshots and video tutorials go a long way. When processes change, they need to update playbooks accordingly and alert the team on new methods.

Reps need to certify on process. They should prove they have absorbed, understood, and are committed to the process. When the design does not match the built reality, they need to speak up and alert ops rather than going quietly through the motions. Reps need to understand the value of data collection and data accuracy to the healthy evolution of the business and work with ops to play the long game.

Sales and HR Alignment

We laid the foundations for Sales and HR alignment when design-building the People System. Both teams need to be in lockstep from the earliest stages of talent acquisition, through interviewing, hiring, and helping the team develop. Ops plays a key supporting role in this relationship, but it really rests on sales and HR leadership to get the rules of engagement down.

HR needs to set the ground rules for sales to follow during the interview process, particularly regarding data collection. Retrospectives are only as good as the available data to look back on. Whether you're using software to collect this or the simple spreadsheet examples used in this book, each candidate's interview performance needs to be meticulously recorded at each step.

HR is also responsible for candidate volume and quality. They play a similar role to sales development reps but are focused on talent versus customer acquisition. Not every candidate does or should convert. Hiring managers should have options for selecting the best fit. Also, through the initial vetting, base qualification criteria for ideal candidate profiles must be established and upheld to maintain efficiency in the downstream interviewing process.

For ongoing team support, HR also plays a key role in providing perspective on the health of the sales team. They check-in 1-on-1 with the team to gather perspectives from a different angle, own the delivery of eNPS surveys, and provide valuable feedback to sales leadership on the strengths of the team and areas of opportunity to improve.

On the sales side, they need to either write or review and edit job descriptions used when recruiting. This is the sales-enablement piece HR will use to attract candidates, and it should be created with care. Commitment to promoting the opening is both on LinkedIn and during sales meetings; beating the drum for referrals is key.

Talent acquisition is a marketing and sales machine, and sales need to help their HR brothers and sisters with talking points and enablement material. Salespeople know what is attractive to other salespeople. Whether it's the company's training and ongoing development investments, culture, career opportunity, or comp plan, share the highlights with HR so that they know the key points to hit. Here sales reps are effectively the case studies of successful clients to the talent-acquisition team.

Throughout the interview process, sales leaders need to follow the process of data recording during the interview process. The discipline here is writing down all scores and notes, even for the candidates you've decided to not move forward with. Recording data only on candidates who advance creates survivor bias and skews the reporting.

As the cycles of conversations, eNPS reports, and employee evaluations progress, sales leadership owns HR detailed action plans for improvement. Tight feedback lookups are key. In this scenario, the sales team is looked at as the internal customer base, HR is customer success, and sales leadership is the product team. Sales need to deliver the roadmap for improving performance and then build and launch the necessary changes.

Sales and Marketing Alignment

Having spent more than a decade working inside marketing technology giants, I learned that the gains of getting marketing and sales on the same page are immense. The cost of not doing so is also extreme. As they are almost always grouped together on the P&L, sales and marketing need to often work not just alongside one another, but also among one another to maximize the value generated from customer-acquisition investments.

Marketing should look at sales as their internal customer. I'm not saying this as a sales guy looking out for self-interest, but rather as a business leader, looking to align marketing's focus on a single priority: revenue. Priority does not mean sole responsibility. Marketing clearly plays key roles in branding, customer enablement, and internal communication. But their top responsibility should be driving customer acquisition.

The measurables for how marketing impacts customer acquisition can vary across different businesses but the need to measure is universal. There may be a host of KPIs that measure marketing inputs, but a single North Star metric should be aligned with sales at the marketing-owned deliverable to the team. In the early days at Rock, we started with total leads/rep. When the value of marketing qualified leads (MQLS) became clearer to us, we evolved the North Star to MQLs/rep. Then again, we got better at localizing valuable channels and MQL criteria that dictated a higher level of quality and predictability. We moved to SQLs/rep or sales-qualified leads.

The goal/rep is key to this relationship. It helps align marketing with what's happening on the ground in sales. A sales organization does not achieve goals in leaps but in baby steps. Teams don't hit targets all at once, but with a collection of everyone doing their job at every level. For that mindset to be baked into the culture of sales and marketing alignment, it needs to be clear in the reporting that each rep has a clear path to victory based on what marketing is delivering.

For the sales team, the mission and the measurables are also clear. Leads need to be worked, worked quickly, and worked through to completion. Time to lead is a key driver of lead-to-opportunity conversion. Sales needs to work with marketing to set the limit of time it will take to get on the lead and hit it. No excuses.

After speed, cadence is the next key deliverable sales owes marketing. How many attempts will be made, using which venues, and by when to effectively complete a comprehensive outreach process, squeezing max value from each marketing-generated opportunity?

There are a host of sales cadence technologies that plug into CRM to systematize this process today. Again, no excuses. As the cadences mature and performance data becomes available, sweet spots for the ideal number of attempts, venues, and message copy/materials will emerge, indicating what gets the best hit rates.

As with all these cross-functional relationships, the devil is in the details, and the details are found in data. Reporting is the glue that holds together the alignment. Ops is the glue factory. The operations team members should play key roles in setting up the tracking and reporting on SLAs (especially between the heavily measured sales and marketing performance) to keep the two teams' performance visible, accountable, and on track.

Sales and Customer Onboarding Alignment

Just as sales is the customer of marketing, onboarding is the customer of sales. Sales supplies the raw material an onboarding team runs on. The quality of that material, and the reporting on that quality, is in direct relation to the quality of output that onboarding is able to achieve.

Onboarding needs to set clear expectations for what they need from their internal vendor (sales). What information do they need from sales and the client? What expectations should be set with the client for how onboarding will unfold? What unique aspects about the client, especially potential risk factors, exist that onboarding should be prepared to address?

Sales needs to take ownership and look at this critical pass-off from the onboarding analyst's perspective. What level of detail and awareness would best serve onboarding and the customer? How should it be communicated? Having a mapped set of criteria inside CRM, which the sales team is responsible for completing to deliver on the Sales-Onboarding SLA, will put guardrails on how this conversation should be structured.

Sales and Customer Success/Support Alignment

Continuing downstream in the customer journey, it's clear that sales has more than one internal client. Customer success (CS) and customer support also depend heavily on how sales aligns expectations with customers and sells good-fit deals.

Similar to onboarding, CS needs to deliberately set specific criteria regarding which information will be critical for building a long-term relationship with the client. Once again, CRM should provide the system of truth for where this information should be captured, stored, transmitted, and measured. CS, with the help of Ops, should work on locking in required fields that salespeople need to fill out as part of a structured order-processing sequence.

Sales should take up the role of SDR for the customer success team. It's not enough to simply pass over a new customer. Sales should prime the customer for continuing the journey with the expectation of deepening the customer-company relationship over time. The key question sales should ask, and answer, isn't "What do I need to do to pass off a good-fit client?" It's "What do I need to do to set up the relationship so that the client will become a customer success story for the business in 6, 12, or 18 months?"

Sales and R&D Alignment

Along with the customer success and support teams, sales is a key channel for info gathering from leads and customers to help shape the future of products and services. They get direct access to live conversations and, when aligned, act as a market-research group for company innovation. The R&D team pays back this info gathering with the delivery of cutting-edge offers that deliver value based on the customer's definition of what value is.

To make this virtuous cycle of offer development work, the product and services teams need to set up the framework for data collection. The need to clearly lay out what type of information offers the highest-value learning and how that information should be collected and passed over.

Most R&D teams want to hear about problems, not solutions. They're curious to know what roadblocks prospects or clients are facing and how the company can build a solution to best solve them. Intelligence on what competitors are offering can add value, to help the R&D teams stay up to speed on where the market is heading and not allow competitive value gaps to open too widely.

For info gathering and reporting, the sales team needs to go no further than the CRM. As with most design-build projects, Sales needs to move out of its build-side mindset. Research and development is the long game, and sales needs to incorporate more long-term thinking as to the value of intelligence gathering. With Ops assistance, one simple way is locking the CRM at the point of moving deals to Lost or Won, requiring reps to fill out critical product and service intel in order to unlock.

The R&D intel checklist items could be:

- Problems uncovered in the sales process for which we do not currently offer a solution.
- Products/services that the customer will maintain, which offer value complementary to our solution.
- Products/services that fit the customer but are not purchased.
- Products/services the client requested that we do not currently offer.
- Products/services the client considered with competition but preferred ours.

Each of these options would need a drop-down menu of options allowing for sortable reporting along with associated open text boxes for reps to elaborate on the selection. Singular data points offer little value when influencing R&D. The best cases are made through the process of multiple attestations. When a variety of sources repeatedly signal areas of missing value in the company's current offer, a much stronger case can be made for investing time, money, and attention in building the solution.

Finance and Sales Alignment

Years ago, forecasting was left to subjective, back-of-the-envelope math made by front-line salespeople. They'd give their gut feels on how confident they were that a customer would buy and report it up the chain of command. Invariably reps would frequently be overly optimistic, routinely missing the mark, or far too conservative, choosing to under-promise and over-deliver. Either way, it made the forecasting inaccurate, unreliable, and thus of little value.

The lack of trustworthy visibility into the revenue expectations came with two big consequences. Financial planning (is there enough money in the bank or are we overextended?) and staffing (do we have enough people or too many people to support the customers coming in?).

The solution: Finance needs to lead a design-build forecasting project, along with sales leadership and ops as contributing stakeholders. An education on why forecasting matters and the consequences of unpredictable finances is a good place to start. (Even really smart people don't know this, or don't very much care until a light is shed on it.)

Next, a forecasting formula should be implemented to align both teams. This means playbook material created for educating the team and holding them accountable to the standard operating procedure of forecasting. A potential forecasting formula option to consider (the one we selected at Rock) is known as forecast triangulation. Forecast data is pulled from three independent sources, CRM conversion rates (just the historical math here), Rep forecast, and Manager forecast. Over time, one of these sources will emerge as a clear winner as the most reliable for forecasting accuracy.

On the sales side of this alignment, a commitment to, and accountability for, accurate forecasting is required. That accountability is backed up by goal setting. If you want to influence a salesperson's behavior, set a goal against it. Reporting on forecasting accuracy in a +/-% off of the projection, stack ranked by each member of the team, is one possible way to get this done. Running the occasional incentive for forecasting accuracy can help shine a light on the process and make it more fun for the team.

Sales and Legal Alignment

Vital to the seamless flow of customer acquisition, sales and legal alignment influences every deal signed. With business regulation and data privacy and cybersecurity needs at an all-time high, it's crucial to the health of the business and health of customer relationships that commercial and legal teams be on the same page.

For legal, the sales team needs speed. This can be delivered in standardized customization, which sounds like an oxymoron. Standardized customization essentially means preapproved versions of the contract, which sales can easily access and send to prospects without the need of approval or other red tape. If there is a single, boilerplate MSA, but clients routinely ask for "item x" to be removed and "item y" to be added, and those edits are always approved, create those additional templates. Standard agreement form, standard – item x, standard + item y, standard – x and + y. When approved customization is needed, an SLA including a rapid turnaround time to reply is key.

Sales needs to fight the good fight. The company contract terms exist for a reason. When sales are done right, enough value has been created where contract terms will not kill the deal. Commit to signing well-aligned customers, not just in product or service expectations, but also in agreement terms. Passing every request for change to legal without this advocacy is lazy and clogs up the legal pipeline, getting in the way of the deals that actually do need customized attention.

The Sacks Cadence

Most growth and evolution happen in small steps over extended periods of time. The 1% better everyday rule. But every so often a pivotal learning comes along that triggers a growth spurt. A new technique, or perspective or approach that accelerates performance in measures of miles not millimeters. For me, one such growth spurt in the realm of internal team alignment came in 2020, in the form of the Sacks Cadence.

Speaking at the SaaStr conference that year David O. Sacks, former COO of PayPal, former CEO of Yammer and Zenefits, and current founding partner of Craft Ventures, taught a master class in the cross-functional alignment. The Sacks Cadence, as he describes it, is "an operating philosophy." When teams scale, siloes are created, walling off functional areas. "The cadence is designed to synchronize the major functions," Sacks says, "so that the team works together in lockstep."[2]

The Cadence puts product, marketing, sales, and finance all working together toward a common quarterly goal. It's a textbook design-build project put on a continuous loop. I advise watching Sack's SaaStr video on the topic (https://www.saastr.com/the-cadence-how-to-turn-your-saas-startup-into-an-army-with-david-sacks-video-transcript/). To summarize the cadence:

- Product works with sales, CS, and marketing to pick high-value product additions to build and launch for the following quarter.
- Marketing works to create campaigns to promote the value of the new product launches and sales enablement material, and plans a launch event for a grand unveiling.
- Sales leverages messaging around the product launch, building excitement around the new value and building urgency to buy.
- Finance manages the quarterly bookkeeping cadence, plans SKU changes if any price increases, or product changes that might alter deal processing.
- Operations manages the cross-functional communications, ensures deliverables are on track, deadlines are met, and performance data is captured accordingly.

From a product standpoint, the cadence doesn't change much the rhythm of their work (many product teams already work on quarterly cycles) but rather their focus and the value. In addition to the small feature and bug-killing work, product is always contributing bigger customer value every quarter. That contribution not only adds fiscal value but also provides a morale boost to the dev team as they see their work consistently moving the needle.

Marketing benefits from the fresh buzz and excitement around new stuff to promote each quarter. The topics for content and ad campaigns get the creative juices flowing, and the ability to flex new messaging muscles all the time keeps the team engaged. Small, quarterly events help anchor the campaigns and provide valuable learning and fast improvement from the rapid succession of the cadence.

Sales wins from the cadence, as they are armed with new value messaging to take confidently to new prospects and use to reawaken older, stale deals. When the product release is paired with a price increase, the organic urgency it creates helps to build urgency and beat the quarterly number.

The Sacks Cadence is design-build modeling at its finest.

Health Check Reporting Inside the Internal Alignment System

The essential health check reporting of the Internal Alignment System is built on the SLAs between teams. Agreements need to be drafted with quantifiable deliverables. And these deliverables need to be measured. Those measures need to be reported on for compliance.

When SLAs are not met and the deliverables compromised, root-cause analysis should be used to identify where and why the breakdown occurred. Assumptions are dangerous and can lead to false narratives. Data assessment is best to bring light to where cracks in the pass-off may be opening up.

Internal Alignment System Rituals

The key ritual for the Internal Alignment System is simple. Assess and revise. Monthly tracking is usually most effective, as it offers a large enough sample size to create a picture of the scenario, within a short enough window to enact swift remedies.

Retrospectives, like those described in the Demand-Generation System, have equal value in maintaining alignment sync. Each month the two functional areas, along with ops, meet to review team performance on the SLA deliverables, run RCA where needed, and craft action plans to improve when needed.

Mistakes I've Made When Constructing the Internal Alignment System

The source of all my mistakes in the Internal Alignment System can be traced back to my initial approach on the subject. It was never top of mind. Setting up the structures of how people should work with one another and teams should collaborate with other teams seemed overly bureaucratic and low on the priority list – something we could just figure out along the way. I was wrong. Not investing in this system early comes at a high price later.

Reactive Alignment

The clearest symptom of my passive mindset toward alignment can be seen in the triage approach I used for years. How should SDRs and Reps collaborate? You guys just work it out among yourselves, how to align on what lead qualification looks like and how to set up the next conversation. Contracts? Let's just get with legal on requests for changes as they come in. Product? Hey, we heard this feature at a competitor keep being mentioned on our calls. Let us know what you think whenever you can.

No processes, no commitments, no plans of action. Reactive alignment guarantees that the same issues will persist and improvement across roles and teams will stagnate. Either you manage the interactions between roles and teams, or they manage you.

Undocumented Alignment

The first step to fixing a problem is admitting you have one. The second step is writing stuff down. The first phase of me addressing my own alignment issues was met mostly with meetings involving the other functional leaders – head of people, head of product, head of legal, and so on. We talked through the issues between teams, agreed on next steps, left meetings with full intention of making progress on issues. It invariably went back to business as usual.

Writing stuff down and signing your name to what you agree to do for someone has a powerful impact on behavior. It makes the agreement more real. Documentation is a physical manifestation of a promise. Your word. At Rock, I started referring to our alignment documentation as the holy trinity of getting things done. Plans needed to have (1) a single owner, (2) a detailed action list of items, and (3) a date for delivery of the next step.

Unmeasured Alignment

"Collaborate better" and "communicate more clearly" and "delivery as expected" are all great aspirations, but also highly subjective. In legal terms these would be called void for vagueness. In my early days at Rock, I was routinely in violation of this doctrine.

Agreements between teams need to be explicit and quantified. Collaborate better? What are we specifically going to do for one another, where we will deliver it, and how will we measure its quality, quantity, and timeliness? Interviews with teams have value but can also be skewed by personal perception and confirmation bias.

One example of this at Rock came in the form of the quality delivery of content by our network team. Freelancers would produce articles; our network team would edit and clean up the text as part of a quality-control process and ship to the customer. Sales had the perception from some loud negative customer feedback that overall quality of our content was poor.

Fortunately, the head of the network team documented customer quality grades. The SLA was that 99% of all content would be accepted by clients upon first review. The team was steadily hitting 99.5% first-review acceptance. It was just 5 low-quality scores out of 1,000 that were getting all the attention. Sales quickly got its confidence back in the team and we had a new data point to talk about with prospects as a sales enablement point of value.

Checkpoint – System 6

Process, demand generation, people and new-hire onboarding, each stacked in sequence, build the core of the sales organization. The Ongoing Improvement System acts as the internal maintenance crew, constantly going over the four core systems to optimize performance over time. Internal alignment hooks up each subsystem into the network of the company like wiring in a power grid.

Leads flow into the sales team at agreed-upon quantities and qualities, and sales delivers measured action on them. Prospects are won or lost, and the intelligence on either is gathered in CRM and passed to marketing and the R&D teams. For won customers, sales delivers quality info and expectations to setup the customer onboarding, success, and support teams for long-term success. Ongoing work with ops, HR, and legal tweaking performance with "holy trinity" projects keep the teams on track.

It's not enough to take care of just yourself. In an integrated business model, the systems are part of a network, not a circuit. As Navy SEALs have swim buddies to look out for, so too should sales teams. Never leave your fellow co-worker behind.

Notes

1. John Rawls, *A Theory of Justice* (Belknap Press, 2005).
2. David Sacks, "The Cadence: How to Operate a SaaS Startup," Craft Ventures, July 1, 2020, https://medium.com/craft-ventures/the-cadence-how-to-operate-a-saas-startup-436aa8099e8.

Conclusion: Takeaways from Design-Building Sales Systems

In 2016, we ran personality assessments on the sales team at Rock, to determine the character of our best salespeople. What we learned was that the quality that our top performers had disproportionately to the rest of the team was planning. Our best salespeople were great planners. They took the time to prepare for sales calls. They did the homework on the client, researched the business case, had well-crafted enablement materials, and asked for help from colleagues who could add value. They thought things through and acted accordingly.

Design-building a sales organization is fundamentally no different. Planning is the core competency needed to effectively build sales systems to last. Sales org constructions start from a holistic vantage point. The entire, end-to-end network of components stacked together and working as one unit.

From there the deconstruction of the network into six smaller systems which own vital subsystems. Each subsystem carries its own weight for the network and, depending on interdependencies, must support follow-on subsystems. Each subsystem has its unique components, measures, and processes. This is the design side.

The build side coordinates the best team to help craft the plan and do the work. Selecting the right people to collaborate on the construction of each subsystem, each component in the process, is the mortar that holds the whole thing together. Systems provide ongoing value. They organize our work and help us make sense of the little worlds in which we operate. But to construct systems effectively, we must plan systems effectively.

Processes and products don't plan. People do. Great systems require great planning. Great planning means great people. If we aim to effectively design-build a sales organization, we must begin with the single greatest element of success: the team. Design building is team building.

About the Author

Matt Doyon is co-founder and CEO of Triple Session, a software company on a mission to make self-improvement, through ongoing practice, standard for everyone. Over his 20+ years in sales, Matt worked his way through the ranks of SDR, rep, account executive, and sales manager. He spent his last eight years as chief revenue officer at Rock Content, where he helped grow the business from a small, early-stage start-up to the largest content marketing company in the world. Matt lives in Newton, Massachusetts, with his wife and three children.

Index